'In this updated 5th edition of *Identity in Adolescence*, Ferrer-Wreder, Sugimura, and Kroger provide a contemporary and up-to-date analysis of pressing issues in identity theory and research. Expanded analysis of the social and cultural contexts that are critical to identity development provides a sophisticated take on an essential developmental task. Updated content addresses timely and relevant issues for youth who are coming of age in a global and digital environment.'

Renee Galliher, *Utah State University, USA*

'A welcome update of this classic text: well-grounded in theory, current in research, and highly readable throughout – is indispensable for students of adolescent development, teachers, researchers, and clinicians.'

James E. Marcia, *Simon Fraser University*, *Canada*

'Identity is relevant to everyone, and this new edition of *Identity in Adolescence* does a wonderful job highlighting its complexity in an accessible way. The updated chapters incorporate a large amount of new state-of-the-art research. What is more, the authors make complex ideas and concepts of identity relatable and understandable by referencing novels, memoirs, and quotes from research. The new chapter on navigating cultures because of immigration is timely and will resonate with people living through such experiences. Whether you're an advanced student who wants to gain a deeper understanding of identity development or a scholar or practitioner who'd like to brush up on their knowledge, this book is an essential source!'

Theo A. Klimstra, *Tufts University*, *USA*

Identity in Adolescence

This fully revised fifth edition of *Identity in Adolescence: The Balance Between Self and Other* presents four theoretical perspectives on identity development during adolescence and young adulthood, and their practical implications for intervention. Ferrer-Wreder, Sugimura, and Kroger consider adolescent identity development as the unique intersection of social and cultural forces in combination with individual factors that each theoretical model stresses in attempting to understand the identity formation process for contemporary adolescents.

Identity in Adolescence addresses the complex question of how identity forms and develops during adolescence and young adulthood, and serves as the foundation for entering adult life. The book is unique in its presentation of four selected models that address this process, along with cutting-edge research and the implications that each of these models holds for practical interventions. This new edition has been comprehensively revised, with one completely new chapter, and seven that have been extensively updated. Special topics are addressed, including ethnic, sexual, and gender identity development, the role of technology in adolescent identity development, bicultural identity development, and ongoing identity development beyond adolescence.

The book is essential reading for advanced undergraduate and graduate students studying adolescent development, self, and social identity within developmental psychology, social psychology, and clinical psychology, as well as practitioners in the fields of child welfare and mental health services, social work, youth and community work, and counseling.

Laura Ferrer-Wreder, Ph.D., is a professor in the Department of Psychology at Stockholm University, Sweden, and at the Institute for Psychology at the University of Agder, Norway. She has published widely, and her current research focuses on advancing the study of positive youth development from a global perspective. She is one of the co-developers of an identity intervention called the Changing Lives Program.

Kazumi Sugimura, Ph.D., is a professor in the Graduate School of Humanities and Social Sciences at Hiroshima University, Japan. Her research focuses on the processes and mechanisms of identity formation among adolescents and young adults in the relational, social, and cultural contexts. She is the past president of the International Society for Research on Identity and Associate Editor of *Identity: An International Journal of Theory and Research.*

Jane Kroger, Ph.D., is Professor Emerita of Developmental Psychology at the University of Tromsø, Norway. Previous works include the books *Identity Development: Adolescence through Adulthood* and *Discussions on Ego Identity*, along with extensive research on identity development during adolescence and adulthood.

Adolescence and Society

Series Editor: John C. Coleman

Department of Education, University of Oxford

In the 20 years since it began, this series has published some of the key texts in the field of adolescent studies. By publishing relatively short, readable books on topics of current interest to do with youth and society, the series makes people more aware of the relevance of the subject of adolescence to a wide range of social concerns. The books do not put forward any one theoretical viewpoint, the authors outline the most prominent theories in the field and include a balanced and critical assessment of each of these. The books summarise, review and place in context current work in the field to interest and engage both an undergraduate and a professional audience.

Adolescent Mental Health
Prevention and Intervention
Terje Ogden and Kristine Amlund Hagen

Adolescent Coping
Promoting Resilience and Well-Being
Erica Frydenberg

Adolescence and Body Image
From Development to Preventing Dissatisfaction
Lina A Ricciardelli and Zali Yager

Sexuality in Adolescence
The Digital Generation
Susan M. Moore and Doreen A. Rosenthal

Adolescent Health and Well-Being
Meeting Challenges Old and New
Melissa Kang, Imelda Coyne, and Nicola J. Gray

Identity in Adolescence
The Balance Between Self and Other
Laura Ferrer-Wreder, Kazumi Sugimura and Jane Kroger

For more information about this series, please visit: https://www.routledge.com/Adolescence-and-Society/book-series/SE0238

Identity in Adolescence

The Balance Between Self and Other

Fifth Edition

Laura Ferrer-Wreder, Kazumi Sugimura and Jane Kroger

Routledge
Taylor & Francis Group
LONDON AND NEW YORK

Designed cover image: Getty Images @Xavier Lorenzo

Fifth edition published 2026
by Routledge
4 Park Square, Milton Park, Abingdon, Oxon, OX14 4RN

and by Routledge
605 Third Avenue, New York, NY 10158

Routledge is an imprint of the Taylor & Francis Group, an informa business

First edition published by Routledge 1989
Fourth edition published by Routledge 2019

British Library Cataloguing-in-Publication Data
A catalogue record for this book is available from the British Library

ISBN: 978-1-032-78138-9 (hbk)
ISBN: 978-1-032-77580-7 (pbk)
ISBN: 978-1-003-48633-6 (ebk)

DOI: 10.4324/9781003486336

Typeset in Times New Roman
by Apex CoVantage, LLC

For my parents, Alice and Tony Ferrer; and for my husband, Richard Wreder and for my children: Sara and Patrick Wreder.
– Laura Ferrer-Wreder

In memory of my former mentor, Toshio Kuze; and for my guide on the path to international research, Jean Phinney.
– Kazumi Sugimura

To those who search and to those who assist along the way.
– Jane Kroger

Contents

Tables

Acknowledgments

We are grateful to the series editor, John Coleman, our editor, Molly Selby, and editorial assistant Shreya Sengupta at Routledge for their responsiveness and support during the development and preparation of this volume. We also greatly appreciate those who have read selected chapters and offered their thoughts on earlier drafts: Lena Adamson, Carolyn Cass Lorente, Shogo Hihara, Takashi Nakao, and Genki Yasui. Their suggestions have significantly improved the coverage and readability of several of the chapters. We also thank Monisha Pasupathi and Deborah Rivas-Drake for agreeing to speak with us and for sharing their biographies and perspectives in this book. And grateful thanks also go to the many students and colleagues over the years whose comments have contributed enormously to the development of the present volume. Finally, to those individuals who participated in research interviews across our varied contexts and provided anonymous statements about their own identity-related concerns that were used as examples in this volume, we express our sincere gratitude.

During the writing of this book, Laura Ferrer-Wreder was supported by research colleagues at Stockholm University and the University of Agder. Her sincere thanks go to Stockholm University's Lilianne Eninger and Radosveta Dimitrova, the University of Bergen's Nora Wiium, and the University of Agder's Siri Håvås Haugland for their steadfast support, which made Laura's work on this book possible. Laura would also like to acknowledge William M. Kurtines for his mentorship. Special thanks also go to Richard Wreder, Alice Ferrer, and the now young adults in Laura's life (Sara and Patrick Wreder), who were patient and helpful in sharing their reflections about the digital life, sexuality, and gender chapters. Finally, our heartfelt thanks go to other family members and friends who have been patient with the many hours that were lost to them through the production of this work.

Kazumi Sugimura would like to express her deepest gratitude to Elisabetta Crocetti, Rita Žukauskienė, Kai Hatano, and Tomotaka Umemura for their fruitful research collaborations with her over the past decade, as well as the many students and colleagues with whom she has engaged in constructive discussions about identity in classrooms and professional societies over the years. These experiences also gave her the opportunity to participate in the revision of this book, which she has cherished ever since embarking on the path of identity research. She would also like to acknowledge Makoto Hiro and Tomoya Ito for their help with editorial corrections. Finally, she would like to express her heartfelt gratitude to Shinichiro Sugimura for his unwavering emotional support throughout the revision process of this book.

Permission Acknowledgment

AI Statement

AI-based tools were not used to produce any of the content of this book in any substantive manner. AI-based tools may have been embedded in search engines used for and format checking of selected chapters. The authors take full responsibility for the originality and validity of this book in accordance with this book's publisher's guidelines and professional scientific standards, according to current American Psychological Association guidelines (APA 7).

Preface to the Fifth Edition

And so a fifth edition of *Identity in Adolescence* now comes into being. I (JK) was joined in the last edition by coauthor Professor Laura Ferrer-Wreder (Stockholm University, Sweden, and University of Agder, Norway) to better incorporate European perspectives on contemporary issues impacting adolescent identity development. For this new, fifth edition, both Laura and I are delighted to welcome our coauthor, Professor Kazumi Sugimura (Hiroshima University, Japan), to expand an understanding of adolescent development further by including Asian perspectives. We hope that our greater international focus in this volume will enhance an appreciation of adolescent identity development beyond those of the more traditional North American shorelines.

I have reviewed the history and development of this volume in the previous (fourth) edition. Let me add here that the unfolding of identity across the lifespan has long been of great interest to me. In the late 1980s, I was fortunate to spend a year as a visiting scholar at the Erik H. and Joan M. Erikson Center in Cambridge, Massachusetts. During the bimonthly evening discussions that I had with other scholars and the Eriksons around their dining room table, concepts from many of Erik Erikson's published and unpublished works were the focus of our exchanges. From these evenings, Erikson's thoughts on the "wider identity" and identity as a move toward greater "wholeness" have stayed with me over the years of authoring or coauthoring the past volumes. And these themes continue to be the foundations for this new volume today.

Erikson framed the idea of one's "wider" and more inclusive identity as one's sense of self in relation to others and within a given place in history and geography. In this volume, we have attempted to implement the idea of one's "wider" identity through examining three different theoretical perspectives on how one's sense of identity emerges (with its biological and psychological origins) within various contemporary contexts (rather different from those of Erikson's original writings) as well as from different geographical locations. And the theme of moving toward greater "wholeness" is approached in this volume through following identity's emergence during adolescence and ongoing evolution through subsequent phases of adult life. Identity foundations, normatively crystallized during adolescence, set a critical foundation for movements through all of adult life – a consistent research finding that we felt important for readers to appreciate.

This new fifth edition of *Identity in Adolescence: The Balance Between Self and Other* is, again, first and foremost, a book about identity development during adolescence and the implications that this development holds for practical response by parents, teachers, youth workers, and others interacting with youths during the second and third decades of their lives. In this book, special care was taken to have a culturally informed perspective on how adolescents in various parts of the world meet the challenges of identity development as well as thrive and contribute to their life contexts. In part, the book aims to capture the many new theoretical and research innovations for some of the existing models of identity development covered in earlier editions of the volume as well as newer approaches in the field of identity studies during adolescence. It has also been sparked by our concern over adults' frequent failure to recognize, meet, and respond optimally to the special needs of adolescents in their various phases of identity development. The wealth of research data that now exists about what constitutes an effective identity intervention during adolescence offers even clearer answers to questions of how effective intervention can be a planned event rather than a chance occurrence. Now, more than ever, it is vital for the adults of today to recognize the strengths and promise of the current generation of youth and to support them in their identity development as a way to better ensure that the next generation is fully equipped to meet the challenges of today and the future. It is hoped that the results of our work with this fifth edition will help promote interests in identity studies, either as a supplementary emphasis to courses on adolescent development or as a field in its own right.

Jane Kroger
Bellingham, Washington, U.S.A.
Laura Ferrer-Wreder
Stockholm, Sweden
Kazumi Sugimura
Hiroshima, Japan

1 Adolescence and the Problem of Identity – Historical, Sociocultural, and Psychosocial Views

> Carsen McCullers's (1946) novel, *The Member of the Wedding*, catalogues the story of Frankie's struggle to define who "she" is, and where she belongs in the world. The scene opens with almost-13-year-old Frankie Addams pondering the strangeness of her existence. While talking with Berenice, the family housekeeper, Frankie realizes that only she can ever be Frankie, and Berenice can only ever be Berenice. And even though they are together, year in and year out, living their lives side by side, Frankie can never be anyone else but Frankie, and Bernice can never be anyone else but Bernice. As Frankie continues her musings, she finds this idea incredibly odd. And ultimately, Frankie realizes that there can only ever be identity enough for one.

Frankie's ruminations address a question that adolescents and social scientists alike have pondered over the preceding decades: When and how does one develop a sense of identity? While the foundations of identity are formed in infancy and childhood through the interactions of caretakers and child, adolescence does seem to be a time, at least in many contemporary, technologically advanced cultures, when one is confronted with the task of self-definition. Frankie can't ever be anything else but herself. However, trying to find out who "she" is and where she "belongs" becomes Frankie's task in McCullers's (1946) novel. The process of identity formation is something that scholars have attempted to understand from a variety of perspectives – historical, sociocultural, and psychosocial. While Frankie, herself, is not concerned with all of these issues, she eloquently gives voice to some of the forces that helped shape her "I," her sense of identity, and her place in the world.

Frankie's story is set during World War II in a small, rural southern town in the United States (U.S.) during a seemingly endless summer. Frankie is painstakingly inching closer and closer to becoming 13 years old, feeling very much betwixt and between meaningful social niches (that summer has a way of exacerbating) and wrestling with the matter of belonging. Given an option, Frankie would have preferred to have been a boy and gone to war as a Marine. However, this was not to be her fate, so she decided instead to give blood (at least a quart a week) to the war efforts. In this way, a part of her would be in the veins of Allies fighting all over the world (the reddest and strongest blood ever – a true medical wonder). Soldiers would return, saying they owed their lives to "Addams" (not "Frankie").

DOI: 10.4324/9781003486336-1

But this scenario was not to be her fate either, for Frankie was too young, and the Red Cross would not take her blood. Thinking about the war for very long made Frankie afraid, not because of the fighting but because the war refused to include her, to give her a place in the world, just as her brother's upcoming wedding would not include her in the wedding party. Actually, thinking for very long, at all, made Frankie afraid as well, for it brought up questions of who she was, of what she could do in the world, and of why she was standing where she was at that moment – alone. Through the trials of trying to adopt a new name (F. Jasmine Addams), a new family, and a new town, Frankie struggled to establish her sense of identity and where she belonged.

The present volume is first and foremost a book about *identity* and its development during *adolescence*. Identity is that which gives meaning and purpose to one's life, allowing one to move with a sense of direction toward expressing one's values and goals. Identity is who and what one believes oneself to be, allowing one to seek and hopefully find meaningful personal expressions of one's psychological needs, interests, talents, and values within a sociocultural context. *Adolescence* has often been defined as the period of life beginning in puberty and ending in culture. By this definition, the biological changes of puberty herald the transformation into an adult body, as well as changes in the emotional, cognitive, and social capabilities that mark the beginning of adolescence. The ending of adolescence has been defined in various ways, but adolescence generally is considered to draw to a close when one is able to take greater responsibility for oneself emotionally, economically, and relationally. One's immediate social and cultural contexts will play an important role in determining when adolescence draws to a close and adulthood proper begins.

The time during which one might be considered adolescent has been greatly lengthening in many parts of the world due to the increased cultural demands for learning the technical skills that are needed to function in that adult world. And so, several decades ago, those who were referred to as "late adolescents" were often young people finishing their educational training and entering the workforce in their late teens or early 20s. However, the current trend toward obtaining further education or training has extended the time of adolescence into emerging[1] or young adulthood, as youth prepare for their future adult roles (Arnett, 2024). This volume thus focuses on issues of identity as they evolve over the course of adolescence through adulthood.

Why Is Identity Important?

There is urgency and value in the scientific effort to advance knowledge about identity development. Identity remains vital to the individual psychological experience, and it continues to have a social and political function that in some cases can work for the benefit or detriment of particular groups of people (Hammack, 2014). For example, many of the worst conflicts in the world are fueled by what Wainryb and Recchia (2014, p. 3) called "polarized collective identities"; such an identity is rooted in

> a belief in the justness of one's ingroup goals, along with a simultaneous negation or delegitimization of the outgroup's perspective, as well as a positive

> collective self-image (e.g., as courageous, fair, and humane) that is juxtaposed against a negative view of the outgroup.
>
> (Wainryb & Recchia, 2014, p. 3)

Polarized collective identity can work as a shield against some of the harm caused when a young person is exposed to the violence and senselessness of war; however, such an identity may perpetuate conflicts for generations to come and can derail a young person's identity development and adaptation in the long run (Wainryb & Recchia, 2014). Although finding oneself may at times appear to be a luxury, it is indeed essential to fostering youth development and harmony between social groups and may even be essential to addressing some of the most pressing problems of the day. In keeping with these ideas, the general aim of this volume is to better understand the essence of adolescent and emerging/young adult identity through a variety of perspectives and special topics in order to encourage informed research and intervention strategies that will facilitate the identity formation process.

Up through the 1960s, much of the literature on adolescent psychology came from psychoanalytic treatment centers. There was often a stress on the "universality of ego weakness" in adolescence and the depiction of an ego "besieged by the drives and unable to rely on the now-dangerous parental ego for support" (Josselson, 1980, p. 188). Such portrayals lay at the heart of the "turmoil" theory of adolescent development, which presented storm and stress as normative features of the teenage years. It was only when researchers of the 1960s and the 1970s (e.g., Douvan & Adelson, 1966; Offer & Offer, 1974) began to find little evidence of psychopathology or even much storm and stress at all among large samples of adolescents in the general population of the U.S. that attention began to shift from clinical to more normative populations for an understanding of the developmental processes occurring during adolescence.

In the following decades, the millennials (the generation born after 1980) began their entrance into late adolescence and early adulthood. These younger members of society were noteworthy both for their ethnic diversity and for their competence with the use of technology (Pew Research Center, 2010), which differentiated them from previous generations. General social attitudes toward adolescents and young adults have also been changing over these years, from considerable negative stereotyping about adolescent behaviors – rebellious, self-centered, and even delinquent ("Generation Me"; Twenge, 2006) – to the growing contemporary focus on youth and their many constructive capacities, likely an influence of several positive frameworks that have advanced what is known about youth development – that is, positive psychology, positive youth development, and social emotional learning (Tolan et al., 2016). Subsequent generations of young people, for example, Generation Z (born late 1990s to early 2000s), are now in young adulthood, and the oldest members of Generation Alpha (born 2010 through 2025) are now entering middle adolescence. These young people are or have grown up in the context of dramatic and sweeping historical changes in the development of digital tools, and at the same time, they have been exposed to very stressful events, such as violence, sexual harassment, and immigration (American Psychological Association, 2018), and more recently, the global pandemic of COVID-19.

Adolescent identity development figures prominently as a target for intervention and change in a diversity of current promotion and prevention intervention efforts with adolescents (e.g., Eichas et al., 2021). Eichas and his colleagues (Eichas et al., 2021) have been involved in developing and evaluating positive youth development interventions that have a particular focus on supporting adolescent identity development, while Umaña-Taylor et al.'s (2018) intervention called the Identity Project has shown positive benefits in adolescents in groups with ethnic minority and majority social positions in the U.S. (Umaña-Taylor et al., 2018) and also in Europe (Juang & Hwang, 2024).

Literature on adolescent and emerging/young adult development has also mushroomed over the past decades, with the creation of journals and societies devoted solely to research on these phases of the life cycle. Additionally, during these life stages, there has been greater specialization in textbooks and popular offerings. A number of supplementary textbooks now deal with selected issues of adolescence and emerging adulthood, including the current volume on identity. Interest in identity has also been evidenced by the appearance of several new journals devoted solely to themes of self and/or identity.

It is the intention of this book to examine prominent theories and special topics related to identity development during adolescence and young adulthood. The task of identity formation, revision, and maintenance is a lifelong challenge, and this volume also highlights the role that adolescent identity resolutions play in ongoing development throughout adulthood. While some less-than-optimal identity outcomes will be presented, the focus of this volume rests primarily on those normative identity changes of adolescence that evolve slowly over time to set the foundations for entry into adult life.

Frankie's own identity struggles that opened this chapter may be understood through a variety of different lenses. Historical, sociocultural, and psychosocial traditions have all arisen to account for various dimensions of identity development during adolescence and beyond. Under these broad labels, a number of specific approaches to understanding identity development have evolved. It is our intention below to note only the general emphases within each basic tradition and to describe aspects of these approaches in more detail in the chapters that follow.

Historical Approaches to Adolescent Identity

Were Frankie born in an earlier *historical* era, her story would probably not have given rise to a literary novel, for self-definition and finding a place in the world would not have been such difficult problems. As Erikson (1975) noted, the issue of identity holds historical relativity; Lifton (as cited in Goren & Alpert, 2017) has also addressed the power that general cultural values and group pressures have in a particular historical context to influence individual identity. Erikson (1975) suggested that identity only became a matter of concern in the U.S. late in the nineteenth century because a new generation of immigrants was attempting to define themselves in a land far removed from their ancestral homes. Baumeister (1986, 1987) and Burkitt (2011) have provided excellent and extensive overviews that illustrate the importance of historical times and forces to how identity is conceived and experienced in America and in other technologically advanced nations over time.

For example, in speaking to the Western European experience, Baumeister (1986, 1987) found that medieval adolescent and adult identities in these societies were defined in a very straightforward manner. The social rank and kinship network into which one was born determined one's place for life. While some changes of title or role were inevitable over time, general possibilities were circumscribed by the clan. In the early modern period, the rise of a middle class began a shift in the standard for self-definition, when wealth rather than kinship ties became the new measure of social status and hence self-definition. The later Protestant split and subsequent decline of the Christian faith gave rise to an era in which individuals became able to accept or reject the religious traditions of their forebears. During the Romantic era, most people still espoused Christian beliefs, but these held less influence over their daily lives. Furthermore, society was often perceived to be oppressive, and the need to reject some of its demands was recognized. By the Victorian era, late adolescents and adults increasingly began to reject Christian dogma, and a focal concern was whether or not morality could survive without religion. Thus, Victorian adolescents had to define their adult identities without clear guidelines in the midst of general cultural uncertainty regarding issues of appropriate values (Baumeister, 1986, 1987).

Such difficulties for adolescents in the U.S. and some Western European nations continued into the twentieth and twenty-first centuries, as the process of self-definition and identity formation became normative developmental tasks (Erikson, 1968). Cushman (1990) further suggested that, at least in the U.S., the absence of community, tradition, and shared meaning created the conditions for an "empty self," a state of being in which adolescents and adults alike experienced chronic emotional hunger. Cushman (1990) argued that the "empty self" attempted to be soothed, to be "filled up" by consumer products, and that advertising and psychotherapy were the two professions that Cushman cited as being most involved in individuals' attempts to heal the "empty self." In the twenty-first century, multiple poly-crises and youth movements advocating for greater equality and unprecedented technological changes (online identity and the unknown impacts of artificial intelligence) and global mobility related to crises and opportunities mark the sociocultural landscape of contemporary identity development for today's youth (e.g., Crocetti et al., 2024).

However, even within the aforementioned challenges, there has also been recent movement, thanks to the influence of positive views on youth development to consider and support adolescents and young adults in their efforts to formulate meaningful identities within their social contexts by focusing on strengths and opportunities for thriving with identity as a focal point (e.g., Eichas et al., 2021; Juang & Hwang, 2024). Thus, in historical terms, the issue of self-definition and identity formation, at least for many adolescents and young adults in the U.S. and in some Western European nations, is a relatively recent phenomenon (Baumeister, 1986, 1987). See Burkitt (2011) for a historical analysis that traces identity and self-related issues further back in time, but also from a Western European social perspective.

Expanding our horizon beyond the West, what identity is and how it has been studied in non-Western contexts has not been well integrated into the study of identity within the field of psychology. Since around 2000, identity formation in different cultural contexts has increasingly gained attention (e.g., Berman, 2011; Schwartz et al., 2012). For instance, Sugimura and Mizokami (2012) argued that the phenomenon of identity formation is clearly observed in contemporary Japan – one of the Eastern countries where young people had traditionally followed the norms given by the society, community, and family to which they belonged. Younger generations after World War II have rapidly moved toward Westernization and enjoyed more individualized lifestyles and, thus, have been striving for their own sense of agency and identity (Sugimura & Mizokami, 2012). At the same time, however, the process of identity formation in Japan (Arnett et al., 2014; Sugimura, 2020) and some other Eastern countries such as China (Sugimura et al., 2021) occurs in the tension between emerging individualism and traditional collectivistic values. Sugimura (2007) found such tension in the narratives of one Japanese adolescent:

> I like psychology, and I want to make use of what I have learned. . . . When I wondered what occupation could make best use of my knowledge of psychology, I found a psychological position in the public service, and that's why it became one of the options. Then, the direction started to be obvious before my parents told me they wanted me to work for the government [not as a psychologist but a government official]. . . . I felt they implied that, and I had to consider that. . . . Their feelings were that they wanted me to get a well secured job. . . . Their auras[2] waft and tell me they want me to get a well-secured job.
>
> (Ayako, Sugimura, 2007, pp. 125–126)

The process of identity formation in non-Western contexts varies considerably across nations, as do the unique histories of respective cultures. Thus, a deeper understanding of identity development in non-Western cultural contexts is currently under active examination (e.g., Adams & van de Vijver, 2021).

Sociocultural Approaches to Adolescent Identity

In her efforts toward self-definition, Frankie voices her intense desire to break free – to be free of her family, town, and many of the sociocultural conditions that constrain her. Berenice, who is African American and the family housekeeper, says that she understands Frankie's longings, but that she, Berenice, is even more "caught" than Frankie because Berenice is Black. Frankie and Berenice are "caught" by the combined facets of their social class and gender as well as the technological influences, societal norms, and legal constraints for adolescents and African Americans living in the South at that historical time. Some would contend that sociocultural conditions of society actually create problems of identity and self-definition in the first place (Baumeister, 1986, 1987).

A variety of theoretical orientations to identity is represented within the general sociocultural approach, ranging from proposals that identity is largely a reflection of an individual's adaptations to social and cultural conditions (e.g., Côté, 2019) to a focus on the reciprocal interactions between person and context (e.g., Galliher et al., 2017; McLean, 2021).

One group of writers working within this general sociocultural framework has focused more strongly on contextual implications that these conditions hold for individual identity formation. Triandis (1989), for example, differentiated "tight" from "loose" societies on the basis of how much opportunity for individual choice a society would allow. Thus, enormous variation may be seen across cultural contexts in how much latitude youth are given for creating or realizing their identity interests. Adolescents in many collectivist societies were not traditionally faced with the choices and decisions that youths in cultures that allow for choice must make in defining their own identities (Côté, 2019). Tupuola (1993) interviewed New Zealand- and Samoan-born youths living in New Zealand in focus groups about their experiences of adolescence. One Samoan-born participant summarized the responses of many as follows:

> I feel I still can't answer the adolescent thing. As a Samoan born, I had never heard of it [adolescence] until I came to New Zealand. I don't think it was part of my life because it is a western concept, and from a non-western society all those development stages didn't relate to me. All I know is that my *aiga* [family] and my community and my culture are important. They determine the way I behave, think, and feel. . . .
>
> (Subject #3, Tupuola, 1993, p. 308)

Cultural conditions for this young woman made the issue of identity formation and finding her place in the social milieu a rather straightforward process. While some of the roles that she was expected to fulfill were not easy, the actual process of identifying suitable roles for herself within the larger society was not, in itself, a complex problem. However, one thing that should be acknowledged here is that sociocultural conditions for adolescent identity development can change over time. In the twenty-first century, many of the collectivist societies are rapidly changing toward valuing individualism amid the era of globalization. Nowadays, each of the traditionally collectivistic societies, such as those in East Asia (e.g., China and Japan), reveals a unique mixture of individualism and collectivism. This shift in cultural values can make adolescents living in such changing contexts increasingly interested in defining their own identities (Sugimura et al., 2021).

Côté (2006, 2015) has nicely summarized a typology of several different and fundamental assumptions that various models of identity development take in describing the nature of the relationship between individual and society. These differences in approach are based on several factors: (1) whether the focus is primarily on the individual or on society in identity's formative process; (2) whether or not social reality is understood as fixed and independent of human consciousness (objectivism) or dependent on social constructions (subjectivism); and (3) whether or not the existing social order is accepted "as is" and represents a universal process or is viewed critically, wherein the researcher assumes that all identity processes are contextually based. All approaches to identity that are overviewed in this volume can be understood in terms of their answers to these basic assumptions. The sociocultural approach highlighted later in this book is one that is highly visible in the field of human development and cultural psychology (e.g., Rogoff, 2016) and is focused on how the individual and context, including culture, come together to produce identity development.

Psychosocial Approaches to Adolescent Identity

Social and historical circumstances have left many present-day teenagers with ambiguous role prescriptions and uncertain social transitions that encourage a struggle with the problem of identity. A number of social scientists, however, have focused more intently on what Frankie described as a changing sense of "I" – on an internal, psychological transformation of the sense of herself and consequent ways of making sense of her life experiences within changing social circumstances. The beginnings of psychological restructuring during adolescence in combination with societal responses have brought Frankie's identity questions to the surface, according to this view. And while sociocultural factors undoubtedly may accelerate, delay, or even arrest this process, this general view argues that sequential changes in the psychological transformation of the self and its way of understanding the world do exist. Changes in biological, cognitive, and affective processes have been deemed accountable for alterations to the subjective sense of identity frequently experienced during life's second decade – at least in those societies where adult identities for youth are not prescribed.

From psychodynamic beginnings, Erik Erikson's work was the first to appreciate the *psychosocial* nature of identity with the important role played by the community in recognizing, supporting, and thus helping to shape the adolescent ego. As a developmental theorist, he distinguished the identity solutions of *introjection* during infancy and *identification* in childhood from the process of *identity formation* during adolescence. It is during adolescence that Erikson saw opportunities for identity resolution through a synthesis that incorporated yet transcended all previous identifications to produce a new whole, based upon yet qualitatively different from that which had gone before:

> The final identity, then, as fixed at the end of adolescence, is superordinated to any single identification with individuals of the past: it includes all significant identifications, but it also alters them in order to make a unique and reasonably coherent whole of them.
>
> (Erikson, 1968, p. 161)

Here, that self of childhood, derived from significant identifications with important others, must, during adolescence, give way to a self based upon, yet transcending, those foundations to create a new whole greater than the sum of its parts. Significant others now become important not merely as potential sources of identification but rather as independent agents, helping to recognize and support the "real me." Erikson appreciated the importance of context to this process. He saw identity development also as a reciprocal relationship between individual and context, a process of recognizing and being recognized by others.

Narrative approaches to adolescent identity also draw many ideas from Erikson's original writings. Although somewhat varied in their emphases, narrative writers commonly underscore the process of autobiographical reasoning and how people make sense of the contents of their past experiences to create a coherent identity in the present that is projected and reevaluated in the future. The stories that one tells about one's life in an attempt to create a coherent identity are not intended to be an accurate portrayal of every life experience; rather, one chooses what is meaningful at a particular point in time and tries to make sense of the content of that experience (McAdams, 2015). Whether or not one has an audience, people work and rework their life experiences through a narrative in an attempt to make some sense of things and to create an identity. Narratives generally aim to integrate questions about who I am now with how I came to be this way and where my life might be going next (McAdams, 2015). McLean (2008) and Fivush et al. (2011) noted that an optimal narrative identity helps individuals find purpose and meaning in life and a sense of coherence and unity within themselves; at the same time, an optimal narrative should be flexible and enable one to incorporate new insights, life lessons, and experiences over time. Coherence in one's narrative likely reflects a sense of identity continuity over time, while "irreconcilable differences between the me-that-was and the me-that-is can be understood as incoherence in identity" (Pasupathi, 2014, p. 21).

Adolescent Identity in the Context of Lifespan Development

While various schools of thought place different emphases on the role of the individual and the social and/or cultural setting in the identity formation process of adolescence and young adulthood, most conceptualize identity formation as a lifelong enterprise. Thus, this volume also emphasizes adolescent and young adult identity development in a manner reflecting this understanding. Just as the significance of a painting cannot be fully grasped without knowledge of its contextual origins and resulting influences on later art, so identity and its development and eventual consolidation during adolescence and young adulthood cannot be fully appreciated without knowledge of its childhood antecedents and consequent adult possibilities.

Identity as the Balance Between Self and Other

Despite the use of different identity-related concepts in contemporary theories of adolescent and young adult identity development, a basic commonality is present as one looks across the general theoretical approaches to the essence of identity. In some way, shape, or form, identity is commonly defined as a balance or interaction between that which is considered to be self and that which is considered to be other. The means by which we differentiate ourselves from other people in our lives as we become aware of our own organic functions constitute the very core of our experiences of personal identity. American novelist Thomas Wolfe struggled through his life to differentiate his own identity from that of the internalized image of his primary caretaker. This intrapsychic battle was replayed in many of his adolescent and adult relationships: "His popularity [as a writer] is partially due to his being a chronicler of the human aspirations for individuation, for the establishment of a real self, as well as of the feelings of loss associated with this search" (Masterson, 1986, speech audio recording). Though using differing terms and concepts, Erikson, McAdams, Pasupathi, Côté, Rogoff, Rivas-Drake, and others all provide descriptions of how the balancing and rebalancing of boundaries between self and other produce more differentiated experiences of identity as well as new forms of relationship with other people and social groups at various life stages. Adolescence encompasses one phase of heightened activity for most in this intrapsychic and interpersonal juggling act.

The Structure of This Volume and Its Chapters

In the preparation for a new edition of any volume, there is a temptation in updating information to delete "older" material, leaving the reader with a clear sense of what research is currently being undertaken but with little or no appreciation for the foundations upon which that current research has been built. In this volume, we certainly have updated new trends in identity theory and research from a variety of perspectives and present the most current information on key topics of contemporary interest in the field, but we have also retained a focus on the origins of these concepts and their development through their conceptions to the present time. In this way, we hope that readers will have a deeper appreciation of the origins of identity concepts and how they have been modified and adapted through the years to arrive at current understandings and research trends, along with the implications that current work holds for social response.

With this long-range overview goal in mind, the initial three chapters of this volume following this introduction begin with theory and view identity development during adolescence and young adulthood with varying emphases placed on the role of the individual and the role of the environment in this process (Chapters 2–4). The following three chapters, Chapters 5–7, concern special identity issues particularly impacting the current generations of youth – those youth navigating globalization and immigration experiences, the challenge of intersectionality as it relates to gender and sexuality, as well as technology, and how each affects and is affected by the identity formation process of adolescence. The concluding chapter, Chapter 8, places the identity formation process of adolescence and young adulthood within the context of lifespan identity development, focusing, in particular, on how the resolutions to identity issues of adolescence may have long-term implications for ongoing developments during adulthood.

The three theoretical chapters (Chapters 2–4) follow a similar pattern of presentation. One major theorist and/or researcher, who has played a key role in the development of the particular approach to identity, is introduced at the chapter's beginning. A brief biographical statement is presented as a way of illustrating the historical context of important ideas in the field, as well as to provide the reader with a sense of the excitement of discovery and striving after innovation that comes from the study of identity development as viewed by that scholar. Key components of identity from this theoretical perspective are presented, followed by a statement of what constitutes an optimal identity from this particular orientation. Criticisms of the construct are detailed as well as an overview of the historical backdrop to key ideas. The focus then turns to research measures that have been developed to assess key dimensions of the adolescent identity formation process within this framework, as well as major research findings that have appeared over time. A section on current trends in identity research follows, and a discussion of the implications that each theory holds for social response in the promotion of optimal identity development for adolescents and young adults concludes each theoretical chapter presented in this volume.

Three subsequent chapters (Chapters 5–7) then turn to explore bicultural identity development, the concept of intersectionality and identity integration with reference to gender and sexual identity, and the use of digital technologies as a context and catalyst for adolescent identity formation. Specifically, Chapter 5 addresses how young people negotiate multiple cultures simultaneously in the context of globalization and/or immigration experiences. The interconnectivity of the world is rapidly changing, and so understanding bicultural identity development among adolescents across multiple cultures and national contexts is an urgent task. In Chapter 6, attention is placed on the particular intersection of adolescent gender and sexuality as an illustration of research that crosses boundaries and offers guidelines for advances in future research practice (Cole, 2009). Intersectionality and the concept of identity integration emphasize the importance of understanding identity in its totality and complexity. In Chapter 7, there is an exploration of the relatively new research field on adolescent identity development in digital landscapes. Even though this is a new field, exciting studies are being launched, and several future directions for research are evident.

A concluding chapter focuses on the role that identity resolutions of adolescence and young adulthood have for ongoing facets of identity development over the course of adulthood. The chapter examines available theory and research across the models examined in this volume to focus on some of the normative changes in identity that are likely to occur through ongoing phases of adult life. The chapter considers dimensions of one's identity formed during adolescence and young adulthood that are likely both to remain stable and to change over time. It also questions whether or not there are different types of contexts that may be associated with different patterns of identity stability and change during adult life. And in conclusion, the chapter considers how adolescent resolutions to identity are likely to impact one's capacity for intimacy, generativity, and integrity during adult life.

Summary

The general aim of this volume is to understand how adolescents and young adults navigate through life, more or less successfully, to develop a sense of who they are and how they can best find personal satisfaction and meaning in the adult world. The volume also highlights the ways in which context interacts with individual factors to shape individual identity pathways. Three models of adolescent identity formation are presented, accompanied by critical comment, reviews of related research, and a discussion of the implications that each theory holds for social response to promote optimal identity development. Each model is based on particular assumptions, focuses on specific understandings of identity, adopts particular research methods, holds particular views about the role of context in development, and describes differing mechanisms for change in addition to differing implications for social response. Immigration experiences are becoming increasingly common globally; contemporary meanings of gender and sexuality as well as technology and social media use play particular roles in the identity formation experience of many adolescents, and some of the impacts of these changing social forces on adolescent identity development are reviewed. A discussion of the place that adolescent identity formation holds in ongoing identity development during adulthood and the role that adolescent identity resolutions have for addressing issues of intimacy, generativity, and integrity during adult life concludes this volume. Einstein once noted that it is the theory that decides what we can observe. It is hoped that the theoretical approaches and special identity topics presented in this volume, however, will in no way set limits to future ways of understanding, researching, and responding to the identity formation process of adolescence.

Notes

1 Emerging adulthood (18–29 years old) was introduced by Arnett (2000). This term is posited to be descriptive of people who delay some aspects of the transition to adulthood, either in terms of their own view of themselves as an adult or in terms of individuals delaying some objective social markers of adulthood (Arnett, 2000, 2024). In Arnett's view, young adulthood refers to chronologically younger individuals who are adults in their cultures, in relation to subjective and objective indicators (Arnett, 2024). However, others writing about identity have used the term "young adulthood" to refer to those in the decade of the 20s or to working or unemployed youths who have completed their years of formal education (e.g., Luyckx and colleagues in some of their identity studies, such as Hatano et al., 2022). We have thus opted to use the terms "emerging" and "young adulthood" interchangeably in this book.

2 The term "aura" is common slang used by young people in Japan for the invisible atmosphere that others are cloaked in. In this narrative, the participant used this term to describe the unspoken but subtle expectations of parents.

References

Adams, B. G., & van de Vijver, F. J. R. (Eds.). (2021). *Non-Western identity: Research and perspectives* (pp. 33–47). Springer. https://doi.org/10.1007/978-3-030-77242-0_3

American Psychological Association. (2018). *Stress in America: Generation Z.* https://www.apa.org/news/press/releases/stress/2018/stress-gen-z.pdf

Arnett, J. J. (2000). Emerging adulthood: A theory of development from the late teens through the twenties. *American Psychologist, 55*, 469–480. 10.1037//0003-066X.55.5.469
Arnett, J. J. (2024). *Emerging adulthood: The winding road from the late teens through the twenties* (3rd ed.). Oxford University Press. 10.1093/oso/9780197695937.001.0001
Arnett, J. J., Žukauskienė, R., & Sugimura, K. (2014). The new life stage of emerging adulthood at ages 18–29 years: Implications for mental health. *The Lancet Psychiatry, 1*(7), 569–576. https://doi.org/10.1016/S2215-0366(14)00080-7
Baumeister, R. F. (1986). *Identity: Cultural change and the struggle for self.* Oxford University Press.
Baumeister, R. F. (1987). How the self became a problem: A psychological review. *Journal of Personality and Social Psychology, 52*(1), 163–176. https://doi.org/10.1037/0022-3514.52.1.163
Berman, S. L. (2011). International perspectives on identity development. *Child and Youth Care Forum, 40*(1), 1–5. https://doi.org/10.1007/s10566-010-9131-5
Burkitt, I. (2011). Identity construction in sociohistorical context. In S. J. Schwartz, K. Luyckx, & V. L. Vignoles (Eds.), *Handbook of identity theory and research, Vol. 1* (pp. 267–283). Springer. https://doi.org/10.1007/978-1-4419-7988-9_12
Cole, E. R. (2009). Intersectionality and research in psychology. *American Psychologist, 64*(3), 170–180. https://doi.org/10.1037/a0014564
Côté, J. E. (2006). Identity studies: How close are we to developing a social science of identity? An Appraisal of the field. *Identity: An International Journal of Theory and Research, 6*(1), 3–25. https://doi.org/10.1207/s1532706xid0601_2
Côté, J. E. (2015). Identity formation research from a critical perspective: Is a social science developing? In K. C. McLean & M. Syed (Eds.), *Oxford handbook of identity development* [E-reader version] (pp. 527–538). Oxford University Press. https://doi.org/10.1093/oxfordhb/9780199936564.013.015
Côté, J. E. (2019). *Youth development in identity societies: Paradoxes of purpose*. Routledge. https://doi.org/10.4324/9780429433856
Crocetti, E., Karataş, S., Branje, S., Bobba, B., & Rubini, M. (2024). Navigating across heritage and destination cultures: How personal identity and social identification processes relate to domain-specific acculturation orientations in adolescence. *Journal of Youth and Adolescence, 53*(2), 397–415. https://doi.org/10.1007/s10964-023-01870-y
Cushman, P. (1990). Why the self is empty. *American Psychologist, 45*(5), 599–611. https://doi.org/10.1037/0003-066X.45.5.599
Douvan, E., & Adelson, J. (1966). *The adolescent experience*. Wiley.
Eichas, K., Montgomery, M. J., Meca, A., Garcia, A. J., & Garcia, A. (2021). Engaging marginalized youth in positive development: The changing lives program. In R. Dimitrova, & N. Wiium (Eds.), *Handbook of positive youth development: Advancing research, policy, and practice in global contexts* (pp. 431–446). Springer Nature Switzerland AG. https://doi.org/10.1007/978-3-030-70262-5_29
Erikson, E. H. (1968). *Identity youth and crisis*. W. W. Norton.
Erikson, E. H. (1975). *Life history and the historical moment*. W. W. Norton.
Fivush, R., Habermas, T., Waters, T. E. A., & Zaman, W. (2011). The making of autobiographical memory: Intersections of culture, narratives and identity. *International Journal of Psychology, 46*(5), 321–345. https://doi.org/10.1080/00207594.2011.596541
Galliher, R. V., McLean, K. C., & Syed, M. (2017). An integrated developmental model for studying identity content in context. *Developmental Psychology, 53*(11), 2011–2022. https://doi.org/10.1037/dev0000299
Goren, E., & Alpert, J. L. (2017). The analyst as witness, historian, and activist: A conversation with Robert J. Lifton. In E. R. Goren & J. L. Alpert (Eds.), *Psychoanalysis, trauma, and community: History and contemporary reappraisals* (pp. 165–187). Routledge. https://lccn.loc.gov/2016022884
Hammack, P. L. (2014). Theoretical foundations of identity. In K. C. McLean & M. Syed (Eds.), *The Oxford handbook of identity development* [E-reader version] (pp. 1–37). Oxford University Press. https://doi.org/10.1093/oxfordhb/9780199936564.013.027

Hatano, K., Luyckx, K., Hihara, S., Sugimura, K., & Becht, A. I. (2022). Daily identity processes and emotions in young adulthood: A five-day daily-diary method. *Journal of Youth and Adolescence, 51*(9), 1815–1828. https://doi.org/10.1007/s10964-022-01629-x
Josselson, R. (1980). Ego development in adolescence. In J. Adelson (Ed.), *Handbook of adolescent psychology* (pp. 186–199). Wiley.
Juang, L. P., & Hwang, C. P. (2024). The importance of ethnic-racialized identities to becoming and being culturally responsive and equity minded educators. *Identity: An International Journal of Theory and Research, 24*(4), 257–268. https://doi.org/10.1080/15283488.2024.2388248
Masterson, J. F. (1986). Creativity as a vehicle to establish a real self: Jean Paul Sartre, Edvard Munch, Thomas Wolfe. In J. F. Masterson (Ed.), *The real self: A developmental and object relations approach* (cassette recording 4). Masterson Group.
McAdams, D. P. (2015). Three lines of personality development: A conceptual itinerary. *European Psychologist, 20*(4), 252–264. https://doi.org/10.1027/1016-9040/a000236
McCullers, C. (1946). *The member of the wedding.* Houghton Mifflin Company.
McLean, K. C. (2008). Stories of the young and the old: Personal continuity and narrative identity. *Developmental Psychology, 44*(1), 254–264. https://doi.org/10.1037/0012-1649.44.1.254
McLean, K. C. (Ed.). (2021). *Cultural methods in psychology: Describing and transforming cultures* [E-reader version]. Oxford University Press. https://doi.org/10.1093/oso/9780190095949.001.0001
Offer, D., & Offer, J. (1974). Normal adolescent males: The high school and college years. *Journal of the American College Health Association, 22*(3), 209–215.
Pasupathi, M. (2014). Autobiographical reasoning and my discontent: Alternative paths from narrative to identity. In K. C. McLean & M. Syed (Eds.), *The Oxford handbook of identity development* [E-reader version] (pp. 1–30). Oxford University Press. https://doi.org/10.1093/oxfordhb/9780199936564.013.002
Pew Research Center. (2010). *Millennials: Confident, connected, and open to change.* Pew Research Center. https://www.pewresearch.org/wp-content/uploads/sites/20/2010/02/millennials-confident-connected-open-to-change.pdf
Rogoff, B. (2016). Culture and participation: A paradigm shift. *Current Opinion in Psychology, 8*(April), 182–189. https://doi.org/10.1016/j.copsyc.2015.12.002
Schwartz, S. J., Zamboanga, B. L., Meca, A., & Ritchie, R. A. (2012). Identity around the world: An overview. *New Directions for Child and Adolescent Development, 2012*(138), 1–18. https://doi.org/10.1002/cad.20019
Sugimura, K. (2007). Transitions in the process of identity formation among Japanese female adolescents: A relational viewpoint. In R. Josselson, A. Lieblich, & D. P. McAdams (Eds.), *The meaning of others: Narrative studies of relationships* (pp. 117–142). American Psychological Association. https://doi.org/10.1037/11580-012
Sugimura, K. (2020). Adolescent identity development in Japan. *Child Development Perspectives, 14*(2), 71–77. https://doi.org/10.1111/cdep.12359
Sugimura, K., & Mizokami, S. (2012). Personal identity in Japan. *New Directions for Child and Adolescent Development, 2012*(138), 123–143. https://doi.org/10.1002/cad.20025
Sugimura, K., Umemura, T., & Nelson, L. J. (2021). Identity development in East Asia. In B. G. Adams & F. J. R. van de Vijver (Eds.), *Non-Western identity: Research and perspectives* (pp. 33–47). Springer. https://doi.org/10.1007/978-3-030-77242-0_3
Tolan, P., Ross, K., Arkin, N., Godine, N., & Clark, E. (2016). Toward an integrated approach to positive development: Implications for intervention. *Applied Developmental Science, 20*(3), 214–236. https://doi.org/10.1080/10888691.2016.1146080
Triandis, H. C. (1989). The self and social behavior in differing cultural contexts. *Psychological Review, 96*(3), 506–520. https://doi.org/10.1037/0033-295X.96.3.506
Tupuola, A. M. (1993). *Critical analysis of adolescent development – a Samoan women's perspective* [Unpublished master's thesis]. Victoria University of Wellington, New Zealand.

Twenge, J. M. (2006). *Generation me: Why today's young Americans are more confident, assertive, entitled – and more miserable than ever before*. Free Press.
Umaña-Taylor, A. J., Kornienko, O., Douglass Bayless, S., & Updegraff, K. A. (2018). A universal intervention program increases ethnic-racial identity exploration and resolution to predict adolescent psychosocial functioning one year later. *Journal of Youth and Adolescence*, *47*(1), 1–15. https://doi.org/10.1007/s10964-017-0766-5
Wainryb, C., & Recchia, H. (2014). Youths' constructions of meanings about experiences with political conflict: Implications for processes of identity development. In K. C. McLean & Syed, M. (Eds.), *The Oxford handbook of identity development* [E-reader version] (pp. 1–33). Oxford University Press. https://doi.org/10.1093/oxfordhb/9780199936564.013.008

2 Adolescence as Identity Synthesis – Erikson's Psychosocial Approach

> Siddhartha reflected deeply as he went on his way. He realized that he was no longer a youth; he was now a man. He realized that something had left him, like the old skin that a snake sheds. Something was no longer in him, something that had accompanied him right through his youth and was part of him: this was the desire to have teachers and to listen to their teachings. He had left the last teacher he had met, even he, the greatest and wisest teacher, the holiest, the Buddha. He had to leave him; he could not accept his teachings.
>
> (Hermann Hesse, *Siddhartha*, 1951, p. 30)

In his novel *Siddhartha*, Hermann Hesse movingly recounted the journey of a man in search of his own identity. The story opened in an idyllic communal setting along a sunny and tranquil riverbank (complete with a fig tree), as Siddhartha sensed the first nuances of inner discontent. Family and friends alike loved and admired Siddhartha, and his destiny as a prince among Brahmins was the fate envisaged for him by all. For Siddhartha, however, knowledge of such a future brought no peace of mind. After a final meditation, the young man announced his intention of joining the Samanas, a wandering group of ascetics who practiced a lifestyle in all ways contrary to the values held dear by childhood friends and mentors. Through such action, Siddhartha's single goal was to let the self die, to become empty, and to become something other than himself. Despite all efforts of self-denial through pain, hunger, thirst, and fatigue, however, Siddhartha could not escape his own existence. After several unsatisfying years with the Samanas, Siddhartha once more sought new hope for peace by testing the way of the Buddha in conquering the self. After a short time, it became clear, however, that such efforts would also fail to bring salvation, and it is at this point that we met Siddhartha ruminating on his newfound learnings in the opening quotation, as he left the grove of the Buddha. It seemed that neither complete identification with childhood's teachers nor their complete banishment from his existence could help Siddhartha to solve the riddle of the self and so structure an identity that would see him through (or at least into) adult life. Perhaps no piece of literature so adequately and accurately anticipates the themes central to Erikson's writings on identity formation during adolescence, and it is to Siddhartha we later return for illumination of Erikson's concepts.

DOI: 10.4324/9781003486336-2

Erik Erikson was the first psychoanalytic writer to inquire seriously into the phenomenon of identity formation during adolescence. His approach was based upon, but diverged in important ways from, Freud's biologically based psychosexual orientation to personality development. Erikson moved beyond classic psychoanalysis with its focus on the id and libidinal drivers of development to emphasize the ego and its adaptive capacities in the environment. Rather than viewing others as objects of cathexis important to intrapsychic functioning, as did Freud, Erikson saw others as interacting with and regulating the ego to provide a context in which the self could find meaning and coherence. Moving beyond Freud's goal of raising human misery to mere unhappiness, Erikson not only painted a more optimistic picture of human capabilities but also shifted the emphasis of psychoanalysis from pathology to healthy functioning. Finally, Erikson recognized that personality development did not end in adolescence but rather continued to evolve throughout the lifespan.

Erikson the Person

Erikson was born in Germany in 1902 to Danish parents. His birth was the result of an affair his mother had following the breakup of her first marriage. Erikson was raised by his mother and German pediatrician stepfather, whom his mother had met when Erik was three years old. Erikson did not learn of the circumstances of his biological parentage until adolescence. However, a sense of being "different," both as a stepson in a reconstituted family and as a blond, blue-eyed Dane growing up in a German Jewish community, pervaded much of Erikson's childhood. Questions regarding his biological father preoccupied Erikson's attentions throughout much of his life (Friedman, 1999). Upon graduating from high school and with no particular career plans, young Erikson was drawn to the role of an artist, a "passing" identity providing some income while still allowing the young man a psychosocial moratorium before choosing his life's work. Additionally, sketching gave him training in the recording of impressions, a skill vital to his later profession. The artist's vocational choice also made a definitive statement to his stepfather about the role in medicine the elder physician had envisaged for his stepson. From late adolescence, Erikson traveled throughout Europe until his mid-20s (Hopkins, 1995). He later responded to Robert Coles's questioning about his youth: "Yes, if ever an identity crisis was central and drawn out in somebody's life, it was so in mine" (Coles, 1970, p. 180).

It was eventually the invitation of childhood friend Peter Blos[1] to join the staff of a small school in Vienna that placed Erikson in a position to meet Freud's inner circle (Friedman, 1999). In Vienna, he was invited by Anna Freud to train and prepare to become a child psychoanalyst. Again, not quite belonging to Freud's community of medical rebels, Erikson's stepson relationship to the psychoanalytic profession did not furnish him with a more settled sense of vocational identity until much later, when his own artistic talents could be integrated with his psychoanalytic practice through theoretical writing – the sketching of impressions through linguistic rather than visual form. It was there in Vienna that Erikson also married

Canadian Joan Serson, who became his intellectual partner and editor for the rest of his life (Hopkins, 1995).

Erikson and Joan left Vienna with their two young sons as Hitler came to power in Germany, and they eventually migrated to Boston, where a psychoanalytic association had recently been formed. It was in this social context that Erikson, one of the society's few nonmedical members, found a professional niche as one of the area's first practicing child analysts (Friedman, 1999). Throughout his impressive career, Erikson accepted appointments at Yale, the University of California, Berkeley, the Austin Riggs Center, and Harvard, all without accruing a single earned academic degree beyond high school. It was in 1950 that Erikson's theoretical framework was adopted in total by the White House Conference on Children, which provided a national charter for child and adolescent development in the United States (U.S.). In 1978, Harvard University awarded Erikson an honorary doctorate and later established the Erik H. and Joan M. Erikson Center to provide a forum for interdisciplinary studies of the life cycle. Erikson died in 1994 following a brief illness, just prior to his 92nd birthday.

It is not surprising that the theme of identity, so central to Erikson's own life, became central in his writings on life-cycle development. Now, with at least ten books and a collection of individual papers dedicated to examining the nature of identity formation during adolescence and the life cycle, Erikson's contributions are an appropriate starting point for inquiries into adolescent identity development.

The Nature of Ego Identity

What then is identity, and how does it develop during adolescence? Erikson first used the term "ego identity" to describe a central disturbance among some returning World War II veterans who were experiencing a loss of sameness and continuity in their lives:

> What impressed me most was the loss in these men of a sense of identity. They knew who they were; they had a personal identity. But it was as if subjectively, their lives no longer hung together – and never would again. There was a central disturbance in what I then started to call ego identity.
>
> (Erikson, 1968, p. 42)

He continued by noting that it was often a decisive yet innocent moment in the lives of these soldiers wherein the needs of a man's social group, those of his biological organism, and those idiosyncratic to his own development and family history met in irreconcilable conflict, heralding the breakdown of personal meaning and life continuity.

Several concepts basic to Erikson's later work emerged from the observation of these veterans. First, identity seemed to be most easily definable through its absence or loss; it was only when one could no longer take for granted the fabric of one's unique existence that identity's foundational threads became exposed and more clearly apparent. It was through such loss of ego identity or its developmental failure that opportunity existed for understanding more normative modes of identity formation and the means by which society could foster optimal development. Erikson's clinical experience also sensitized him to questions of how identity formed and developed for the wider non-patient population.

Furthermore, the soldiers' tales brought the tripartite nature of identity into view. Freud had left psychoanalysis focused on the role played by biology in personality development. However, a somewhat dissatisfied Erikson believed that traditional psychoanalysis could not capture the real meaning of identity, for it did not have a means to understand the impact of the environment on individual personality development (Erikson, 1968). While biology was important to individual biography, so too were an individual's life history as well as the presiding cultural and historical context, argued the analyst. For one medical officer veteran who came to Erikson's attention, it was the combination of lowered group morale in his unit followed by group panic over loss of leadership (social and historical context), physical fatigue and illness (biological state), and his lifelong denial of anger following a traumatic childhood incident (individual life history) that culminated in his loss of ego identity and eventual treatment. Erikson conceptualized and defined identity in an interdisciplinary way; he believed that biological endowment, personal organization of experience, and cultural milieu all interact to give meaning, form, and continuity to one's unique existence.

Following his initial statements on identity, Erikson was persuaded to expand and elaborate on the construct. As a psychosocial phenomenon, he saw identity rooted both within the individual and within the communal culture (Erikson, 1970). Subjectively, the theorist suggested what it feels like to have a sense of identity by citing a letter from William James to his wife:

> A man's character is discernible in the mental or moral attitude in which, when it came upon him, he felt himself most deeply and intensely active and alive. At such moments there is a voice inside which speaks and says: "*This* is the real me!"
>
> (James, as cited in Erikson, 1968, p. 199)

For the individual, identity is partly conscious and partly unconscious. It gives one's life a feeling of sameness and continuity, purpose and direction, yet also a "quality of unselfconscious living"; it is also taken for granted by those in possession of it. Identity involves conflict. During adolescence, identity development involves a time when biological endowment and intellectual processes must eventually meet societal expectations for a suitable display of adult functioning. Identity depends upon the past and determines the future; rooted in childhood, it serves as a base from which to meet later life tasks (Erikson, 1970). Erikson (1968) did not elaborate in similar detail on the "social" side of the psychosocial partnership, though he did stress the importance of the social context in providing the child with something to value and adhere to. Erikson also viewed identity as a generational issue, pointing to the responsibility of adults to provide an ideological framework for youth (if only for the purpose of giving adolescents a structure against which to rebel and forge their own values).

Identity: Development and Resolutions

Perhaps Erikson's most concise account of how identity develops is to be found in *Toys and Reasons*: "[T]he process of identity formation depends on the interplay of what young persons at the end of childhood have come to mean to themselves and what they now appear to mean to those who become significant to them" (Erikson, 1977, p. 106). This deceptively simple statement is based upon a number of developmental principles basic to Erikson's concept of identity. The theorist distinguished identity formation, which generally occurs during adolescence, from the childhood processes of introjection and identification. That first sense of "I," he suggested, emerged only through the trustful interplay with a parental figure during infancy (Erikson, 1968). It was in the experience of a safe relationship that the child came to know itself as distinct from its beloved developmental partner. At this point, *introjection*, or the incorporation of another's image, operated and prepared the way for more mature forms of identity resolution. During childhood, "being like" admired others and assuming their roles and values reflects the mechanism of *identification* as the primary means by which the self is structured. It is only when the adolescent is able to select some and discard other childhood identifications in accordance with his or her interests, talents, and values that *identity formation* occurs. Identity formation involves a synthesis of these earlier identifications into a new configuration, based upon but different from the sum of its individual parts. It is a process also dependent on social response; identity formation relies on the way society "identifies the young individual, recognizing him as somebody who had to become the way he[2] is and who, being the way he is, is taken for granted" (Erikson, 1968, p. 159). Thus, identity does not first emerge during adolescence but rather evolves through earlier stages of development and continues to be reshaped throughout the life cycle.

Erikson used the term *epigenesis* to describe this property of identity development as well as broader aspects of personality change. Meaning literally "upon" (*epi*) "emergence" (*genesis*), epigenesis implies that "one item develops on top of another in space and time" (Evans, 1967, p. 21, 22). Suffice it to say at this point that identity formation during adolescence emerges from what young people (through their introjections and identifications) at the end of childhood come to know as their selves. Yet it also transcends these earlier forms in the individual's realization and society's recognition of personal interests and talents.

To return now to Siddhartha and his beleaguered quest: In his journey, this Brahmin's son tried many means by which Erikson suggested identity resolution was possible. Through his childhood years, Siddhartha successfully appeared to have internalized and identified with his father and the later vocational, ideological, and sexual roles he was expected to play as an up-and-coming Brahmin priest. We are told of his father's happiness in watching the son grow up to become a great priest among Brahmins. A psychosocial *foreclosure* appeared well on the way, whereby Siddhartha seemed prepared to step into predetermined roles in his family and culture. While Erikson did not detail this identity solution, it has been elaborated through empirical research, which will be presented in a later section of this chapter.

Soon, however, shadows passed across Siddhartha's eyes, and restlessness made its presence known as he began to feel the beginnings of discontentment within. The late adolescent's decision to join a group of wandering ascetics whose values presented a diametric contrast to all those of his own heritage seemed to be a choice of *negative identity*. Such a solution for Siddhartha illustrates the ego's attempt to adhere to something distinctly other than its past, to go beyond the bounds of given experience, and to begin anew. Here, there was no synthesis of previous identifications to give some foundation to later identity but rather an effort to jettison all identifications and start the task of creating a self completely different from its origins. Siddhartha attempted to cancel his previous self through the denial of physical needs and the self-destructive infliction of pain. Erikson commented on such a form of negative identity resolution:

> Such vindictive choices of a negative identity represent, of course, a desperate attempt at regaining some mastery in a situation in which the available positive identity elements cancel each other out. The history of such a choice reveals a set of conditions in which it is easier for the patient to derive a sense of identity out of a total identification with that which he is least supposed to be than to struggle for a feeling of reality in acceptable roles which are unattainable with his inner means.
>
> (Erikson, 1968, p. 176)

For some troubled adolescents, it is better to be somebody totally other than what existed during childhood rather than struggle to reintegrate the past into a present and future having some continuity with one's previous existence. There is often much relief following the choice of a negative identity, however destructive that solution may ultimately be.

For Siddhartha, however, that relief did not come. His realization came that complete immersion in the "contra-culture" of the Samanas' community and later the Buddhist collective failed to solve the riddle of his existence. He departed, and it is at this point that the young man continued his ruminations that opened this chapter:

> The reason why I do not know anything about myself, the reason why Siddhartha has remained alien and unknown to myself is due to one thing, to one single thing – I was afraid of myself, I was fleeing from myself. . . . I wished to destroy myself . . . in order to find in the unknown innermost, the nucleus of all things. . . . But by doing so, I lost myself on the way. . . . [Now] I will learn from myself, be my own pupil; I will learn from myself the secret of Siddhartha.
>
> (Hesse, 1951, pp. 30–31)

At this point, Siddhartha entered a *moratorium* that carried him in search of different roles that allowed greater possibilities for synthesizing and integrating all that had gone before. Anxiety, however, soon became his companion:

> [A]n icy chill stole over him. . . . Previously when in deepest meditation, he was still his father's son, he was still a Brahmin of high standing, a religious man. Now he was only Siddhartha . . .
>
> (Hesse, 1951, p. 33)

Siddhartha's realization brought with it a new challenge for development: to *achieve* an identity, a sense of self that synthesized earlier identifications into a new whole that was now uniquely his own.

Siddhartha's life is a case study of the evolution of identity from adolescence to old age. After experiencing many roles and building various lifestyles that fit his innermost needs at the time, Siddhartha returned in his old age to the river over which many of his earlier life journeys had crossed and beside which he eventually found peace. Through many inward and external travels in adult life, Siddhartha demonstrated how the achievement of an identity does not remain fixed, resolved once and for all, but rather is constantly open to change through shifting needs and circumstances:

> Such a sense of identity is never gained nor maintained once and for all. Like a good conscience, it is constantly lost and regained, although more lasting and more economical methods of maintenance and restoration are evolved and fortified in late adolescence.
>
> (Erikson, 1956, p. 74)

An Optimal Sense of Identity

If soma, ego, and society have done their jobs, what should be present by the end of adolescence and the beginning of early adulthood? Subjectively, there should be a sense of well-being: "Its most obvious concomitants are a feeling of being at home in one's body, a sense of 'knowing where one is going' and an inner assuredness of anticipated recognition from those who count" (Erikson, 1968, p. 165). With its psychosocial connotation, optimal identity formation should show itself through commitment to those work roles, values, and sexual orientations that best fit one's own unique combination of needs and talents within a context that both recognizes and supports these choices. It is these more directly observable commitment features of ego identity that have been at the heart of most empirical attempts to address some of identity's many properties.

Identity as a Stage in the Life-Cycle Scheme

As hinted previously, identity has a past. Erikson portrayed identity as the fifth stage in an eight-act sequence of life conflicts one encounters along the road from birth to death in old age. While the primary focus in this chapter is on identity, it is nevertheless important to appreciate the contribution that both earlier and later acts make to the complete life drama.

Erikson conceptualized the life cycle as a series of stages, critical periods of development that involved bipolar conflict that must be addressed and resolved before one can proceed unhindered. According to the epigenetic principle, each stage had a critical time of emergence, which contributed, in turn, to the functional whole. There is a proper rate and sequence of development; the child must crawl before she can walk.

The polarity of each stage presented a crisis, a crucial turning point where development must make a move for better or for worse as one orients to the physical environment as well as social and historical context: "Each successive stage and crisis has a special relation to one of the basic elements of society, and this for the simple reason that the human life cycle and man's institutions have evolved together" (Erikson, 1963, p. 250). The developmental possibilities of each stage do not demand "either/or" resolutions but rather some dynamic balance of "more or less" between the poles; hopefully, that balance favors the positive end. Erikson described his fifth stage, which came to the fore during adolescence, as that of *identity versus role confusion*. Here, as mentioned earlier, the young person is faced with the psychosocial dilemma of synthesizing yet transcending earlier identifications of childhood to realize aptitudes in social roles, while the community, in turn, provides its recognition and contribution to an individual's sense of self. Ironically, it may be one's willingness to undergo times of temporary uncertainty that gives the achievement resolution its ultimate strength. Stage resolutions should not be regarded as achievement scales based only on the more positive pole; they represent a balance between positive and negative poles that determine an individual's characteristic mode of adapting to the environment. One does not, however, enter the life drama during the fifth identity formation act. Identity versus role confusion has been preceded by four earlier stages, each having a necessary place in the unfolding chain of life-cycle tasks. All of Erikson's eight stages are now briefly reviewed to illustrate their relationships to the identity crisis of adolescence.

Trust Versus Mistrust/Hope

As the opening scene in the life-cycle production, *trust versus mistrust* sets the stage for all that is to follow. It is during infancy that the developmental crisis of trust is met, based in part on Freud's biological concern with early oral experience. Through the mutual regulation and interaction between caretaker and infant, a rudimentary sense of ego identity is born. The child comes to know itself in relation to another and gains a sense of inner continuity, sameness, and trust in itself and its developmental partner.

Somewhere between the polar extremes of trust and mistrust, most of us find an adaptive balance; neither complete trust nor complete mistrust of the world is ultimately beneficial. An optimal resolution to this infant crisis has the scales tipped more firmly toward the trusting pole, leading to *hope*, which in turn is the basic ingredient for later survival. It is also through this dynamic balance that a sense of

"I," as one who can hope, emerges to serve as the very rudimentary foundation for identity in adolescence.

Autonomy Versus Shame and Doubt/Will

Following the sense of basic trust, life's next developmental hurdle during the second and third years is that of developing autonomy. Again, finding a biological base in Freud's anal stage of development, Erikson's sense of autonomy is characterized by the child's increasing awareness of its self through control of bodily functions and expression of other motor and linguistic skills (performing in concert with the expectations of important others in the social milieu).

Holding on to or letting go of body wastes is one of the child's earliest opportunities to exercise complete control over the outcome of events, regardless of parental desire. Such auspicious occasions as toilet-training episodes provide toddlers with an experience of *will*, something that originates from within in response to social conditions and highlights the issue that wills of developmental partners can differ. With *trust* in order, it is now possible to risk one's own *will* against the response that such self-expression might bring. This "counterpointing of identities" again carries the rudiments of later adolescent identity.

Newfound linguistic and locomotor skills conspire to aid the development of autonomy during toddlerhood. By the age of two and a half years, the child is using the personal pronoun "I" (as well as the declarative "no") to give further evidence of will. Now possessing the motoric status of "one who can walk," one is also in a position to encounter social response, for better or worse.

Like all of Erikson's stages, an adaptive balance between the two extremes is necessary for optimal development. When the scale is weighted toward shame and doubt, one retains a sense of inferiority, of being "not good enough," through all of life's later stages. As a corollary, however, it is knowledge that one is fallible and capable of evoking a less than favorable social response that tempers absolute autonomy and serves to regulate the self in a social order.

Initiative Versus Guilt/Purpose

The third act of Erikson's life drama is met during the preschool years and coincides with Freud's phallic stage of development; pleasure in infantile genitality gives rise to Erikson's social as well as sexual sense of being "on the make" in the stage of *initiative versus guilt*. Now adept at mastering such skills as playing Batman on a tricycle and more complicated gender roles, the preschooler possesses the ability to imagine. This capacity, so central to early childhood play, carries with it the seeds for *initiative* in the translation of thoughts to action. Only from an autonomous position is it possible to initiate; in knowing *that* one is, it is then possible to learn *what* one is. Issues such as what kind of person to become and what kinds of gender roles to adopt now become critical questions. From initiative grows a sense of purpose and ambition that are vital to tasks of adolescence and adulthood. It is an initiative that "sets the direction toward the possible and the tangible which permits the dreams of early childhood to be attached to the goals of an active adult life" (Erikson, 1963, p. 258).

Locomotor skills and language continue to develop. One is now able to move and expend energy, finding out what this status of one who walks means and how moving can be used for purposes other than pleasure alone to accomplish more far-reaching goals. Language becomes a tool for communication with others in sorting out the often complex and confusing state of world affairs, or at least those of the preschool playground.

In sum, identity in adolescence has roots in the purposeful activities of early childhood. Out of initiative comes the ability to fantasize about and experiment with social and gender roles of critical importance to adolescent and young adult life. At this stage, however, the potential for guilt exists. A tip of the scales toward this negative end may leave the individual immobilized in taking future action through guilt or fear. An optimal balance would see boundless gender and social initiative tempered by an awareness of the possibilities for social criticism and sanctions. Such a balance can best be obtained by a social environment aware of its role in fostering curiosity within the limits of cultural convention.

Industry Versus Inferiority/Competence

According to Freud, the primary school years were marked by a shift from libidinal energy focused on bodily zones to a time of sexual latency; attention becomes channeled outward toward the world of the schoolyard and neighborhood. In contrast to Freud's focus on sexual latency, Erikson viewed the primary school years as ones in which the practicing of skills and completion of tasks, anticipating those of later adult work roles, were life's main focus. Industry was described as an apprenticeship to life; feelings of competence and achievement were the optimal results here. Thus, it is only through the *initiative* of an *autonomous* self, which *trusts* the social milieu, that the challenge of *industry versus inferiority* can be addressed. Social recognition for a job well done is the milieu's contribution to fostering development at this stage.

Crucial to this sense of industry is identification with others who know how to do and make things. One special teacher in the lives of many individuals has often been credited as the spark that ignited outstanding later achievements (Erikson, 1968). Finding one's special skills and talents during the phase of industry may have long-range implications for later vocational identity. Wise parents, teachers, or other important identification figures play a critical role in fostering a sense of industry or inferiority.

Erikson (1968) observed a child's possible negative resolution of this stage, involving a sense of estrangement from one's self as well as one's work. A home environment insufficiently preparing the child for life outside its boundaries, or failure of the wider cultural milieu to recognize and reward real accomplishments of its younger members, may precipitate inferiority. Again, a healthy resolution to the *industry versus inferiority* conflict sees a ratio favoring industry. At the same time, feelings of limitless competence must be checked by an awareness of one's genuine limitations in order for optimal development to occur.

Identity Versus Role Confusion/Fidelity

Moving away from Freud's biological orientation to personality development during puberty, Erikson saw physiological change as only one aspect of a more pervasive adolescent dilemma:

> But even where a person can adjust sexually in a technical sense and may at least superficially develop what Freud called genital maturity, he may still be weakened by the identity problems of our era . . . fully developed genitality is not a goal to be pursued in isolation.
>
> (Erikson, as cited in Evans, 1967, p. 29)

Identity, to Erikson, incorporated yet transcended the endocrinological revolution of puberty to include psychosocial issues. It was finding a "feeling of reality" in socially approved roles. Drawing upon resolutions to earlier stages, one now approaches the task of identity formation. Erikson suggested fidelity to be the essence of identity. To become faithful and committed to some ideological worldview was the task of this stage; to find a cause worthy of one's vocational energies and reflecting one's basic values was the stuff of which identity crises are made. It is ultimately to affirm and be affirmed by a social order to which identity aspires.

Some possible ways of negotiating life's identity conflicts during the fifth act were described through Siddhartha's quest. Suffice it to say here that the stage of *identity versus role confusion* is one of life's critical crossroads in the transition to adult life; not only must this stage incorporate a *trustworthy* "I" who has evolved as an *autonomous* individual capable of *initiating* and completing (through *industry*) satisfying tasks modeled by significant others, but it must also transcend such identifications to produce an "I" sensitive to its own needs and talents and capable of finding its own niche in the surrounding social landscape.

In contrast to Freud, the curtain on development for Erikson did not fall at this point. With a favorable resolution to the identity crisis of adolescence, it is now and only now possible to proceed to the stage of *intimacy* – that meeting of an "I" with an "I," each firm in one's own unique identity foundations. The remaining three acts of the life-cycle production, however, involve a shift of developmental focus from "I" to "we."

Intimacy Versus Isolation/Love

For Erikson, intimacy in young adulthood encompasses far more than sexual fulfillment; in fact, sexual activity might be used in the service of an identity conflict rather than as a reflection of *love*. "Intimacy is the ability to fuse your identity with somebody else's without fear that you're going to lose something yourself" (Erikson, cited in Evans, 1967, p. 48). Intimacy involves the desire to commit oneself to a relationship, even when such commitment might call for personal sacrifice or compromise. Intimacy involves communion and can occur in a variety of forms – in same-sex and opposite-sex friendships, in love, in sexual union, and even in relationships with oneself or one's life commitments (Evans, 1967).

To Erikson, genuine intimacy was not possible until issues of identity were reasonably well resolved. Relationships of earlier adolescence often served only the purpose of self-definition rather than intimacy; another person might be used merely as a mirror to reflect a form less visible to their owner. Relationships might also involve attempts to find one's own identity through merger with another – efforts that similarly preclude intimacy. In these cases, ultimately, there is only enough identity for one.

Drawing upon Martin Buber's concepts of "I" and "Thou," Moustakas captured the character of genuine intimacy in the following passage:

> Growth of the self requires meetings between I and Thou, in which each person recognizes the other as he is; each says what he means and means what he says; each values and contributes to the unfolding of the other without imposing or manipulating. And this always means some degree of distance and independence. It does not depend on one revealing to another everything that exists within, but requires only that the person be who he is, genuinely present.
>
> (Moustakas, 1974, p. 92)

Here, the identities of "I" and "Thou" must be assured in order for such a relationship of mature, unselfish love to occur.

Isolation is the psychosocial alternative, creating conflict at this stage. If true "engagement" with another is elusive, one might "isolate . . . and enter, at best, only stereotyped and formalized interpersonal relations; or one may, in repeated hectic attempts and dismal failures, seek intimacy with the most improbable partners" (Erikson, 1968, p. 167). Isolation can occur in the context of a relationship just as intimacy can exist in the physical absence of a partner. An ideal balance between intimacy and isolation results in a relationship that allows time for both withdrawal and communion between partners. It is the recognition of one's ultimate aloneness that gives intimacy its base, and it is one's capacity for security in that aloneness that makes genuine intimacy possible.

Generativity Versus Stagnation/Care

The next task for that "we" to meet during adulthood is taking a place in society at large and *caring* – for one's offspring, productions, social contributions, and future generations. Erikson again noted the limitations of Freud's psychosexual scheme with its emphasis on genital maturity as the epitome of development:

> I would go even further than that and say that Freud, by paying so much attention to the prepubertal impediments of the genital encounter itself,

> underemphasized the procreative drive as also important to man. I think this is a significant omission, because it can lead to the assumption that a person graduates from psychoanalytic treatment when he has been restored to full genitality. As in many movies, where the story ends when lovers finally find one another, our therapies often end when the person can consummate sexuality in a satisfactory, mutually enriching way. This is an essential stage but I would consider generativity a further psychosexual stage, and would postulate that its frustration results in symptoms of self-absorption.
>
> (Erikson, as cited in Evans, 1967, p. 52)

Erikson's concept here does not imply that generativity could be met only in parenting; it resides also in the desire of an *autonomous* "I" as part of an *intimate* "we" to contribute to the present and future well-being of other life cycles. Such generative individuals provide the figures necessary for introjection and identification by younger members of a society.

The counterpart to generativity is stagnation or self-absorption, whereby personal comfort becomes the primary motivator for action. When this resolution occurs, individuals "often begin to indulge themselves as if they were their own – or one another's – one and only child; and where conditions favor it, early invalidism, physical or psychological, becomes the vehicle of self-concern" (Erikson, 1963, p. 267). Alternatively, procreation or other forms of production are not necessarily the expression of generativity; true care must take root for generativity to flourish.

Again, an optimal balance between generativity and self-absorption is necessary. One needs to be selective of those people and projects to nurture in the interests of self-preservation; unlimited energy and resources are not available to one through life's passages, and some attention to self-interest is crucial in perpetuating a generative life attitude. As in all previous life stages, the ratio needs to favor the more positive pole for healthy development to proceed.

Integrity Versus Despair/Wisdom

The final act of the life drama requires facing the developmental task of balancing *integrity* with *despair*. More difficult to define than preceding stages, integrity "is the acceptance of one's one and only life cycle as something that had to be and that, by necessity, permitted of no substitutions. . . . In such final consolidation, death loses its sting" (Erikson, 1963, p. 268). One gauge of integrity is the ability to accept one's own mortality. A life lived in contributing one's guidance, gifts, and talents to future generations is not regretted, and death is not feared as time shortens before the last curtain call. An old age favoring integrity is characterized by the *wisdom* of mature judgment and a reflective understanding of one's own "accidental" place in the historical scheme of things.

On the other hand, the potential for despair in old age exists to counterpoint integrity. In a life culminating in despair, one is unable to identify a different path toward a more comfortable and satisfying conclusion.

Identity themes are thus met again in old age, where the sense of the "I" that has developed and established itself in social contexts through earlier stages of development must rest content (or not) on what it *is*.

> [A] sense of "I" becomes a most sensitive matter again in old age, as an individual's uniqueness gradually and often suddenly seems to have lost any leeway for further variations such as those which seemed to open themselves with each previous stage. Now, non-Being must be faced "as is."
>
> (Erikson, 1984, p. 102)

The favorable balance of integrity with despair again gives wisdom its ultimate strength. Remaining open to existential issues of being and nonbeing as well as Kierkegaard's sense of dread presents very real opportunities for despair. Willingness to address sobering questions such as the meaning of one's existence and the inevitability of one's own death makes the tranquility that integrity brings deeper.

Identity is thus an ingredient of all stages of the human life cycle. Having roots in infant trust, identity is also present in the *integrity-versus-despair* conflict of old age. Identity formation during adolescence reflects developmental resolutions to all preceding stages and serves as a base for personality development that lies ahead. In adolescence, however, identity assumes a change in form. Through a process different from the internalizations and identifications during earlier psychosocial stages, identity's configuration now evolves into a new structure, different from (but related to) the sum of its parts. Through the synthesis of all earlier childhood identifications, the "I," like Siddhartha's sense of self, is now ready to move forward, no longer looking backward.

Analysis of Erikson's Identity Concept

Erikson's definition of identity has been criticized on a number of grounds. Unclear or imprecise formulations of identity have been the source of numerous difficulties for many readers of Erikson. The analyst himself suggested that the concept should be defined from different angles, and he proceeded to use the term to emphasize different issues at different points. At times, identity referred to a structure or a configuration; at other times, it referred to a process. Still, on other occasions, identity was viewed as both a conscious subjective experience and an unconscious entity. Roazen (2000, p. 438) noted that despite Erikson's capacity for insight, his writing could also be "subtle, elusive, and sometimes hard to follow." In a rather candid comment given during a radio interview, Erikson himself stated, "I think one could be more precise than I am, or than I am able to be. I very much feel that scientific training and logic would have helped a lot" (Erikson, as cited in Stevens, 1983, p. 112). Yet it is this very breadth of phenomena captured through Erikson's formulations of identity that many social scientists have suggested makes the construct more amenable to research than much of psychodynamic theory. Wallerstein (2014) argued that Erikson's life-cycle stage scheme should regard optimal stage resolutions as aspirational end points, rather than essential steps toward optimal functioning; varying degrees of success in this process, he suggested, give rise to our uniquely individual characters.

Empirical validation of the psychosocial issues addressed at different stages that were described by Erikson has been questioned by some critics. Ciaccio (1971) was one of the first investigators to test whether or not conflicts purported by Erikson to be inherent in some of the early developmental stages were actually at issue for groups of boys aged five, eight, and 11 years. Although psychosocial strengths or attitudes did seem to progress with age in the sequence described by Erikson, the negative aspects (or crises) of the stages did not find such confirmation. Additional research raised questions regarding Erikson's proposed timing of development; issues of focal concern at specific ages have varied across samples, possibly reflecting the influence of different cultural and/or historical factors (Schwartz, Adamson, et al., 2015). While finding empirical support for central propositions of Erikson's theory, Côté and Levine (2015) suggested that identity formation is a much more gradual process for most than Erikson's concept of "identity crisis" implies.

Erikson's views on womanhood and the inner space have drawn equally sharp responses from critics. To Erikson, anatomy was destiny, as behavior reflected sexual morphology; boys emphasized outer space in their predominantly aggressive and intrusive play, while girls focused on the inner space in their more peaceful, passive activities. The scientific validity of this observation was questioned shortly after its publication by Caplan (1979), who failed to replicate results from Erikson's single experiment in any of the findings from a series of studies. Furthermore, many in the following decades attacked the idea that women could not attain their identity until a suitable partner was found and "welcomed to the inner space." Now, however, Erikson's comments on women's identity are recognized as a likely product of the cultural attitudes toward women in the U.S. at the time of his writing.

Additionally, Erikson's epigenetic scheme of identity formation, many have argued, reflects cultural bias. It would seem that conditions for identity crises could only be ripe in cultural contexts that allow choice as to social, ideological, and vocational roles. Now, many researchers share the perspective that there can be no single, unified path to healthy identity development among youth living in diverse cultural contexts (e.g., Rogers et al., 2020) due to variation in adaptation and ecological demands across place and time. Further, it is the task of scholars to empirically document how healthy or adaptive identity development progresses under a variety of life circumstances and conditions. Despite such limitations, however, Erikson's theory continues to offer important insights and has sparked an array of empirical inquiries in various parts of the world into identity formation during and beyond adolescence.

Measuring Ego Identity

Erikson's vivid descriptions of the adolescent identity formation process have presented a challenge to researchers attempting to examine and understand the phenomenon empirically. In a frequently cited definition of ego identity, Erikson (1959, p. 116) described many different dimensions of identity's structure and functions: "[Ego identity is] an evolving configuration of constitutional givens, idiosyncratic libidinal needs, favored capacities, significant identifications, effective defenses, successful sublimations, and consistent roles." It is not surprising, then, that different research approaches have emerged to examine various dimensions of the identity formation experience. Erikson himself never wished to undertake empirical studies to validate his theory and hence devised no measures of ego identity to enable researchers to explore its many properties.

Later investigators have focused on specific dimensions of Erikson's identity concept. The bulk of research attention over the past decades has elaborated exploration and commitment processes in the identity formation task of adolescence, though a growing body of research also has examined such issues as resolutions to "identity versus role confusion" in relation to other life-cycle stages (e.g., Hearn et al., 2012), "identity synthesis versus confusion" (e.g., Schwartz et al., 2009), the role that identity distress may play in life-cycle development (e.g., Berman et al., 2014), narrative approaches to identity development (e.g., McLean & Syed, 2016), micro-level processes of identity development (e.g., Van der Gaag et al., 2017), identity control theory (e.g., Kerpelman et al., 1997), cognitive styles associated with various identity statuses (e.g., Berzonsky & Papini, 2015), and quality of identity commitments (Waterman et al., 2013) to name a few areas of investigation. Narrative approaches to identity drawn from Erikson's and others' writings have now attracted sufficient research interest so that they will be elaborated in Chapter 3 of this volume.

Erikson's virtue of fidelity, however, has drawn a tremendous amount of research attention, and this line of inquiry was originally initiated in studies conducted by James Marcia (1966, 1967; Marcia et al., 1993/2011). Marcia (2004) described how his interest in Erikson's (1959) concept of identity arose during his clinical internship. Marcia was assigned to undertake a psychodiagnostic review of a 16-year-old boy, a new admission to the hospital. The boy's psychological tests indicated a severe thought disorder, indicative of schizophrenia. However, six months later, the youth was released from the hospital with no signs of this illness; it was likely that this young man had undergone a severe identity crisis. Marcia reflected on this experience as he selected a dissertation topic: the construct validation of Erikson's identity construct. With many false starts and amused skepticism from peers and professors, Marcia constructed the identity statuses. Over the years of his career, Marcia wished to make Erikson more accessible to the social science community. With his construct now reviewed in most major textbooks on adolescent development, Marcia has certainly succeeded in accomplishing that goal.

In the model developed by Marcia, the processes of identity exploration and commitment have been most fully examined. Indeed, Marcia's identity status model has now generated over 900 studies during the past five decades, not including dissertations. Marcia's original approach and recent expansions of Marcia's exploration and commitment processes will be overviewed in the next section of this chapter. Ongoing research advances using these expanded identity process models will be presented in the "Current directions in identity research" section of this chapter.

Marcia's Identity Statuses

On the basis of Erikson's writings on identity, Marcia (1966, 1967) developed the Identity Status Interview (ISI). This interview has been revised and expanded over several decades, and early, mid-, and late adolescent versions, as well as an adult version, are available with interview guidelines and scoring instructions (Marcia et al., 1993/2011). The interview consists of domains deemed to be salient to the adolescent in question. For the late adolescent, areas commonly examined are vocational plans, religious and political values, sexual expression, and sex role values. Semi-structured questions are designed to assess any current identity-defining commitments the individual might hold, how stable those are, and how any commitments have been or are being undertaken. If commitments are not present, the interview questions also probe whether or not the respondent is attempting to make any such decisions. Interviews generally last 30 to 45 minutes and are recorded for later assessment. Interrater reliability has generally been about 80–85% agreement between two raters. Among studies that have corrected for chance agreements, this percentage far exceeds agreements expected by chance. Expected patterns of relationships with other variables have helped to establish construct validity of the ISI (for reviews, see Kroger & Marcia, 2011, 2022).

Marcia reasoned that fidelity or commitment to a vocation, a set of meaningful values (religious and political beliefs), and a sexual identity (sexual expression and sex role values) that Erikson had described are the observable cues indicative of a more or less successful identity resolution for those in many Western contexts. From Marcia's observations, however, commitment or fidelity comes in several forms. While Erikson saw identity as a balance between commitment and confusion about one's values and roles in society, Marcia identified two distinct types of commitment and two types of noncommitment. Individuals adopting an achievement or foreclosure orientation have both made commitments to various social roles and values. However, *identity-achieved* individuals have done so following a decision-making period, while *foreclosures* have bypassed the identity formation process to simply adopt the roles and values of childhood identification figures. Similarly, moratorium and diffusion individuals both lack commitment to a place in the social context. However, *moratoriums* are undergoing an evaluative process (ego synthesis) in search of suitable social roles and values for themselves, while *diffusions* are not. These commitment types or identity statuses were empirically validated as four distinct modes of dealing with identity-defining issues during adolescence, and expected patterns of relationships with other variables helped to establish construct validity of the ISI (for a review, see Marcia et al., 1993/2011).

A paper-and-pencil measure of identity status was developed by Adams and colleagues (Adams, 1999). The Objective Measure of Ego Identity Status II (EOM-EIS-II) was composed of 64 items presented in a Likert-scale format that assessed the degree of identity achievement, moratorium, foreclosure, and diffusion an individual demonstrated within eight identity-defining domains. Occupational, political, religious, and philosophy of life values constituted the general ideological domain, while friendship, dating, sex roles, and recreational values comprised a general interpersonal domain. Reliability was established over a number of studies via measures of internal consistency. Cronbach's alphas were generally around 0.66. Test–retest reliability studies showed an average correlation of 0.76. Efforts to establish construct, predictive, and concurrent validity generally produced moderate-to-high relationships between the EOM-EIS-II and associated measures (Adams, 1999). Afterward, Schwartz, Adamson, et al. (2015) examined the utility of the EOM-EIS-II across several cultural contexts. While finding the internal structure of the instrument to be consistent across settings, their results also suggested that identity content areas and item wording may need to be altered to be more culturally meaningful in particular contexts.

Similar to adolescents in Western contexts, Marcia's identity status model has been used in samples living in non-Western contexts (e.g., for a review of studies in Japan, see Sugimura & Mizokami, 2012). Yet it is clear that the full picture of identity formation in non-Western contexts has not been captured (Klimstra & Adams, 2021). For instance, salient domains of identity resolution may vary across cultures. Indeed, in Japanese youth, vocation is a leading life area for identity resolution (Sugimura & Mizokami, 2012), but religious beliefs may be optional (Sugimura et al., 2019). Understanding salient life domains and steps of identity resolution from both Western and non-Western perspectives is absolutely vital to providing a comprehensive and contextualized knowledge about identity.

Extensions of Marcia's Model

Two currently popular, additional paper-and-pencil measures were developed to extend Marcia's concepts of the exploration and commitment processes: the Dimensions of Identity Development Scale (DIDS; Luyckx et al., 2006; Luyckx, Schwartz, Berzonsky, et al., 2008) and the Utrecht-Management of Identity Commitments Scale (U-MICS; Crocetti, Rubini, & Meeus, 2008; Crocetti, Rubini, Luyckx, et al., 2008). The DIDS is a 25-item instrument presented in a five-point Likert-scale format, with three scales reflecting different forms of identity exploration (*exploration in breadth, exploration in depth*, and *ruminative exploration*) and two scales reflecting different forms of identity commitment (*commitment making* and *identification with commitment*). *Exploration in breadth* corresponds to Marcia's exploration concept, whereby the degree to which adolescents have explored alternative roles and values is assessed, while *exploration in depth* looks at the extent to which existing commitments have been reexamined and refined against the respondent's internal interests and values. *Ruminative exploration* refers to the possibility of a "perpetual moratorium" process, whereby the individual remains "stuck" in ongoing identity exploration, unable to make meaningful identity choices; this process is most likely to be dysfunctional. *Commitment making* is similar to Marcia's commitment concept, referring to the degree to which adolescents adopt meaningful identity-defining roles and values. *Identification with commitment* reflects the degree to which individuals feel certain about or identify with the identity commitments they have made. Each of the five scales is composed of five items. Cronbach's alphas for the five scales ranged from 0.79 to 0.86 for two initial samples, while internal construct validity for the five scales and external construct validity for the three exploration scales were in line with predictions (Luyckx et al., 2006).

The 13-item U-MICS (Crocetti, Rubini, & Meeus, 2008) is composed of three scales (*commitment, in-depth exploration*, and *reconsideration of commitment*) using a Likert-scale format. The *commitment* (five items) and *in-depth exploration* (five items) scales correspond to the same dimensions of identity described earlier for the DIDS instrument. The *reconsideration of commitment* scale (three items) refers to abandoning initial identity choices and evaluating possible alternatives. Two domains were examined in initial studies – education and friendship; each of these two domains contains the 13 items noted earlier and is presented in a Likert-scale format. "My education/best friend gives me certainty in life" is found on the *commitment* scale, while "I often reflect on my education/best friend" is found on the *in-depth exploration* scale. Internal construct validity was supported by a three-factor solution, while external validity was established in predicted directions with various personality and relational variables. Later studies have indicated moderate-to-good internal reliabilities (0.63 to 0.82) for each scale across samples living in seven European countries (Dimitrova et al., 2016) and similar levels of reliability (0.67 to 0.92) for the scale of education in samples living in ten nations in Europe, the Middle East, and Asia (Crocetti et al., 2015).

These elaborations of exploration and commitment processes have brought valuable insights into the process of identity development and produced a wealth of studies on the types of and steps in identity exploration and commitment processes. Clusters or profiles[3] from both the DIDS and U-MICS have been extracted, also purporting to reflect Marcia's identity statuses. However, this procedure may be problematic for a number of reasons that Waterman (2015) detailed, and he indicated caution when trying to interpret results from studies utilizing identity status clusters derived from these more recent instruments. For example, in contrast to the Identity Status Interview (Marcia et al., 1993/2011) and the EOM-EIS-II (Adams, 1999), which assessed identity exploration and commitment through past and present circumstances across a number of identity-defining domains, both the DIDS and U-MICS phrase items were in the present tense only. This present-tense wording makes evaluation of previous exploration impossible to assess; knowledge of any past identity exploration is necessary to accurately differentiate Marcia's foreclosure and achievement statuses.[4] Also, based on psychometric analyses, Johnson, de Moor, et al. (2022) noted that DIDS and U-MICS items may capture narrow/specific parts of exploration and commitment processes and may not convey the same meaning across different samples (e.g., adolescents speaking Dutch vs. English). While there are noted variations and problems comparing what is measured across identity status measures, the DIDS and U-MICS instruments have made a more nuanced examination of identity exploration and commitment processes possible and have stimulated much research. Further, from an intervention perspective, these present-oriented indicators of identity commitment and exploration (e.g., mean level or continuous changes in the *amount* of exploration and/or commitment) could be useful for capturing incremental changes in identity development and thereby inform the structuring of identity-related interventions.

Research Findings on Adolescent Identity Exploration and Commitment Processes

While identity and its development during adolescence have been examined from many angles, Marcia's (1966; Marcia et al., 1993/2011) identity status approach has either generated or served as a springboard for the largest body of investigations to date, and the brief review below will focus on studies using this approach; the "Current directions in identity research" section will focus on recent efforts that examine exploration and commitment processes in greater detail. Early research with the identity statuses through the 1970s, 1980s, and 1990s focused on individual personality, cognitive, and relational differences associated with the different identity statuses, while subsequent work has examined developmental patterns of change over time, as well as gender and ethnic/cultural/contextual factors associated with the identity statuses. Identity status clusters derived from more recent instruments have also examined a number of these issues, though some problems with this approach have been noted by Waterman (2015), which were described earlier in this chapter. Because the identity statuses remain a focus of many past as well as current approaches to adolescent identity, the profiles of each identity status, based upon findings from five decades of research, are described briefly below.

Identity-achieved adolescents have been through a thoughtful, decision-making process of searching for and finding meaningful psychosocial roles and values that "fit" with their own interests and needs. From meta-analytic studies, identity-achieved youths are less reliant on the opinions of others to make their decisions and score consistently higher on measures of "internal locus of control" compared with other identity status groups (Lillevoll et al., 2013a). Identity-achieved individuals function well under stress and use more planful, rational, and logical decision-making strategies compared to people described by other identity statuses (Boyes & Chandler, 1992; Marcia et al., 1993/2011). No significant differences in intelligence, however, have appeared across the identity statuses as assessed in various studies by at least six different intelligence measures (Marcia et al., 1993/2011). The identity achieved and foreclosed individuals have shown the highest levels of self-esteem compared with other statuses from meta-analytic results and are satisfied with the way they are (Makros & McCabe, 2001; Ryeng et al., 2013a; Schwartz et al., 2011). Meta-analyses also indicated that the identity-achieved individuals are most likely to be at post-conformist levels of ego development as well as post-conventional levels of moral reasoning (Jespersen et al., 2013a, 2013b). Identity achievements have tended to be intimate in their close relationships and more secure in their attachment patterns (Årseth et al., 2009; Beyers & Seiffge-Krenke, 2010). Achievements are also able to perceive parental strengths and weaknesses and come from families in which parents support their autonomy (Grotevant & Cooper, 1985; Willemsen & Waterman, 1991). In general, more positive mental health outcomes have been found among those identity-achieved individuals who explored and synthesized identity possibilities into an identity configuration that is uniquely their own (for a review, see Kroger & Marcia, 2011).

Moratorium adolescents and young adults are in the throes of trying to make decisions about important identity questions, and they are anxious, changeable, and intense in their personal relationships. While possessing the capacity for intimacy, they have tended to shy away from the commitments demanded by it (Dyk & Adams, 1990; Josselson, 2017; Orlofsky et al., 1973). In many ways, moratoriums resemble identity achievements in their cognitive complexity, higher levels of moral reasoning, and ego development (Jespersen et al., 2013a, 2013b; Slugoski et al., 1984). Moratoriums also have demonstrated greater degrees of skepticism than other identity statuses (Boyes & Chandler, 1992), as well as greater openness to experience and experiential orientation (Stephen et al., 1992; Tesch & Cameron, 1987). Parents of moratorium youths have tended to foster independence in their child-rearing practices (Frank et al., 1990; Grotevant & Cooper, 1985).

Foreclosure adolescents have adopted strong, identity-defining commitments based on identifications with important others rather than their own identity explorations. Meta-analytic studies have found foreclosures of both sexes to be more authoritarian in attitude compared with other identity statuses (Ryeng et al., 2013b). These individuals have tended to seek the approval of others and have based their actions on what others think. Perhaps as a result of their rigid adherence to authoritarian values, studies have found foreclosures to be less anxious compared with other identity status groups (Lillevoll et al., 2013a) and least open to new experiences (Stephen et al., 1992; Tesch & Cameron, 1987). If there is no openness or willingness to question life commitments, there is little room for anxiety to enter. Foreclosures also have used less complex cognitive styles (Slugoski et al., 1984), though meta-analytic studies have found those in the foreclosed identity status to be more mixed in their levels of moral reasoning and ego development compared to achievement and moratorium individuals (Jespersen et al., 2013a, 2013b). In interpersonal relationships, foreclosures have tended to be "well-behaved" and engaged in stereotypic or merger styles of relationships with significant others (Dyk & Adams, 1990; Levitz-Jones & Orlofsky, 1985). Youths who have remained foreclosed over the course of late adolescence are more nonsecure (anxious or detached) in attachment profiles than youths of any other identity status group (Kroger & Haslett, 1988; Papini et al., 1989). Foreclosures have reported very close relationships with parents, while their parents, in turn, have encouraged conformity and adherence to family values (Frank et al., 1990; Grotevant & Cooper, 1985; Willemsen & Waterman, 1991).

Diffusion adolescents and young adults are less homogeneous as a group than the other identity statuses. The inability to make identity commitments may have resulted from cultural conditions (producing few viable identity options) as well as developmental deficits. Diffusions have been unlikely to be involved in intimate relationships and lack any real sense of self to contribute to others (Josselson, 2017). Meta-analytic studies have shown lower levels of self-esteem to be associated with the uncommitted moratorium and diffusion statuses (Ryeng et al., 2013a).

Furthermore, diffusions have shown high levels of an "external locus of control" and low levels of an "internal locus of control" in comparison with other identity statuses (Lillevoll et al., 2013b). The diffusions have used less complex cognitive styles than moratoriums and achievements (Slugoski et al., 1984). In terms of interpersonal relationships, diffusions have tended to be distant and withdrawn, most likely to be stereotyped or isolated in their relationships with others (Orlofsky et al., 1973). Their reports of parents' child-rearing practices have indicated caretakers who were distant and rejecting (Josselson, 2017); diffusions, furthermore, have shown a lack of awareness of family issues (Gfellner & Bartoszuk, 2015). In general, diffusions have exhibited more troubled or risky behaviors in comparison with those of other identity statuses (Josselson, 2017; Schwartz et al., 2011).

Developmental Patterns of Change

Marcia et al. (1993/2011) intended the identity statuses to reflect "snapshots" at a particular point in time of how individuals were attempting (or not) to make key, identity-defining decisions. Questions thus arose regarding the length of time one was likely to remain in any given identity status and the course of the most common trajectories of both identity status change and stability, as well as events that were most likely associated with identity status change and stability over time.

Investigations of identity status change during adolescence and young adulthood have identified common patterns of progressive movement from foreclosure and diffusion positions to moratorium and achievement statuses among those individuals who do change over this time frame. Meta-analyses of a number of both longitudinal and cross-sectional studies of identity status change during adolescence and young adulthood have been undertaken (Kroger et al., 2010). Among results from meta-analyses of longitudinal studies, a little over one-third of individuals (36%) showed some type of progressive identity status change (defined as diffusion to foreclosure, moratorium, or achievement; foreclosure to moratorium or achievement; and moratorium to achievement) over an average range of three years. Some 15% of participants showed regressive identity status change, while, surprisingly, almost half (49%) of individuals were found to be in the same identity status over this same period of time. Among results from cross-sectional studies across the years of late adolescence and young adulthood, the mean proportion of identity achievements increased steadily over time, though only about one-third of the sample (34%) had reached identity achievement by the age of 22 years. Foreclosure and diffusion statuses declined across high school years but fluctuated throughout late adolescence and young adulthood. It appears that identity achievement remains elusive for many individuals during the time frame in which Erikson suggested identity formation is a key developmental task, leaving considerable scope for identity development through the adult years of life.

Subsequent developmental studies of identity status change have produced similar findings. During the late adolescent and young adult years, diffusion and foreclosure clusters or profiles have generally decreased or remained stable, while the identity-achieved cluster or profile has either increased or remained stable (e.g., a cross-sectional study in Belgium: Verschueren et al., 2017; a longitudinal study in the Netherlands: Meeus et al., 2010; and a longitudinal study in Japan: Hatano & Sugimura, 2017). In a cross-sectional study in Trinidad, the identity-achieved cluster was most commonly found in middle age, compared with adolescence, emerging adulthood, and young adulthood years (Arneaud et al., 2016). In a longitudinal study of Swedish young adults, Carlsson et al. (2015) found that about half of their participants were coded in the same identity status from ages 25 to 29 years, except for those in the moratorium status, which decreased. In a longitudinal study in the U.S., Cramer (2017) found a modest increase in identity achievement scores between ages 18 and 35, as well as a decrease in moratorium and foreclosure scores; little change in diffusion scores was found over this interval. Josselson's (2017) longitudinal study with women in the U.S. found similar stability in the diffusion status from late adolescence through mid-adulthood. In general, identity appears to be a long, slowly developing process that occurs throughout adolescent and young adult life; at the same time, there also may be considerable identity status stability, particularly in diffusion and foreclosure statuses from late adolescence through early and middle adulthood years. More comments will be made about ongoing identity development from adolescence to adulthood in Chapter 8.

Where identity change has occurred, perceived conflict and/or stressful life events, both positive and negative emotional experiences, readiness for change, planfulness, using resources, and intentional behavior appear to be key elements associated with an identity exploration process (Anthis, 2011; Kunnen, 2023; Luyckx & Robitschek, 2014). The use of narrative methods to gain new insights into identity development over time has also made steady progress over the past decade (e.g., McLean et al., 2020); this trend will be described in Chapter 3.

Gender and Ethnicity in Identity Status Research

Questions have been frequently asked about the possibility of gender and ethnic differences in the adolescent identity formation process, and these issues will be examined in greater detail in Chapters 4 and 6 of this volume. The focus here will be on investigations that have emerged through studies of identity exploration and commitment processes.

A number of studies have examined the possibility of gender differences in identity status within particular identity domains as well as in overall identity assessments. In a narrative analysis, Kroger (1997) found few gender differences in identity status distributions for general or domain ratings of identity status as well as in the timing of the developmental process itself. The studies reviewed were primarily from North American contexts. More recent studies from a diversity of cultural settings, however, produced somewhat more diverse findings in response to identity-defining domains as well as developmental timing of identity status changes (e.g., in Sweden: Carlsson et al., 2015; in South Africa: Alberts & Bennett, 2017; and in Japan: Hatano et al., 2023). It may be that different cultural norms for the two genders in more diverse settings can at least partially account for the more mixed findings.

A further question that has been of great interest to identity researchers has been potential gender differences in the sequential ordering of Erikson's identity and intimacy tasks of adolescence and young adulthood. Through past decades, many writers have suggested that the Eriksonian tasks of *identity versus role confusion* and *intimacy versus isolation* may codevelop for women, rather than following a sequential order, as Erikson proposed. Meta-analytic research does indicate that this pattern of co-development may exist for some, but not all, women and a few men (Årseth et al., 2009). Details of this research will be discussed in Chapter 8 of this volume.

One's *ethnicity* is an aspect of identity that involves both membership in an ethnic group and the assumption of the values and attitudes of that group (Phinney, 2006). Over the past decades, research on ethnicity and cultural context in the identity formation task of adolescence and young adulthood has increased exponentially. Identity, ethnicity, and cultural context are interdependent, and greater contact among people of various cultural backgrounds has led to the need for many to develop a bicultural identity (Vedder & Phinney, 2014). As Schwartz et al. (2012) have noted, though, many youths in cultural majority groups take their ethnicities for granted and do not consider ethnicity as a key, identity-defining element. However, the same cannot be said for ethnic minority youths.

Through the 1990s, much research on ethnic identity confirmed a model of ethnic identity development proposed by Phinney (1989) that was based on Marcia's identity status model. Phinney's work suggested three stages in ethnic identity development:

1. an initial stage with little or no questioning of ethnic identity and its meaning (foreclosure/diffusion);
2. a moratorium stage that questioned preexisting ethnic attitudes and the place of one's ethnicity in present life circumstances; and
3. an achieved ethnic identity, in which one attained a secure, positive sense of one's identity as a member of an ethnic group, with an acceptance of other groups.

Subsequent longitudinal work has indicated a significant change to more complex levels of ethnic identity development over time for late adolescents and young adults of various ethnic minority groups (e.g., Syed & Azmitia, 2009; Vedder & Phinney, 2014).

Further research regarding adolescent ethnic identity development over the past two decades has focused on a number of issues, including cultural and subcultural variations in the ethnic identity formation process, the question of how a bicultural identity develops, dimensions of social contexts that facilitate and impede positive ethnic identity development, and immigration and acculturation in the ethnic identity formation process. These issues will be elaborated more fully in Chapters 4 and 5.

Current Directions in Identity Research

Within the past two decades, identity research based on Erikson's writings has seen developments in a number of new directions. Perhaps the largest area of expansion has come through efforts to elaborate and refine identity exploration and commitment processes (for reviews, see Branje et al., 2021; Meeus, 2023). DIDS (Luyckx et al., 2006) and U-MICS (Crocetti, Rubini, & Meeus, 2008) studies have generated findings describing detailed patterns of change in identity exploration and commitment processes. For example, a longitudinal study by Klimstra, Hale III, Raaijmakers, et al. (2010) of adolescents aged 12–20 years found that levels of identity commitment did not change much over this time, while reconsideration of commitments changed substantially (as one would expect). Additionally, exploration in depth increased in the 16–20-year age range. Increases in exploration in depth during late adolescence from this study were also replicated by Luyckx and Robitschek's (2014) cross-sectional study, alongside exploration in breadth.

A takeaway from these identity process-oriented studies is that forming an initial sense of identity stability through commitment is an important step for many younger adolescents, while more reflective identity explorations and subsequent commitments are the purview of many older adolescents. Among college students about 18–22 years old, commitment making, exploration in breadth, and exploration in depth increased, while identification with commitment first decreased but increased again toward the end of a longitudinal study (Luyckx, Schwartz, Goossens, et al., 2008). Studies of older adolescents and young adults have shown a general pattern of progressive identity development, though there may be regressive changes, as well as large individual differences in developmental trends (for a review, see Klimstra & van Doeselaar, 2017). The study of exploration and commitment dimensions over time allows many insights into the complexities of identity commitment, blockages, and revision processes during adolescence and young adulthood.

Further, clusters or profiles extracted from both the DIDS and U-MICS added interesting information about identity progression (as noted with data collected from a present-day-in-the-moment view of identity work) – that is, identifying some potentially new types of identity work that involve ongoing reexamination of one's commitments over time. The DIDS (Luyckx, Schwartz, Berzonsky, et al., 2008) differentiated the "classical" or troubled[5] diffusion found by Marcia from a "carefree diffusion" status. Individuals in troubled diffusion, characterized by high ruminative exploration, appeared stuck in their identity development due to overwhelming choices and/or fears of making a wrong choice, having unrealistic expectations, or perfectionism. This finding suggests that those showing ruminative exploration were characterized as ready for change but lacking the ability to make realistic plans or show intentional behaviors (Luyckx & Robitschek, 2014). When examining young adults at three points in time during a one-year period, Luyckx et al. (2013) found troubled diffusions attempted some exploration of identity issues over time, albeit in a haphazard and unsystematic way, while carefree diffusions were not motivated to undertake any identity exploration at all. Troubled diffusions also evidenced far lower levels of self-esteem and community integration over time than other identity groups.

Meanwhile, using the U-MICS (Crocetti, Rubini, Luyckx, et al., 2008), Crocetti and colleagues differentiated Marcia's "classical" moratorium from a "searching moratorium" profile. Adolescents in searching moratorium were characterized by high commitment, in-depth exploration, and reconsideration of commitment, looking for new choices from a secure base of current commitments. Although searching moratoriums and moratoriums were similar in the lower levels of adaptive personality traits and interpersonal relationships than other identity profiles, the moratorium group showed high levels of psychosocial problems and was much more troubled than the searching moratorium adolescents. By readdressing his own team's longitudinal studies on adolescent (12–20 years) identity (Meeus et al., 2010; Meeus, 2018), he concluded that both moratorium and searching moratoriums are the transient identity groups in the developmental continuum from diffusion to closure[6] and from searching moratorium and moratorium to closure and achievement.

Mechanisms of Identity Development

These process-oriented models have called researchers' attention to mechanisms that underlie developmental changes in identity commitment and exploration. The central notion is that long-term identity development is assumed to result from short-term direct experiences, repeated over many occurrences (Bosma & Kunnen, 2001; Kunnen, 2019). Many researchers currently recognize the role of microlevel or short-term processes (e.g., minutes, days, or weeks) as a potential mechanism of macro-level or long-term development (e.g., months, years, or decades) in identity exploration and commitment (Kunnen & Sugimura, 2021).

Here, longitudinal relations between microlevel identity processes (e.g., day-to-day fluctuations in identity exploration and commitment) are examined in relation to macro-level identity development (e.g., yearly levels of identity exploration and commitment). For instance, Klimstra, Luyckx, Hale III, et al. (2010) found that, in education and friendship domains, a more stable daily identity (i.e., little day-to-day fluctuations) predicted higher levels of commitment and lower levels of reconsideration of commitment across three years. Even in the context of these advances, Klimstra and Schwab (2021) argued that it is important to investigate how "concrete actions and experiences" are important to identity formation, due to the inherent difficulty of assessing thoughts and reflections while they happen.

Van der Gaag et al. (2017) illustrated the benefits of taking this more experiential approach to short-term processes. In this study, researchers asked adolescents every week to report an important positive and negative emotional experience and their levels of exploration and commitment in the educational domain over several months. They found that not only positive but also negative emotional experiences were related to increases in educational commitment. In a qualitative study, Sugimura et al. (2022) observed adolescents' behaviors of exploration in real-time interactions with their peers. They found three overarching interaction patterns that advanced exploration and helped adolescents to discover emerging commitments: creating a safe environment for exploration, clarification, and elaboration of an idea, and finding a keyword and repeating it. These studies provide new directions for advancing our understanding of how daily life plays a role in long-term developmental change.

A recent avenue of promising research links identity exploration and commitment processes to their neurological underpinnings. Some researchers focused on brain areas and others on brain activities. They offer a new step toward understanding how and why identity develops during adolescence and individual differences appear in the process. Becht and colleagues (Becht et al., 2018, 2020) were interested in the question of how changes in brain areas associated with certain behaviors during adolescence might actually facilitate elements of the identity formation process. The researchers wished to test whether individual differences in initial levels of and structural changes in the brain's gray matter volume might be linked with certain identity-related behaviors during adolescence.

Specifically, the researchers addressed whether NAcc (nucleus accumbens in the limbic regions that have been linked to the pursuit of valued and long-term goals) and PFC (prefrontal cortex gray matter that has been linked with cognitive control and information-seeking behaviors) might be linked with goal-directedness and information-seeking behaviors in the identity formation process. Decreasing gray matter volume in the brain is normal in brain maturation, though there are large individual differences in initial levels of gray matter and in the extent of changes over time. The researchers combined self-reported questionnaires and brain imaging data to test whether individual differences in initial level and structural changes of NAcc and PFC gray matter volume predicted later identity commitments, in-depth exploration, and reconsideration of commitments. They hypothesized that a more prolonged developmental trajectory of both NAcc and PFC gray matter volume would allow more time for identity exploration and predict a more mature adolescent identity over time. Findings confirmed that adolescents with higher goal pursuit self-report and higher NAcc volume showed stronger identity commitments with less uncertainty about them over time. Adolescents with higher PFC volume and more prolonged PFC volume development indicated more reflection on their identity commitments in the service of strengthening and maintaining them over time. The importance of PFC for identity development was further confirmed in their subsequent study (Becht et al., 2020).

Another research team was interested in individual differences in brain activity linked to a synthesized or confused sense of identity (Sugimura et al., 2021). They focused on the intrinsic dynamics of the resting-state brain activity, which are not entirely random over time but display a certain degree of temporal self-consistency, known as long-range temporal correlations (LRTC). Individuals who showed stronger responses in the LRTC in the resting-state frontocentral alpha band (8–13 Hz) of electroencephalography (EEG) exhibited higher temporal consistency in occupational preference judgments (e.g., Nakao et al., 2019). This finding suggests that stronger LRTC is associated with a more clearly established understanding of one's traits, values, and beliefs, implying a potential link between LRTC and identity. Therefore, Sugimura and colleagues combined self-report questionnaires assessing identity synthesis and confusion (Schwartz et al., 2009) with EEG data and expected that frontocentral alpha-range LRTC would be positively correlated with identity synthesis (a temporally consistent sense of the self across time) and/or negatively correlated with identity confusion (a temporally changeable and fragmented sense of the self). As expected, young adults with a higher alpha-range LRTC – less random noise in intrinsic brain activity – showed a lower level of identity confusion, indicating a link between the temporal consistency of intrinsic brain activity and that of one's sense of identity.

Identity Content

In the past decade, researchers have not only delved into the processes of identity development ("how" individuals develop their identities), but they also have been increasingly interested in the content of identity ("what" identity consists of) (Galliher et al., 2017). Attention to both the processes and contents of identity leads to a more comprehensive understanding of identity development in context.

In the original (Marcia, 1966) and expanded (e.g., Crocetti, Rubini, & Meeus, 2008) identity models, researchers have selected identity domains such as vocational plans, religious, political, and sexual values as relevant or salient areas to see how identity development proceeds. Adolescents themselves are key informants as to important identity contents, particularly when identity is studied across different sociocultural contexts. From this perspective, Johnson, Odjakjian, et al. (2022) took a participant-driven approach using a shortened version of the Twenty Statements Test (TST: 20 answers to the question "Who am I?") and investigated what identity content was important in a sample of adolescents living in the U.S. Results indicated that traditionally examined identity domains (e.g., occupation, religion, and friendship) as well as novel content elements were important and included (e.g., physical characteristics, emotions, and personality characteristics). Interestingly, many of these content elements included adolescents' own self-evaluations (ascribing content with positive, negative, or neutral values).

The finding that identity content can be infused with ascriptions of social values is consistent with findings from recent research on "negative identity" (identifications with socially undesirable or dangerous roles, Erikson, 1968). Hihara and colleagues (2022) identified the content valence of Japanese young adults' TST responses as positive (socially desirable identity content in the Japanese social context), negative (socially undesirable identity content), and neutral (neither positive nor negative identity content) and showed that negative and positive content valences were associated with maladaptive and adaptive functioning, respectively, over time. These studies of identity contents in the U.S. and Japan show that adolescents' spontaneous reports vary considerably across contexts. Further, Hihara et al. (2021) reported bidirectional positive associations between identity commitment and positive identity content valence over time, which is an important first step in understanding the interplay between identity processes and contents within a given context.

Identity Development in Contexts

A number of issues related to the contexts of identity development are also being examined in greater detail. The role of contexts, generally, in the identity formation process has been described at both theoretical and empirical levels. Côté (1996) attempted theoretically to describe ways in which culture and identity are interrelated. Furthermore, he tested the relationship between agency and identity formation, inspiring more interdisciplinary approaches to understanding the identity formation process across diverse settings (e.g., Côté & Schwartz, 2002; Côté et al., 2016). Galliher et al. (2017) carried this interdisciplinary notion further by proposing a general framework for the study of identity and identity domains within historical, cultural, and political contexts and described ways to evaluate identity development in circumstances of shifting cultural norms, values, and attitudes.

One of the recent important research directions aims to understand identity development in non-Western contexts (Klimstra & Adams, 2021). Identity formation is a necessary developmental task but could be stressful for adolescents in cultural contexts that have traditionally valued social harmony and expectations of parents and emphasized less personal agency and individualization, such as in East Asia (for a detailed discussion, see Sugimura et al., 2021). A relatively large number of findings from studies in Japan have been accumulating. For instance, Hatano and colleagues (Hatano & Sugimura, 2017; Hatano et al., 2020) have found remarkable characteristics of identity formation among adolescents in Japan through longitudinal studies using the U-MICS and DIDS. While their findings from two studies showed identity maturation with age, Hatano et al. (2020), through use of the U-MICS, reported a very high prevalence of moratorium types of identity status trajectories (moratorium and searching moratorium) in both education and friendship domains and the absence of a foreclosure trajectory that was the most prevalent trajectory in Dutch adolescents (Meeus et al., 2010). Moreover, the researchers (Hatano & Sugimura, 2017) found that, through the use of DIDS, the vast majority of Japanese adolescents were classified within the diffusion types of trajectories (e.g., troubled diffusion and carefree diffusion) and none in a foreclosure trajectory, which contrasted with findings from Belgian youth (Luyckx et al., 2013). Further, in these two studies, Hatano and colleagues reported transient identity status trajectories, including adaptive (e.g., diffusion–moratorium) and maladaptive (e.g., diffusion–moratorium–diffusion), that clarified development patterns within a trajectory (Meeus, 2018). Thus, they presented the uncertain and unstable features of identity development in Japanese adolescents that might be due to the paradoxical situation where Japanese society demands adolescents both develop a unique identity and live up to conventional social norms (for a more detailed discussion, see Sugimura, 2020). These studies reporting unique features of development that differ from Western adolescents are important to expand our knowledge of how identity is differentially shaped in diverse cultural contexts.

For more proximal contexts, one of the growing topics of interest is the role of school systems and experiences in identity development (for a review, see Negru-Subtirica, 2024). School is a pivotal place that offers adolescents various opportunities to find, reflect on, and try out aspects of the self, future possibilities, and roles in society. Many researchers who are interested in school contexts have conducted longitudinal studies, with a particular focus on adolescents "who are on the edge between study and work" (Kunnen, 2023, p. 379). For instance, increasing attention is being directed to adolescents in work-bound or vocational high schools who have been relatively neglected and marginalized compared to those in university-bound or academically oriented high schools. For example, vocational school students' strong interest in their education (e.g., professional practical training: Negru-Subtirica & Pop, 2018, in Romania) and affiliation with groups of people who have the same majors (e.g., engineering and agriculture: Sugimura et al., 2025, in Japan) are crucial predictors of their healthy identity development. This phenomenon is likely because vocational students' present education is directly linked to their future vocational choices and professional careers. Studies focusing on professional practical training among university students have shown nuanced relationships between emotional experiences (positive or negative) during the training that enhanced or reduced the levels of exploration and/or commitment, such as clinical internships for psychology students in the Netherlands (Kunnen, 2023) and teaching practicums for teacher training program students in Japan (Iwasa et al., 2022).

Further, the transition from secondary school to work/tertiary education has been increasingly recognized as an impactful event in which identity appears to play a key role in adolescent adjustment during the transition. Longitudinal studies covering adjustment before and after the transition have generally shown that favorable identity development during adolescence is related to adaptive characteristics during the transition, such as less anxiety among prevocational/scientific education students in the Netherlands (Christiaens et al., 2021) and high work/academic engagement after the transition among vocational high school students in Japan (Sugimura et al., 2023). These studies suggest that we pay careful attention to country-specific educational systems for understanding adolescent identity development.

Analysis of the Identity Status Construct

Schwartz, Luyckx, et al. (2015) have argued for newer models and methods to study identity development during adolescence. The increasing volume of studies employing the DIDS (Luyckx et al., 2006) and the U-MICS (Crocetti, Rubini, & Meeus, 2008) has generated considerable discussion in the identity literature as to whether it may be most beneficial to focus on identity exploration and commitment as independent processes or to retain a "person-centered approach" by focusing on identity status clusters derived from the paper-and-pencil instruments described earlier (see, e.g., the debate on this issue in McLean & Syed, 2015; Waterman, 2015). Recent longitudinal studies using these process-oriented models have extracted identity status "trajectories" and found multiple trajectories that showed development within a trajectory (for details of these clusters, see Meeus, 2018).

Crocetti and Meeus (2015) argued for the use of both person- and variable-centered approaches, although particular research questions should ultimately determine the choice of method; person-centered approaches may be best suited for capturing identity development through various identity status pathways, for example, as researchers try to find predictors and consequences of various identity status transitions. A focus on exploration and commitment measures alone, however, can provide useful information about how incremental exploration and commitment dynamics may impact long-term identity goals (Klimstra & Schwab, 2021).

Syed and McLean (2016) noted that the idea of identity integration is understudied in identity research, particularly with its theoretical and practical importance to Erikson's (1968) theory of lifespan development (for a more recent criticism focusing on adulthood, see Mitchell et al., 2021). Marcia's identity status construct, they observed, placed heavy emphasis on personal agency rather than fully appreciating the restrictions that context and opportunity may impose on an individual. Furthermore, in the identity status approach, they pointed out, there has been little research undertaken to understand the relations among identity domains and how they become integrated into one's general sense of identity. Syed and McLean observed that some research focused exclusively on individual identity domains (e.g., ethnicity, vocation, and religion) and how they developed, rather than on how these domains developed in relation to each other, which they believed would be a more productive approach. There are some examples that examined the integration of two domains, such as educational and friendship domains in emerging adulthood (Hihara et al., 2020) and work and family domains in young adults (Gyberg et al., 2019). Yet it is clear that more research attention directed to the issues of the coordination of more than three identity domains and the interplay between identity processes and contents within varied contexts will advance the field.

Implications for Social Response

Social response is intimately linked to identity development through all eight of Erikson's life-cycle stages. From the mutual recognition and regulation of infant and caretaker behavior to the definition of identity through social roles and supportive contexts in adolescence to reflection over one's engagements and social participation in the integrity tasks of old age, recognition from both a developmental partner and a larger social group has been critical to resolving the conflict of each stage in a favorable direction. Assuming that more or less favorable solutions have been found to the conflicts of preceding eras, parents, close associates, and the educational, employment, recreational, religious, health, political, and legal systems of one's cultural context have a vital role to play in the formation of identity during adolescence. All such contexts help to regulate attitudes and behaviors of their younger members, and all are capable of becoming too cooperative in the provision of labels that may not ultimately serve the best interests of youths seeking identity definition. It is through social willingness *not* to predetermine roles and to allow youths a moratorium period that identity formation is best facilitated; it is social tolerance for role experimentation without labeling that eventually benefits all concerned (Erikson, 1968).

Erikson himself cited numerous examples of ways in which the psychiatric profession and legal system could provide youths with labels that offered a ready identity to troubled adolescents but did not allow optimal resolution to the conflicts of this stage. Just as an adolescent psychiatric patient may "choose the very role of patient as the most meaningful basis for an identity formation" (Erikson, 1968, p. 179), others might gratefully adopt the role of "criminal" or "delinquent" that courts and psychiatric agencies could so easily and cooperatively confer. Society's *refusal* to provide ready role definitions for such adolescents and *not* to treat their experimentations as the final identity are in the best interests of the entire community.

Systematic research on group-implemented, universal (i.e., for everyone) identity intervention programs has expanded greatly over the past decades. Markstrom-Adams et al.'s (1993) study was one of the first studies to provide evidence that short-term intervention training strategies in social perspective taking might facilitate ideological identity achievement. Kurtines and colleagues have continued this line of inquiry (e.g., Berman et al., 2024; Eichas et al., 2015; Meca et al., 2014) and developed and tested identity intervention programs to facilitate positive identity development based on Erikson's (1968) identity concepts.

One example of such an intervention is by Berman et al. (2024), who administered the Making Life Choice Intervention Program to university students enrolled in an elective personal growth psychology course. The program facilitated small group discussions each week for an hour and a half over a 16-week semester on identity issues important to group members, following readings on how to resolve identity issues through critical thinking and discussion and a short survey on how to apply the readings to their lives. Intervention outcomes from 2015 to 2023 were evaluated and indicated that students' improvements in identity exploration and commitment were associated with decreased identity distress and positive changes in self-esteem, purpose in life, locus of control, self-actualization, and ego strength.

A review of this and other programs by Ferrer-Wreder et al. (2014) concluded that it is possible to influence the process of identity development among adolescents and that the most promising identity intervention strategies appear to have the following three key elements:

1. expanding self-understanding through identity exploration;
2. teaching critical thinking and problem-solving skills; and
3. helping youth learn to take control and accept responsibility for their own life decisions.

Ferrer-Wreder and colleagues (2014) also addressed the issue of whether or not concerned adults should try to influence the identity development process. From studies to date, they concluded an unequivocal "yes." Their review showed that positive youth identity development interventions promoted healthy psychosocial functioning and reduced or protected against adjustment difficulties. A recent meta-analysis reported several concrete strategies to enhance educational and professional identity (Crocetti et al., 2025). The examples of effective components included mentoring, group-based activities (e.g., discussions and sharing experiences), and reflections (e.g., writing) that could promote key elements presented by Ferrer-Wreder et al. (2014). The importance of these and other school-based identity intervention programs is currently viewed as particularly valuable for ethnic minority youths to develop their ethnic–racial identities in both Europe and the U.S. (for a review, see Juang & Hwang, 2024); this topic is elaborated in Chapter 4.

Summary

Ego identity as conceptualized by Erik Erikson is a psychosocial construct that can be understood only through the interaction of biological foundations, ego organization, and social context. During adolescence, features of identity, which have formed through more or less favorable resolutions to earlier stages of developmental conflict, must now evolve into a new configuration, different from yet based upon the earlier introjections and identifications of childhood. Furthermore, the balance achieved during the identity versus role confusion conflict of adolescence will affect all developmental stages encountered during adult life. Marcia has empirically elaborated Erikson's identity-versus-role confusion conflict, describing four identity resolutions based on attitudes of exploration of and commitment to particular social roles and values. Subsequent research has elaborated these exploration and commitment processes. The identity statuses and various types of exploration and commitment processes have implications for effective educational, counseling, and psychotherapeutic interventions.

Notes

1 Peter Blos (1903–1997) was a psychoanalyst and theorist who built a psychodynamic model of the intrapsychic separation and individuation process during adolescence. His "separation–individuation" model describes adolescence as a time of relinquishing the old intrapsychic arrangement of that which has been considered self (the parental introjects) and creating a new psychological structure, distinct from the old introjects and individuated in the expression of a person's own genuine interests and desires (Blos, 1967).

2 In this chapter, the use of "he" is retained from original writings when quoted but should be understood in the sense of "people" more generally.

3 In this chapter, the term "identity cluster, profile, or trajectory" instead of "identity status" is used when describing findings from the extended models (DIDS and U-MICS). This is because, based on Waterman's (2015) arguments (see the "Extensions of Marcia's Model" section in this chapter), the extended models measure slightly different conceptual aspects of identity from more traditional measures (ISI and EOM-EIS-II); direct compatibility of the findings of those models with findings from ISI and EOM-EIS-II is difficult.

4 These problems have been discussed by several researchers (Carlsson et al., 2024; Kroger & Marcia, 2022; Negru-Subtirica & Klimstra, 2022; Waterman, 2015).

5 Troubled diffusion was termed "diffused diffusion" in Luyckx, Schwartz, Berzonsky, et al. (2008). They changed it to "troubled diffusion" to make a clearer contrast with "carefree diffusion," characterized by a seemingly untroubled approach toward identity (Luyckx et al., 2013).

6 The "closure" cluster termed by Meeus (2018) means "passive" maintenance of strong commitments (i.e., high commitment, low in-depth exploration, and low reconsideration of commitment). This cluster includes two types of adolescents: those who begin in the classic "foreclosure" state and remain there over time and those who have explored different commitments and are not engaged in in-depth exploration of present commitments (Meeus et al., 2010).

References

Adams, G. G. (1999). *The objective measure of ego identity status: A manual on theory and test construction* [Unpublished manuscript]. Department of Family Relations and Applied Nutrition, University of Guelph.

Alberts, C., & Bennett, M. J. (2017). Identity formation among isiXhosa-speaking adolescents in a rural Eastern Cape community in South Africa: A brief report. *Journal of Psychology in Africa, 27*(2), 198–202. http://dx.doi.org/10.1080/14330237.2017.1303128

Anthis, K. (2011). The role of conflict in continuity and change: Life events associated with identity development in racially and ethnically diverse women. *Identity: An International Journal of Theory and Research, 11*(4), 333–347. https://doi.org/10.1080/15283488.2011.613588

Arneaud, M. J., Alea, N., & Espinet, M. (2016). Identity development in Trinidad: Status differences by age, adulthood transitions, and culture. *Identity: An International Journal of Theory and Research, 16*(1), 59–71. https://doi.org/10.1080/15283488.2015.1121818

Årseth, A. K., Kroger, J., Martinussen, M., & Marcia, J. E. (2009). Meta-analytic studies of identity status and the relational issues of attachment and intimacy. *Identity: An International Journal of Theory and Research, 9*(1), 1–32. https://doi.org/10.1080/15283480802579532

Becht, A. I., Bos, M. G. N., Marieke, G. N., Nelemans, S. A., Peters, S., Vollebergh, W. A. M., Branje, S. J. T., Meeus, W. H. J., & Crone, E. A. (2018). Goal-directed correlates and neurobiological underpinnings of adolescent identity: A multi-method multi-sample longitudinal approach. *Child Development, 89*(3), 823–836. https://doi.org/10.1111/cdev.13048

Becht, A. I., Klapwijk, E. T., Wierenga, L. M., van der Cruijsen, R., Spaans, J., van der Aar, L., Peters, S., Branje, S., Meeus, W., & Crone, E. A. (2020). Longitudinal associations between structural prefrontal cortex and nucleus accumbens development and daily identity formation processes across adolescence. *Developmental Cognitive Neuroscience, 46*(May), 100880. https://doi.org/10.1016/j.dcn.2020.100880

Berman, S. L., Hall, J., Andrion, C., & Stuckey, A. L. (2024). Making life choices: An evaluation of a university-based identity intervention program. *Identity: An International Journal of Theory and Research, 25*(2), 305–315. https://doi.org/10.1080/15283488.2024.2389431

Berman, S. L., Ratner, K., Cheng, M., Li, S., Jhingon, G., & Sukumaron, N. (2014). Identity distress during the era of globalization: A cross-national comparative study of India, China, and the United States. *Identity: An International Journal of Theory and Research, 14*(4), 286–296. https://doi.org/10.1080/15283488.2014.944698

Berzonsky, M. D., & Papini, D. R. (2015). Cognitive reasoning, identity components, and identity processing styles. *Identity: An International Journal of Theory and Research, 15*(1), 74–88. https://doi.org/10.1080/15283488.2014.989444

Beyers, W., & Seiffge-Krenke, I. (2010). Does identity precede intimacy? Testing Erikson's theory on romantic development in emerging adults of the 21st century. *Journal of Adolescent Research, 25*(3), 387–415. https://doi.org/10.1177/0743558410361370

Blos, P. (1967). The second individuation process of adolescence. *Psychoanalytic Study of the Child, 22*, 162–186. https://doi.org/10.1080/00797308.1967.11822595

Bosma, H. A., & Kunnen, E. S. (2001). Determinants and mechanisms in ego identity development: A review and synthesis. *Developmental Review, 21*(1), 39–66. https://doi.org/10.1006/drev.2000.0514

Boyes, M. C., & Chandler, M. (1992). Cognitive development, epistemic doubt, and identity formation in adolescence. *Journal of Youth and Adolescence, 21*(3), 277–304. https://doi.org/10.1007/BF01537019

Branje, S., de Moor, E. L., Spitzer, J., & Becht, A. I. (2021). Dynamics of identity development in adolescence: A decade in review. *Journal of Research on Adolescence, 31*(4), 908–927. https://doi.org/10.1111/jora.12678

Caplan, P. J. (1979). Erikson's concept of inner space: A data-based reevaluation. *American Journal of Orthopsychiatry*, *49*(1), 100–108. https://doi.org/10.1111/j.1939-0025.1979.tb02590.x

Carlsson, J., Wängkvist, M., & Frisén, A. (2015). Identity development in the late twenties: A never ending story. *Developmental Psychology*, *51*(3), 334–345. https://doi.org/10.1037/a0038745

Carlsson, J., Wängqvist, M., Syed, M., & Frisén, A. (2024). Lost in translation: The conceptual drift from the identity status interview to questionnaire measures. *Journal of Adult Development*. Advance online publication. https://doi.org/10.1007/s10804-024-09506-6

Christiaens, A. H. T., Nelemans, S. A., Meeus, W. H. J., & Branje, S. (2021). Identity development across the transition from secondary to tertiary education: A 9-wave longitudinal study. *Journal of Adolescence*, *93*(1), 245–256. https://doi.org/10.1016/j.adolescence.2021.03.007

Ciaccio, N. V. (1971). A test of Erikson's theory of ego epigenesis. *Developmental Psychology*, *4*(3), 306–311. https://doi.org/10.1037/h0030969

Coles, R. (1970). *Erik H. Erikson: The growth of his work*. Little Brown.

Côté, J. E. (1996). Identity: A multidimensional analysis. In G. R. Adams, R. Montemayor, & T. Gullotta (Eds.), *Psychological development during adolescence: Progress in developmental contextualism* (pp. 130–180). Sage.

Côté, J. E., & Levine, C. G. (2015). *Identity formation, youth, and development: A simplified approach*. Psychology Press. https://doi.org/10.4324/9780203767047

Côté, J. E., Mizokami, S., Roberts, S. E., & Nakama, R. (2016). An examination of the cross-cultural validity of the Identity Capital Model: American and Japanese students compared. *Journal of Adolescence*, *46*(1), 76–85. https://doi.org/10.1016/j.adolescence.2015.11.001

Côté, J. E., & Schwartz, S. J. (2002). Comparing psychological and sociological approaches to identity: Identity status, identity capital, and the individualization process. *Journal of Adolescence*, *25*(6), 571–586. https://doi.org/10.1006/jado.2002.0511

Cramer, P. (2017). Identity change between late adolescence and adulthood. *Personality and Individual Differences*, *104*, 538–543. https://doi.org/10.1016/j.paid.2016.08.044

Crocetti, E., Cieciuch, J., Gao, C.-H. H., Klimstra, T., Lin, C.-L. L., Matos, P. M., Morsünbül, Ü., Negru, O., Sugimura, K., Zimmermann, G., & Meeus, W. (2015). National and gender measurement invariance of the Utrecht-Management of Identity Commitments Scale (U-MICS): A 10-nation study with university students. *Assessment*, *22*(6), 753–768. https://doi.org/10.1177/1073191115584969

Crocetti, E., De Lise, F., Pagano, M., Bobba, B., Maratia, F., Meeus, W., & Bacaro, V. (2025). What's your vocation? A meta-analysis of interventions tackling youth educational and professional identity. *Identity: An International Journal of Theory and Research*, *25*(2), 197–215. https://doi.org/10.1080/15283488.2024.2394861

Crocetti, E., & Meeus, W. (2015). The identity statuses: Strengths of a person-centered approach. In K. C. McLean & M. Syed (Eds.), *The Oxford handbook of identity development* (pp. 97–114). Oxford University Press. https://doi.org/10.1093/oxfordhb/9780199936564.013.016

Crocetti, E., Rubini, M., Luyckx, K., & Meeus, W. (2008). Identity formation in early and middle adolescents from various ethnic groups: From three dimensions to five statuses. *Journal of Youth and Adolescence*, *37*(8), 983–996. https://doi.org/10.1007/s10964-007-9222-2

Crocetti, E., Rubini, M., & Meeus, W. H. J. (2008). Capturing the dynamics of identity formation in various ethnic groups: Development and validation of a three-dimensional model. *Journal of Adolescence*, *31*(2), 207–222. https://doi.org/10.1016/j.adolescence.2007.09.002

Dimitrova, R., Crocetti, E., Buzea, C., Jordanov, V., Kosic, M., Tair, E., Taušová, J., van Cittert, N., & Uka, F. (2016). The Utrecht-Management of Identity Commitments Scale (U-MICS): Measurement invariance and cross-national comparisons of youth from seven

European countries. *European Journal of Psychological Assessment*, *32*(2), 119–127. https://doi.org/10.1027/1015-5759/a000241

Dyk, P. H., & Adams, G. R. (1990). Identity and intimacy: An initial investigation of three theoretical models using cross-lag panel correlations. *Journal of Youth and Adolescence* *19*(2), 91–109. https://doi.org/10.1007/BF01538715

Eichas, K., Meca, A., Montgomery, M. J., & Kurtines, W. M. (2015). Identity and positive youth development: Advances in developmental intervention science. In K. C. McLean & M. Syed (Eds.), *Oxford handbook of identity development* (pp. 337–354). Oxford University Press. https://doi.org/10.1093/oxfordhb/9780199936564.013.020

Erikson, E. H. (1956). The problem of ego identity. *Journal of the American Psychoanalytic Association*, *4*(1), 56–121. https://doi.org/10.1177/000306515600400104

Erikson, E. H. (1959). *Identity and the life cycle.* Psychological Issues Monograph 1. International Universities Press.

Erikson, E. H. (1963). *Childhood and society* (2nd ed). Norton.

Erikson, E. H. (1968). *Identity, youth, and crisis.* Norton.

Erikson, E. H. (1970). Autobiographic notes on the identity crisis. *Daedalus*, *99*(4), 730–759. https://www.jstor.org/stable/20023973

Erikson, E. H. (1977). *Toys and reasons: Stages in the ritualization of experience.* Norton.

Erikson, E. H. (1984). Reflections on the last stage – and the first. *Psychoanalytic Study of the Child*, *39*(1), 155–165. https://doi.org/10.1080/00797308.1984.11823424

Evans, R. I. (1967). *Dialogue with Erik Erikson.* Harper & Row.

Ferrer-Wreder, L. A., Montgomery, M. J., Lorente, C. C., & Habibi, M. (2014). Identify interventions for adolescents: Promoting optimal identity development in adolescents. In T. P. Gullotta & M. Bloom (Eds.), *Encyclopedia of primary prevention and health promotion* (pp. 1278–1287). Springer Science + Business Media. https://doi.org/10.1007/978-1-4614-5999-6_183

Frank, S. J., Pirsh, L. A., & Wright, V. C. (1990). Late adolescents' perceptions of their relationships with their parents: Relationships among de-idealization, autonomy, relatedness, and insecurity and implications for adolescent adjustment and ego identity status. *Journal of Youth and Adolescence*, *19*(6), 571–588. https://doi.org/10.1007/BF01537177

Friedman, L. J. (1999). *Identity's architect: A biography of Erik H. Erikson.* Scribner.

Galliher, R. V., McLean, K. C., & Syed, M. (2017). An integrated developmental model for studying identity content in context. *Developmental Psychology*, *53*(11), 2011–2022. https://doi.org/10.1037/dev0000299

Gfellner, B. M., & Bartoszuk, K. (2015). Emerging adulthood in North America: Identity status and perceptions of adulthood among college students in Canada and the United States. *Emerging Adulthood*, *3*(5), 368–372. https://doi.org/10.1177/2167696815595555

Grotevant, H. D., & Cooper, C. R. (1985). Patterns of interaction in family relationships and the development of identity exploration in adolescence. *Child Development*, *56*(2), 415–428. https://doi.org/10.1111/j.1467-8624.1985.tb00116.x

Gyberg, F., Frisén, A., & Syed, M. (2019). "Being stuck between two worlds" – Identity configurations of occupational and family identities. *Identity: An International Journal of Theory and Research*, *19*(4), 330–346. https://doi.org/10.1080/15283488.2019.1681997

Hatano, K., Hihara, S., Sugimura, K., & Mizokami, S. (2023). Identity formation with gender differences in university students: A three-wave longitudinal study. *Current Psychology*, *42*(34), 30174–30186. https://doi.org/10.1007/s12144-022-04036-4

Hatano, K., & Sugimura, K. (2017). Is adolescence a period of identity development for all youth? Insights from a longitudinal study of identity dynamics in Japan. *Developmental Psychology*, *53*(11), 2113–2126. https://doi.org/10.1037/dev0000354

Hatano, K., Sugimura, K., Crocetti, E., & Meeus, W. H. J. (2020). Diverse-and-dynamic pathways in educational and interpersonal identity formation during adolescence: Longitudinal links with psychosocial functioning. *Child Development*, *91*(4), 1203–1218. https://doi.org/10.1111/cdev.13301

Hearn, S., Saulnier, G., Strayer, J., Glenham, M., Koopman, R., & Marcia, M. (2012). Between integrity and despair: Toward construct validation of Erikson's eighth stage. *Journal of Adult Development, 19*(1), 1–20. https://doi.org/10.1007/s10804-011-9126-y
Hesse, H. (1951). *Siddhartha*. New Directions Publishing Corp.
Hihara, S., Ishibashi, I., Umemura, T., & Sugimura, K. (2020). Roles of configurations of multiple identity domains in adaptive and maladaptive functioning in Japanese emerging adults: Using a culturally relevant index. *Emerging Adulthood, 8*(5), 373–381. https://doi.org/10.1177/2167696819858457
Hihara, S., Sugimura, K., Umemura, T., Iwasa, Y., & Syed, M. (2022). Positive and negative valences of identities: Longitudinal associations of identity content valences with adaptive and maladaptive functioning among Japanese young adults. *Development and Psychopathology, 34*(4), 1516–1530. https://doi.org/10.1017/S0954579421000043
Hihara, S., Umemura, T., Iwasa, Y., Saiga, S., & Sugimura, K. (2021). Identity processes and identity content valences: Examining bidirectionality. *Developmental Psychology, 57*(12), 2265–2280. https://doi.org/10.1037/dev0001275
Hopkins, J. R. (1995). Erik Homburger Erikson (1902–1994). *American Psychologist, 50*(9), 796–797. https://doi.org/10.1037/0003-066X.50.9.796
Iwasa, Y., Hihara, S., Umemura, T., Tazume, H., & Sugimura, K. (2022). Identity formation and school experience among university students in a teacher training program: A four-wave longitudinal study during the teaching practicum. *Identity: An International Journal of Theory and Research, 22*(3), 183–197. https://doi.org/10.1080/15283488.2021.1954520
Jespersen, K., Kroger, J., & Martinussen, M. (2013a). Identity status and ego development: A meta-analysis. *Identity: An International Journal of Theory and Research, 13*(3), 228–241. https://doi.org/10.1080/15283488.2013.799433
Jespersen, K., Kroger, J., & Martinussen, M. (2013b). Identity status and moral reasoning: A meta-analysis. *Identity: An International Journal of Theory and Research, 13*(3), 266–280. https://doi.org/10.1080/15283488.2013.799472
Johnson, S. K., de Moor, E. L., Chung, J. M., den Boer, L., & Klimstra, T. A. (2022). An item response theory analysis of two frequently used measures of identity development. *Psychological Assessment, 34*(11), 1047–1061. https://doi.org/10.1037/pas0001171
Johnson, S. K., Odjakjian, K., & Park, Y. (2022). I am whatever I say I am: The salient identity content of U.S. adolescents. *Journal of Research on Adolescence, 32*(2), 737–755. https://doi.org/10.1016/j.neuroimage.2019.116015
Josselson, R. (2017). *Paths to fulfillment: Women's search for meaning and identity*. Oxford University Press.
Juang, L. P., & Hwang, C. P. (2024). The importance of ethnic-racialized identities to becoming and being culturally responsive and equity minded educators. *Identity: An International Journal of Theory and Research, 24*(4), 257–268. https://doi.org/10.1080/15283488.2024.2388248
Kerpelman, J. L., Pittman, J. F., & Lamke, L. K. (1997). Toward a microprocess perspective on adolescent identity development. *Journal of Adolescent Research, 12*(3), 325–346. https://doi.org/10.1177/0743554897123002
Klimstra, T. A., & Adams, B. G. (2021). Perspectives on personal identity development in Western and non-Western contexts. In B. G. Adams & F. J. R. van de Vijver (Eds.), *Non-Western identity: Research and perspectives* (pp. 217–231). Springer. https://doi.org/10.1007/978-3-030-77242-0_13
Klimstra, T. A., Hale III, W. W., Raaijmakers, Q. A. W., Branje, S. J. T., & Meeus, W. H. J. (2010). Identity formation in adolescence: Change or stability? *Journal of Youth and Adolescence, 39*(2), 150–162. https://doi.org/10.1007/s10964-009-9401-4
Klimstra, T. A., Luyckx, K., Hale III, W. W., Frijns, T., van Lier, P. A. C., & Meeus, W. H. J. (2010). Short-term fluctuations in identity: Introducing a micro-level approach to identity formation. *Journal of Personality and Social Psychology, 99*(1), 191–202. https://doi.org/10.1037/a0019584

Klimstra, T. A., & Schwab, J. R. (2021). Time and identity: An evaluation of existing empirical research, conceptual challenges, and methodological opportunities. *Identity: An International Journal of Theory and Research, 21*(4), 275–288. https://doi.org/10.1080/15283488.2021.1924722

Klimstra, T., & van Doeselaar, L. (2017). Identity formation in adolescence and young adulthood. In J. Specht (Ed.), *Personality development across the lifespan* (pp. 293–308). Elsevier. https://doi.org/10.1016/B978-0-12-804674-6.00018-1

Kroger, J. (1997). Gender and identity: The intersection of structure, content, and context. *Sex Roles, 36*(11–12), 747–770. https://doi.org/10.1023/A:1025627206676

Kroger, J., & Haslett, S. J. (1988). Separation-individuation and ego identity status in late adolescence: A two-year longitudinal study. *Journal of Youth and Adolescence, 17*(1), 59–79. https://doi.org/10.1007/BF01538724

Kroger, J., & Marcia, J. E. (2011). The identity statuses: Origins, meanings, and interpretations. In S. J. Schwartz, K. Luyckx, & V. Vignoles (Eds.), *Handbook of identity theory and research* (pp. 31–53). Springer. https://doi.org/10.1007/978-1-4419-7988-9_2

Kroger, J., & Marcia, J. E. (2022). Erikson, the identity statuses, and beyond. In M. Bamberg, C. Demuth, & M. Watzlawik (Eds.), *The Cambridge handbook of identity* (pp. 215–237). Cambridge University Press. https://doi.org/10.1017/9781108755146.012

Kroger, J., Martinussen, M., & Marcia, J. E. (2010). Identity status change during adolescence and young adulthood: A meta-analysis. *Journal of Adolescence, 33*(5), 683–698. https://doi.org/10.1016/j.adolescence.2009.11.002

Kunnen, E. S. (2019). Identity development from a dynamic systems perspective. In E. S. Kunnen, N. M. P. de Ruiter, B. F. Jeronimus, & M. A. E. van der Gaag (Eds.), *Psychosocial development in adolescence: Insights from the dynamic systems approach* (pp. 146–159). Routledge. https://doi.org/10.4324/9781315165844-9

Kunnen, E. S. (2023). The role of emotional experiences in commitment development in internship students. *Identity: An International Journal of Theory and Research, 23*(4), 379–393. https://doi.org/10.1080/15283488.2023.2235392

Kunnen, E. S., & Sugimura, K. (2021). Real-time identity processes: Theories and methods. *Identity: An International Journal of Theory and Research, 21*(4), 271–274. https://doi.org/10.1080/15283488.2021.1985845

Levitz-Jones, E. M., & Orlofsky, J. L. (1985). Separation–individuation and intimacy capacity in college women. *Journal of Personality and Social Psychology, 49*(1), 156–169. https://doi.org/10.1037/0022-3514.49.1.156

Lillevoll, K. R., Kroger, J., & Martinussen, M. (2013a). Identity status and anxiety: A meta-analysis. *Identity: An International Journal of Theory and Research, 13*(3), 214–227. https://doi.org/10.1080/15283488.2013.799432

Lillevoll, K. R., Kroger, J., & Martinussen, M. (2013b). Identity status and locus of control: A meta-analysis. *Identity: An International Journal of Theory and Research, 13*(3), 253–265. https://doi.org/10.1080/15283488.2013.799471

Luyckx, K., Goossens, L., Soenens, B., & Beyers, W. (2006). Unpacking commitment and exploration: Preliminary validation of an integrative model of late adolescent identity formation. *Journal of Adolescence, 29*(3), 361–378. https://doi.org/10.1016/j.adolescence.2005.03.008

Luyckx, K., Klimstra, T. A., Schwartz, S. J., & Duriez, B. (2013). Personal identity in college and the work context: Developmental trajectories and psychosocial functioning. *European Journal of Personality, 27*(3), 222–237. https://doi.org/10.1002/per.1903

Luyckx, K., & Robitschek, C. (2014). Personal growth initiative and identity formation in adolescence through young adulthood: Mediating processes on the pathway to well-being. *Journal of Adolescence, 37*(7), 973–981. https://doi.org/10.1016/j.adolescence.2014.07.009

Luyckx, K., Schwartz, S. J., Berzonsky, M. D., Soenens, B., Vansteenkiste, M., Smits, I., & Goossens, L. (2008). Capturing ruminative exploration: Extending the four-dimensional model of identity formation in late adolescence. *Journal of Research in Personality, 42*(1), 58–82. https://doi.org/10.1016/j.jrp.2007.04.004

Luyckx, K., Schwartz, S. J., Goossens, L, Soenens, B., & Beyers, W. (2008). Developmental typologies of identity formation and adjustment in female emerging adults: A latent class growth analysis approach. *Journal of Research on Adolescence, 18*(4), 595–619. https://doi.org/10.1111/j.1532-7795.2008.00573.x

Makros, J., & McCabe, M. P. (2001). Relationships between identity and self-representations during adolescence. *Journal of Youth and Adolescence, 30*(5), 623–639. https://doi.org/10.1023/A:1010404822585

Marcia, J. E. (1966). Development and validation of ego identity status. *Journal of Personality and Social Psychology, 3*(5), 551–558. https://doi.org/10.1037/h0023281

Marcia, J. E. (1967). Ego identity status: Relationship to change in self-esteem, "general maladjustment," and authoritarianism. *Journal of Personality, 35*(1), 118–133. https://doi.org/10.1111/j.1467-6494.1967.tb01419.x

Marcia, J. E. (2004). Why Erikson? In K. R. Hoover (Ed.), *The future of identity: Centennial reflections on the legacy of Erik Erikson* (pp. 43–59). Lexington Books. https://doi.org/10.5771/9780739155417

Marcia, J. E., Waterman, A. S., Matteson, D. R., Archer, S. L., & Orlofsky, J. L. (2011). *Ego identity: A handbook for psychosocial research.* Springer. https://doi.org/10.1007/978-1-4613-8330-7 (Original work published 1993)

Markstrom-Adams, C., Ascione, F. R., Braegger, D., & Adams, G. R. (1993). Promotion of ego identity development: Can short-term intervention facilitate growth? *Journal of Adolescence, 16*(2), 217–224. https://doi.org/10.1006/jado.1993.1020

McLean, K. C., & Syed, M. (Eds.). (2015). *The Oxford handbook of identity development.* Oxford University Press. https://doi.org/10.1093/oxfordhb/9780199936564.001.0001

McLean, K. C., & Syed, M. (2016). Personal, master, and alternative narratives: An integrative framework for understand identity development in context. *Human Development, 58*(6), 318–349. https://doi.org/10.1159/000445817

McLean, K. C., Syed, M., Pasupathi, M., Adler, J. M., Dunlop, W. L., Drustrup, D., Fivush, R., Graci, M. E., Lilgendahl, J. P., Lodi-Smith, J., McAdams, D. P., & McCoy, T. P. (2020). The empirical structure of narrative identity: The initial Big Three. *Journal of Personality and Social Psychology, 119*(4), 920–944. https://doi.org/10.1037/pspp0000247

Meca, A., Eichas, K., Quintana, S., Maximin, B. M., Ritchie, R. A., Madrazo, V. L., Harari, G. M., & Kurtines, W. M. (2014). Reducing identity distress: Results of an identity intervention for emerging adults. *Identity: An International Journal of Theory and Research, 14*(4), 312–331. https://doi.org/10.1080/15283488.2014.944696

Meeus, W. (2018). The identity status continuum revisited: A comparison of longitudinal findings with Marcia's model and dual cycle models. *European Psychologist, 23*(4), 289–299. https://doi.org/10.1027/1016-9040/a000339

Meeus, W. (2023). Fifty years of longitudinal research into identity development in adolescence and early adulthood: An overview. In L. J. Crockett, G. Carlo, & J. E. Schulenberg (Eds.), *APA handbook of adolescent and young adult development* (pp. 139–157). American Psychological Association. https://doi.org/10.1037/0000298-009

Meeus, W., van de Schoot, R., Keijsers, L., Schwartz, S. J., & Branje, S. (2010). On the progression and stability of adolescent identity formation: A five-wave longitudinal study in early-to-middle and middle-to-late adolescence. *Child Development, 81*(5), 1565–1581. https://doi.org/10.1111/j.1467-8624.2010.01492.x

Mitchell, L. L., Adler, J. M., Carlsson, J., Eriksson, P. L., & Syed, M. (2021). A conceptual review of identity integration across adulthood. *Developmental Psychology, 57*(11), 1981–1990. https://doi.org/10.1037/dev0001246

Moustakas, C. E. (1974). *Portraits of loneliness and love.* Prentice-Hall.

Nakao, T., Miyagi, M., Hiramoto, R., Wolff, A., Gomez-Pilar, J., Miyatani, M., & Northoff, G. (2019). From neuronal to psychological noise – Long-range temporal correlations in EEG intrinsic activity reduce noise in internally-guided decision making. *NeuroImage*, *201*, 116015. https://doi.org/10.1016/j.neuroimage.2019.116015

Negru-Subtirica, O. (2024). Educational identity processes in adolescence: An analysis of longitudinal evidence and the role of educational systems. *Child Development Perspectives*, *18*(2), 97–103. https://doi.org/10.1111/cdep.12504

Negru-Subtirica, O., & Klimstra, T. (2022). Synthesized or confused field?: A critical analysis of the state-of-the-art in identity status research methods. In M. Bamberg, C. Demuth, & M. Watzlawik (Eds.), *The Cambridge handbook of identity* (pp. 388–413). https://doi.org/10.1017/9781108755146.021

Negru-Subtirica, O., & Pop, E. I. (2018). Reciprocal associations between educational identity and vocational identity in adolescence: A three-wave longitudinal investigation. *Journal of Youth and Adolescence*, *47*(4), 703–716. https://doi.org/10.1007/s10964-017-0789-y

Orlofsky, J. L., Marcia, J. E., & Lesser, I. M. (1973). Ego identity status and the intimacy versus isolation crisis of young adulthood. *Journal of Personality and Social Psychology*, *27*(2), 211–219. https://doi.org/10.1037/h0034787

Papini, D. R., Micka, J. C., & Barnett, J. K. (1989). Perceptions of intrapsychic and extrapsychic functioning as bases of adolescent ego identity status. *Journal of Adolescent Research*, *4*(4), 462–482. https://doi.org/10.1177/074355488944005

Phinney, J. S. (1989). Stages of ethnic identity development in minority group adolescents. *Journal of Early Adolescence*, *9*(1–2), 34–49. https://doi.org/10.1177/0272431689091004

Phinney, J. S. (2006). Ethnic identity exploration in emerging adulthood. In J. Arnett & J. L. Tanner (Eds), *Emerging adults in America: Coming of age in the 21st century* (pp. 117–134). American Psychological Association. https://doi.org/10.1037/11381-005

Roazen, P. (2000). Review of "Ideas and identities: The life and work of Erik Erikson". *Psychoanalytic Psychology*, *17*, 437–442.

Rogers, L. O., Kiang, L., White, L., Calzada, E. J., Umaña-Taylor, A. J., Byrd, C., Williams, C. D., Marks, A., & Whitesell, N. (2020). Persistent concerns: Questions for research on ethnic-racial identity development. *Research in Human Development*, *17*(2–3), 130–153. https://doi.org/10.1080/15427609.2020.1831881

Ryeng, M. S., Kroger, J., & Martinussen, M. (2013a). Identity status and self-esteem: A meta-analysis. *Identity: An International Journal of Theory and Research*, *13*(3), 201–213. https://doi.org/10.1080/15283488.2013.799431

Ryeng, M. S., Kroger, J., & Martinussen, M. (2013b). Identity status and authoritarianism: A meta-analysis. *Identity: An International Journal of Theory and Research*, *13*(3), 242–252. https://doi.org/10.1080/15283488.2013.799434

Schwartz, S. J., Adamson, L., Ferrer-Wreder, L. A., Dillon, F., & Berman, S. L. (2015). Identity status measurement across contexts: Variations in measurement structure and mean levels among White American, Hispanic American, and Swedish emerging adults. *Journal of Personality Assessment*, *86*(1), 61–76. https://doi.org/10.1207/s15327752jpa8601_08

Schwartz, S. J., Beyers, W., Luyckx, K., Soenens, B., Zamboanga, B. L., Forthun, L. F., Hardy, S. A., Vazsonyi, A. T., Ham, L. S., Kim, S. Y., Whitbourne, S. K., & Waterman, A. S. (2011). Examining the light and dark sides of emerging adults' identity: A Study of identity status differences in positive and negative psychosocial functioning. *Journal of Youth Adolescence*, *40*(7), 839–859. https://doi.org/10.1007/s10964-010-9606-6

Schwartz, S. J., Luyckx, K., & Crocetti, E. (2015). What have we learned since Schwartz (2001)? A reappraisal of the field of identity development. In K. C. McLean & M. Syed (Eds.), *The Oxford handbook of identity development* (pp. 539–561). Oxford University Press. https://doi.org/10.1093/oxfordhb/9780199936564.013.028

Schwartz, S. J., Zamboanga, B. I., Meca, A., & Ritchie, R. A. (2012). Identity around the world: An overview. *New Directions in Child and Adolescent Development*, *2012*(138), 1–18. https://doi.org/10.1002/cad.20019

Schwartz, S. J., Zamboanga, B. L., Wang, W., & Olthuis, J. V. (2009). Measuring identity from an Eriksonian perspective: Two sides of the same coin? *Journal of Personality Assessment, 91*(2), 143–154. https://doi.org/10.1080/00223890802634266

Slugoski, B. R., Marcia, J. E., & Koopman, R. F. (1984). Cognitive and social interactional characteristics of ego identity statuses in college males. *Journal of Personality and Social Psychology, 47*(3), 646–661. https://doi.org/10.1037/0022-3514.47.3.646

Stephen, J., Fraser, E., & Marcia, J. E. (1992). Moratorium–achievement (Mama) cycles in lifespan identity development: Value orientations and reasoning system correlates. *Journal of Adolescence, 15*(3), 283–300. https://doi.org/10.1016/0140-1971(92)90031-Y

Stevens, R. (1983). *Erik Erikson: An introduction*. Open University Press.

Sugimura, K. (2020). Adolescent identity development in Japan. *Child Development Perspectives, 14*(2), 71–77. https://doi.org/10.1111/cdep.12359

Sugimura, K., Gmelin, J.-O. H., van der Gaag, M. A. E., & Kunnen, E. S. (2022). Exploring exploration: Identity exploration in real-time interactions among peers. *Identity: An International Journal of Theory and Research, 22*(1), 17–34. https://doi.org/10.1080/15283488.2021.1947819

Sugimura, K., Hihara, S., Hatano, K., & Crocetti, E. (2023). Adolescents' identity development predicts the transition and the adjustment to tertiary education or work. *Journal of Youth and Adolescence, 52*(11), 2344–2356. https://doi.org/10.1007/s10964-023-01838-y

Sugimura, K., Hihara, S., Hatano, K., Umemura, T., & Crocetti, E. (2025). The interplay between personal identity and social identity among vocational high school students: A three-wave longitudinal study. *Journal of Youth and Adolescence, 54*(2), 454–467. https://doi.org/10.1007/s10964-024-02073-9

Sugimura, K., Iwasa, Y., Kobayashi, R., Honda, T., Hashimoto, J., Kashihara, S., Zhu, J., Yamamoto, K., Kawahara, T., Anno, M., Nakagawa, R., Hatano, K., & Nakao, T. (2021). Association between long-range temporal correlations in intrinsic EEG activity and subjective sense of identity. *Scientific Reports, 11*(1), 1–11. https://doi.org/10.1038/s41598-020-79444-2

Sugimura, K., Matsushima, K., Hihara, S., Takahashi, M., & Crocetti, E. (2019). A culturally sensitive approach to the relationships between identity formation and religious beliefs in youth. *Journal of Youth and Adolescence, 48*(4), 668–679. https://doi.org/10.1007/s10964-018-0920-8

Sugimura, K., & Mizokami, S. (2012). Personal identity in Japan. *New Directions for Child and Adolescent Development, 2012*(138), 123–143. https://doi.org/10.1002/cad.20025

Syed, M., & Azmitia, M. (2009). Longitudinal trajectories of ethnic identity during the college years. *Journal of Research on Adolescence, 19*(4), 601–624. https://doi.org/10.1111/j.1532-7795.2009.00609.x

Syed, M., & McLean, K. C. (2016). Understanding identity integration: Theoretical, methodological and applied issues. *Journal of Adolescence, 47*(1), 109–118. https://doi.org/10.1016/j.adolescence.2015.09.005

Tesch, S. A., & Cameron, K. A. (1987). Openness to experience and development of adult identity. *Journal of Personality, 55*(4), 615–630. https://doi.org/10.1111/j.1467-6494.1987.tb00455.x

Van der Gaag, M. A. E., Albers, C. J., & Kunnen, E. S. (2017). Micro-level mechanisms of identity development: The role of emotional experiences in commitment development. *Developmental Psychology, 53*(11), 2205–2217. https://doi.org/10.1037/dev0000336

Vedder, P., & Phinney, J. S. (2014). Identity formation in bi-cultural youth: A developmental perspective. In V. Benet-Martinez & Y. Y. Hong (Eds.), *The Oxford handbook of multicultural identity* (pp. 335–354). Oxford University Press. https://doi.org/10.1093/oxfordhb/9780199796694.013.003

Verschueren, M., Rassart, J., Claes, L., Moons, P., & Luyckx, K. (2017). Identity statuses throughout adolescence and emerging adulthood: A large-scale study into gender, age, and contextual differences. *Psychologica Belgica, 57*(1), 32–42. https://doi.org/10.5334/pb.348

Wallerstein, R. S. (2014). Erik Erikson and his problematic identity. *Journal of the American Psychoanalytic Association*, *62*(4), 657–674. https://doi.org/10.1177/0003065114547637

Waterman, A. S. (2015). What does it mean to engage in identity exploration and to hold identity commitments? A methodological critique of multidimensional measures for the study of identity processes. *Identity: An International Journal of Theory and Research*, *15*(4), 309–349. https://doi.org/10.1080/15283488.2015.1089403

Waterman, A. S., Schwartz, S. J., Hardy, S. A, Kim, S. Y., Lee, R. M., Armenta, B. E., Whitbourne, S. K., Zamboanga, B. L., Brown, E. J., Williams, M. K., & Agocha, V. B. (2013). Good choices, poor choices: Relationship between the quality of identity commitments and psychosocial functioning. *Emerging Adulthood*, *1*(3), 163–174. https://doi.org/10.1177/2167696813484004

Willemsen, E. W., & Waterman, K. K. (1991). Ego identity status and family environment: A correlational study. *Psychological Reports*, *69*(3_suppl), 1203–1212. https://doi.org/10.2466/pr0.1991.69.3f.1203

3 Identity as Life Story – Narrative Understandings of Adolescent Identity Development

One day, a granddaughter asked her grandmother to tell her about her life. At the time, the granddaughter was moving from adolescence to adulthood. The grandmother, Sara, was nearing the end of her life. Sara gave her granddaughter a look as if to say, "Do you really want to hear this?" The look back from her granddaughter was encouragement enough, and it was time for a story to be told and heard. Sara began her story about her life, not with her own childhood, but instead by explaining how her parents came to live in Cuba.[1] As Sara spoke, people appeared and exited her story – their ways of life, dispositions, motivations, and values were sketched out as she continued.

Sara said her father was easygoing but strong and warm. He was also hardworking, lucky, and an adventurer. The adventurer part was not completely by choice because Sara's father was a second-born son. During that time, it was the custom in Spain for only the firstborn son to receive the family fortune. As a second-born son, Sara's father would have to find his own way in the world. He left home at 14 for Argentina and then returned to Spain when he was 18 years old. He was lucky enough to get the number 13 for his conscription number, which meant he was released from military service. So he left Spain again, but this time, he went to Cuba.

The stories that Sara told that day were nuanced, and the emotional tone ranged from the comical and joyous to tragic and inconsolable, and they gave glimpses of memorable times such as her mother's trip from Spain to Cuba by ship – she was seasick and vowed never to be on the ocean again – as well as what everyday life was like for Sara growing up in the Cuban countryside before the revolution. Her story touched on influential characters like her father, mother, and brother – her mother was loving but had a temper, and her brother was always in a hurry and loved gambling so much that his mother said that he would come home one day with no pants on (because he lost them to gambling).

For the part of Sara's story that is retold below, the insights that her granddaughter had were tacit and twofold. It should be expected that if a person lived long enough, unexpected things were likely to happen, and that meant that a person should value the moments and relationships that they have today because they could be gone tomorrow. In terms of the unexpected, for instance, Sara's father's story had several moments where chance played a role – he was born a second son

DOI: 10.4324/9781003486336-3

and was unexpectedly released from military service – free to go to Cuba when he did. Chance also collided with Sara's will when she told the story of trying to get back to Cuba to see her mother.

Sara said that when she heard that her mother had died, she tried to get back to the far east of Cuba – to Guantanamo – before her mother was buried so she could see her face one last time. But it seemed like everything was working against her. She went from Miami to Havana in heavy rain by plane. She landed and wanted to take a second flight to Guantanamo. Sara was a new mother at the time and had her son, Tony, with her (the granddaughter's father). The pilot of the second flight told her that there was no way they were flying to Guantanamo that night because of the weather, so Sara took the train and in time reached home. Sara's mother had recently been buried when she arrived. The gravedigger and her father asked her if she wanted them to break the concrete covering her mother's grave so Sara could see her again, but she decided against it.

Except for starting her narrative in an unexpected place, Sara's story had many events that had a temporal coherence or order to them (McAdams & McLean, 2013), and her story had several themes that ran through it. To make meaning out of one's life, a person engages in cognitive and emotional processes like autobiographical reasoning, which involves connecting life events to psychological changes or stability in one's self and can involve deriving wider life lessons and insights from life events[2] (Habermas & Köber, 2014). Life stories contain depictions of important moments and people. They speak to the roles of chance and a person's will (i.e., agency), goals, and values, as well as the larger push and pull of history, culture, and tradition in everyday people's lives and how losses are weathered, sometimes conquered, or left unresolved. Narrative identity researchers would say that Sara's story and the act of Sara telling her story to her granddaughter are typical, even necessary, ways for family members to bond and communicate, for the older generation to model values and insights that can be of help to the next generation, as well as a way for narrators to continue to make sense of themselves and their lives across a lifetime (McAdams & McLean, 2013). Indeed, it has been noted that the intergenerational narration of life stories creates an entrée into a family's identity, as well as demonstrating,

> . . . for children that telling and sharing the past is an important social activity. They [narrators] also convey that there are certain ways to tell these kinds of stories, focusing not just on what happened but why it was interesting, important, and emotional.
>
> (Fivush et al., 2011, p. 324)

Different types of studies have been used to investigate narrative identity in adolescence and emerging adulthood, including those that document normative trends and how relationships are important to narrative identity development, as well as studies that clarify how narrative identity relates to other psychological constructs and outcomes. A number of innovative scholars have advanced the field of adolescent narrative identity development, among them, Monisha Pasupathi.

Pasupathi the Person

Monisha Pasupathi, professor of developmental psychology at the University of Utah, is a leading scholar in the narrative identity field. She has conducted innovative research in several areas, such as a series of studies that map out the dynamic interaction between narrators and listeners. She has also been examining how these social processes relate to wider ideas about how narrative identity develops (Pasupathi et al., 2021). As she remarked, "what captivates me is the way people use narrating to build an identity" (Pasupathi, personal communication, July 11, 2018).

Pasupathi was born on the East Coast of the United States (U.S.) but grew up in the American Midwest, in Ohio. Her parents were both Southerners. Her mother was from the Deep South of the U.S., and her father was born in southern India. Pasupathi completed her undergraduate degree in psychology and English literature at Case Western Reserve University in Ohio and then went on to complete a doctoral degree in psychology at Stanford University. Following that time, she completed a postdoctoral research fellowship investigating wisdom at the Max Planck Institute in Berlin, Germany, before taking on a faculty position at the University of Utah.

In discussing professionally formative life events, she told a story about how a temporary holiday from her doctoral project led her to pursue an abiding interest in studying conversations, listeners, narrators, and the social construction of narrative identity.

> I was in grad school. . . . I was in a personality program, studying emotional regulation across the adult development and aging . . . yet I kept hanging around with a psycholinguist named Herb Clark. . . . He was interested in communication and the way that a speaker forms an utterance . . . Herb was working on this joint action model of language use. I loved this idea, and it had nothing to do with my dissertation work, but I just could not really let it go. And, I would go to Herb's lab meetings and one month he brought in a friend – her name was Janet Bavelas – who was also a psycholinguist. And he said, "Hey, I want you to come and meet Janet, and I want you to come and listen to her presentation – I know you guys are going to like each other because you both wander around all the time with your dogs." It is true, I had this Australian Shepherd who went everywhere with me in graduate school. So, I went to Janet's talk and she talked about a study in which people were asked to tell another person about a close call, a story about a time when they almost died. And what Janet did was change whether the person they were talking to paid attention or not. What she was able to show was that even though there was not a lot of back and forth – it was a monologue – the speaker is so dependent on the listener to be able to tell that story, that if you disrupt the listener's attention, the speaker is not able to tell the story . . . I was completely blown away, could not stop talking about it. I was with

> a friend in the stairwell after that talk, a fellow graduate student and said it probably not only changes the story but also changes how they remember the story, and how they think about themselves over time. And that was the moment . . . the thing that captivated me was this talk from a very different discipline. They did not want to understand memory or the self or identity; they wanted to answer a particular question, how you produce a sentence . . . But being exposed to that work really changed everything in my life. I am forever grateful, and I don't know if I have to be grateful to Herb, Janet, or the dog?
> (Pasupathi, personal communication, July 11, 2018)

After her early inspiration from theory and experiments conducted by psycholinguists, Pasupathi has worked systematically to shed considerable light on ways that listeners help to co-construct personal narratives and to develop new ideas about other potential processes of change possibly involved in narrative identity development that not only include but also go beyond autobiographical reasoning[3] (Pasupathi et al., 2022).

In asking her about the cutting edge of narrative identity research, Pasupathi was excited about three ideas as follows:

> One of the front edge issues in narrative identity research is about understanding how narrative identity looks when we think more broadly about the types of experiences people narrate and the settings in which they do that narration – if we look more broadly, what do we see that our initial emphasis on emotion-based (in childhood) and major life event narratives (in adulthood) may have obscured or overlooked? Another front edge, to me, is around implications of narrative identity variations – to look beyond indicators of psychological well-being and to consider what narrative identity is related to in terms of individual decisions around education/career, in terms of values. You could consider this last question one around links between narrative identity and other concerns of identity writ broadly (value commitments, political identities, career/occupational identities and commitments). Finally, for me, in this historical moment it's hard to avoid asking about relationships between self and other – are there implications of narrative identity for avoiding or developing what my young adult daughter calls "main character syndrome."
> (Pasupathi, personal communication, August 2, 2025)

Pasupathi's ideas and research are referred to throughout this chapter, but for detailed research examples of her and other scholars' research in conversational narrative identity studies, see the later chapter section titled "Spill the tea! The social construction of narrative identity."

The Nature of Narrative Identity

The stories that make up narrative identity are not a faithful rendering of every moment of our lives (Adler et al., 2016; McAdams, 2019). We choose what is meaningful to us and work on our life stories in order to make some sense of it all (McAdams, 2019).

> [The life story] is not synonymous with a case study; it is not simply any old thing that a person says when asked to talk about the self in a psychological experiment. The life story, instead, is an internalized and evolving structure of the mind – an integrative story about who I am, how I came to be, and where my life may be going.
>
> (McAdams & Manczak, 2015, p. 425)

In the story of Siddhartha, which is referred to in Chapter 2, Siddhartha also considered what it means not only to seemingly change one's sense of identity as time passes across a lifetime but also to remain the same in some essential ways. Siddhartha's new insights about the presence of the past and the future in one's identity experience in the here and now were gained by working as a ferryman along with his friend Vasudeva to help travelers cross a river later in his life (Hesse, 1951).

Optimal Narrative Identity

An optimal narrative identity is thought not only to help people find increasing meaning and purpose in life and a sense of unity within themselves across time and situations but also to allow enough room for change so that new life experiences, lessons, and insights can be incorporated along the way (Fivush et al., 2011).

> Identity matters for people's functioning in the world – identities help people to see themselves moving from past to future, make commitments meaningful, and find common ground with others. Problems of continuity can be understood as incoherence in identity over time – irreconcilable differences between the me-that-was and the me-that-is.
>
> (Pasupathi, 2014, p. 21)

Narrative identity development acts as a conduit by which adolescents can move into a more adult-like space that values responsibility and purpose in one's life, as well as self-insight, understanding of life in general, and a sense of direction and purpose that guides one's future (de Silveira & Habermas, 2011). Later in this chapter, the theoretical proposition about what comprises optimal adolescent narrative identity development is examined in light of the available research evidence.

Narrative Identity as Part of Lifespan Personality Development

Since the 1980s, several psychologists have developed theories and advanced the use of methods to document different aspects of narrative identity. One prominent framework is the three-layer model of personality development, which was put forward by Dan P. McAdams and colleagues (e.g., McAdams, 2015, 2019; McAdams & Manczak, 2015; McAdams & Olson, 2010; McAdams & Pals, 2006).

The three-layer framework aims to bring a greater synthesis between developmental and personality psychology (McAdams, 2019) and derives key concepts and research priorities from William James and Erik Erikson (e.g., the individual's search for continuity across time; Hammack, 2014). The framework also draws from Erikson's emphasis on lifespan developmental change (McLean & Pratt, 2006), as well as from classic and contemporary personality theorists such as Gordon Allport, Henry Murray, Paul Costa, and Robert McCrae (McAdams, 2019; McLean & Syed, 2014). The framework sets for itself an ambitious task in attempting to integrate a diverse set of more specific theories and research findings, some of which were intended to test and expand the framework and others that were not (McAdams & Olson, 2010). The three-layer framework explains how change takes place across different developmental domains and considers person–context interactions across different settings – all with the aim of proposing a comprehensive framework for the study of lifespan personality development (McAdams, 2019).

Historically, it has been more typical that a body of knowledge would emerge for one of the framework layers (e.g., traits) without a concerted attempt to sort out distinctions and intersections between allied features and mechanisms involved in different facets of personality development (McAdams, 2015). Stated differently, the ingredients (i.e., psychological constructs and conceptions of how developmental change takes place) that make up the three-layer framework are a mix of the novel (e.g., narrative identity) and the familiar (e.g., traits or motives) within the discipline of psychology; the way that these ingredients are combined and integrated in the three-layer model is original and eclectic (McLean, 2017). In the history of psychology, eclectic frameworks have not always been successful, in that they have not always yielded the anticipated knowledge production and staying power. However, McAdams (1996) reflected on the value of the three-layer framework early in its development and the merits of trying to strike a successful balance between what McAdams (1996, p. 378) called "parochialism and the most promiscuous forms of eclecticism."

Specifically, in the three-layer framework, personality is conceptualized as being made up of traits, motivations/goals, and narrative identity (McAdams, 2019; McAdams & Olson, 2010). These personality features or metaphorical layers in the framework have been called the self as a social actor (i.e., a noticeable, socially important constellation of traits that typify a person), the self as an agent (i.e., a person acting in the world to fulfill goals based on motivations such as agency or connection), and the self as an autobiographical author (i.e., a person who is in the process of co-constructing a narrative identity; McAdams, 2019).

The Three Layers of Personality – Traits

The metaphor of three layers – one personality feature stacked on top of the other with traits at the bottom, motivation/goals (also called characteristic adaptations) in the middle, and narrative identity on top – paints a picture of the nature and development of these distinct yet intersecting personality features (McLean, 2017). Traits are at the foundation of the framework, and they are thought to develop earlier in comparison to other layers and are posited to emerge out of temperament (McAdams & Manczak, 2015). Temperament has been conceptualized as an early developing building block of personality and consists of the usual ways that infants behave as well as how infants experience and express their emotions (negative to positive) as they interact with others and the environment (showing low-to-high impulsivity/control or regulation as well as low-to-high reactivity; Groh et al., 2017). Other ongoing psychological and social processes at work in the development of traits include how adept individuals are at social cognition, including forming attributions of others and impression management (McAdams, 2015).

Traits develop in childhood and become more solidified in adolescence and adulthood (McAdams & Olson, 2010). Traits are thought to be the substance of a person's individuality and provide a basis for one's social roles and reputation (McAdams & Olson, 2010). Theory and research about Costa and McCrae's (2017) big five trait theory have been used in descriptions of the three-layer framework (e.g., McAdams & Olson, 2010). In the big five theory, the essential traits are **c**onscientiousness, **a**greeableness, and **n**euroticism (CAN traits are important to the constancy or reliability of personality), as well as **o**penness to experience and **e**xtraversion (OE traits are involved in the adaptability or plasticity of personality, i.e., CANOE), and each trait is a multidimensional construct made up of several facets (Costa & McCrae, 2017; McAdams, 2015).

Traits are dispositions that people can experience or exhibit in abundance or in moderation or only sporadically (relative to others), and together, core traits, such as those in the big five, are predictive of a person's usual ways of thinking, feeling, and acting across a diversity of situations (Costa & McCrae, 2017). Traits are thought to help us meet the demands of human social life (Costa & McCrae, 2017). Traits represent cues to let others know in rapid ways the kind of person they may be encountering (McAdams, 2015, p. 255; "the streamlined reputational signatures through which actors initially know each other and sort each other out"). While the idea of a trait, historically, has implied continuity, a meta-analysis of longitudinal studies has shown significant mean-level changes in some traits in adulthood (e.g., Bleidorn et al., 2022; Roberts et al., 2006). For example, it is not uncommon that as one moves from adolescence to middle adulthood, conscientiousness and agreeableness are likely to increase for the typical person along with a decline in neuroticism (e.g., normative changes in CAN traits – this research finding has been called the maturity principle, e.g., Roberts et al., 2006). Such changes are thought to be precipitated by the demands of and more experience with adult social roles (McAdams & Olson, 2010).

The Three Layers of Personality – Motives, Goals, and Characteristic Adaptations

The next layer in the middle of the three-layer framework of personality development addresses how people act on their needs, motivations, and values/goals

(McAdams, 2015). Important developmental processes and transitions that have been hypothesized to make a motivated agent possible include children developing an understanding that other people can have their own unique wishes and thoughts and that, in general, wishes and thoughts can be a reason why people behave, think, or feel as they do (i.e., theory of mind; Tompkins et al., 2025). Additionally, the age five to seven shift, which heralds a noticeable transition, which many children show through their behaviors, is evidence of increasingly integrated and efficient cognitive, emotional, and social competencies that come with age (Sameroff & Haith, 1996).

> By age 8 or 9 years, many children have developed and articulated personal goals, and they see themselves as more or less self-determining, goal-directed agents . . . Layered over the actor's developing dispositional profile is a slowly evolving motivational agenda, a program for striving that eventually will come to encompass personality's most salient goals, plans, values, and life projects.
>
> (McAdams & Manczak, 2015, p. 428)

People certainly have their own agendas in life, ranging from the esoteric to the normative, that may, in turn, correspond to a person's phase in the lifespan. Unlike the layer of the model that involves traits, this middle layer not only describes what is normative or to be expected for most people but also pays substantial attention to the individual person's development (i.e., a person's goals, which can be one of a kind; McAdams, 2015). Further, this middle layer has an emphasis on how values support the goals that people formulate for themselves (McAdams, 2015). For example, when people pursue a particular set of goals, their selection and efforts to actualize their goals in part reflect what values they hold (McAdams, 2015).

The Three Layers of Personality – Narrative Identity

A concise but far-reaching description of narrative identity is as follows:

> Narrative identity is the story that a person composes about how he or she came to be the person he or she is becoming – a selective reconstruction of the past integrated with the imagined future, providing a life in full with a sense of meaning, purpose, and temporal continuity. . . .
>
> (McAdams, 2015, p. 259)

Another formulation, which emphasized other nuances, was given by Hammack (2010, p. 184) as follows: "Our personal narratives become cognitive and affective anchors for the life course – filters through which we make sense of the social world and our experience in it." Life stories and other personal narratives can be private at times and the object of introspection, but most stories end up going public at some point (McLean & Pasupathi, 2011). Once shared, our personal narratives end up on a metaphorical editor's desk (i.e., important people in our lives and our culture play this editorial role). The editor hears our tale and gives us a decision as to whether or not to reject, accept, or revise and resubmit our story (i.e., retell our story again, but this time with some changes). Of course, we can then protest or accept the editor's decision. The cultural aspect of this editing job is called a master narrative (Hammack, 2008).

In the three-layer framework, narrative identity is viewed as the top layer in the framework – the metaphor here is the self as the autobiographical author or storyteller (McAdams, 2015). While narrative identity is present and measurable in studies with adolescents, the full, nuanced expression of one's narrative identity is not typically realized until sometime during adulthood (McAdams, 2015). Narrative identity is complex and has many features and processes involved in it. Narrative identity has been measured by analyzing life stories as well as personal narratives of different types such as self-defining memories (e.g., McLean, 2005). Autobiographical/episodic memory and narration skills are examples of some of the cognitive and sociocultural processes that can drive narrative identity development from childhood onward (i.e., narration skills concern knowing how a story is told in one's culture and being able to execute that story with an audience; McLean, 2017). Narration and interpretative skills are fostered by reminiscence and storytelling about life events in the context of conversations with important others such as parents and friends (McLean & Jennings, 2012).

Processes that come to the forefront of narrative identity development, particularly in adolescence, include formal operational thinking (i.e., having a flexible command of deductive and inductive reasoning and abstract reasoning, for example, about time and causality) and autobiographical reasoning, which is more commonly used by adolescents than children (Fivush et al., 2011). Autobiographical reasoning spans cognitive and emotional domains of development; it is hypothesized to be a main driver of changes in narrative identity development and involves remembering one's life (i.e., the who, what, and where), but it also demands active organizing, reflecting, interpreting, and making meaning of one's life experiences (McLean, 2017).

To firmly grasp what narrative identity is in terms of how it is conceptualized and studied in the psychological research literature, it is helpful to consider how many researchers collect narratives from study participants. What are the questions and prompts used by narrative researchers, and how are narratives typically analyzed? What is singled out as the main object of the analysis? These issues are described later in the chapter by considering different types of measures used in the field as well as by an in-depth description of a selection of illustrative research studies.

The Three Layers of Personality – Distinctions and Intersections

In terms of distinctions, the timing of the developmental emergence of the layers in the framework and the mechanisms of change at work in the layers in some cases differ. Take, as a case in point, autobiographical reasoning, which is a driver of change in the development of narrative identity. Autobiographical reasoning is not directly at work in the emergence and functioning of traits; instead, early temperament, social interactions, and evolutionary forces are posited to be essential to trait development (McAdams, 2015).

Another distinction has to do with time orientation and which aspects of time (the past, present, and future) are emphasized in each layer. The present is thought to be important to all of the personality features in the framework (McAdams, 2015). Considering the present in relation to the future is hypothesized to be most relevant to the motivated agent who is in the process of formulating goals as well as autobiographical authors who also have to consider their story in light of what is likely to happen in the future (McAdams, 2015). A reflection on and integration of experiences in the past and present in relation to what is expected in the future (i.e., the full gamut of time orientations) is thought to be most pressing for the autobiographical author who is working on a narrative identity (McAdams, 2015).

Additional distinctions deal with research/knowledge emphasis, for example, whether the ambition is to explain personality development at the individual and/or group level. Traits concern nomothetic or group-oriented personality features (i.e., traits upon which we all vary). The layer concerning motivations and goals (i.e., self as agent) and narrative identity (i.e., the self as storyteller working on a narrative identity) attests to the uniqueness of individual development. In other words, this layer combines an idiographic, single-person-focused view, in terms of personality development explained at the individual level, one person and life at a time, with more shared processes of importance. For example, in the case of narrative identity, different forms of coherence (e.g., causal motivational coherence) can act as a shared universal driver of narrative identity development, but the meaning that is made of one's life story can be completely unique (i.e., "no one else has exactly the same collection of life experiences or ways of telling about those experiences"; Reese et al., 2017, p. 613). In terms of intersections, the layers are thought to come together to produce a "one of a kind person" (McAdams & Olson, 2010).

Some empirical evidence has supported intersections between the layers (e.g., McAdams et al., 2021; McAdams & Mayukha, 2024). An illustration of such an intersection was represented by the co-development of the trait and motivation/goals layers. Individuals have been found to formulate major life goals consistent with their personality traits and, conversely, invest in goals related to trait change (e.g., Atherton et al., 2021). Another study revealed that adaptive traits (agreeableness, conscientiousness, and extraversion) were associated with narrative identity during high points, and some traits (openness and agreeableness) were more connected to narrative identity during low points in life (McLean et al., 2020). Thus, in the three-layer framework, personality development is best understood by not only appreciating the distinctions but also empirically seeking to document potential intersections among these personality features (McAdams, 2019).

Analysis of the Three-Layer Framework Including Narrative Identity

How Do the Layers Work?

It has been posited that layers in the three-layer framework of lifespan personality development may interact in a reciprocal manner in some instances (Lilgendahl, 2014). Research on how the three layers are distinct and interact is a relatively new area (Adler et al., 2016; McAdams et al., 2021; McLean, 2017). Beyond the intersections noted in the prior section, other examples of what has been found thus far are some evidence for the distinctiveness of the trait, motivation/goals, and narrative identity layers (Adler et al., 2016; Atherton et al., 2021). Consider several studies in which there is a simultaneous comparison of the association between the two layers (i.e., traits and narrative identity) and well-being; results tend to show that each layer has a unique and nonredundant association with well-being (Adler et al., 2016; McLean, 2017). McLean (2017) concluded that people elevated on particular traits, such as neuroticism and openness to experience, are more likely to have a more negative emotional tone and more complexity in their personal narratives, respectively, based on findings across relevant studies. While the overall three-layer framework of personality development is conceptually innovative and has inspired many new research studies designed to expressly test the framework, more longitudinal research is needed in order to elaborate on how each of the three layers functions during adolescence.

Methodology

Another challenge to the field has been the concern that the life story interview may artificially elicit autobiographical reasoning and the movement toward self-continuity, rather than capture a naturally occurring and necessary change process. In other words, ". . . the core identity attributes of stability and continuity may not be latent properties of personal narratives but instead are artifacts of the interview/event itself" (Seaman et al., 2017, p. 2031). A potential approach to address this concern is to have more frequent inclusion of naturalistic (non-laboratory-based) storytelling occasions as a complement to structured interviews in a laboratory-based setting (Adler et al., 2016). In this way, one would obtain a wider sampling of personal narratives under different situations. Another recent approach captures a person's interpretations of their life story rather than the researchers' interpretations (Lind et al., 2025) to minimize the possibility of an artificial self-continuity created by an outsider's perspective. Yet there is debate as to whether this approach, which seeks to capture the participants' interpretation of their own narrative by using a 20-item scale called the Narrative Identity Self-Evaluation (NISE) questionnaire, can be taken as a substitute for rater-coded and generated assessments of narrative identity (Lind et al., 2025). Further research is needed to clarify the similarities and differences between the two methods (i.e., coded by researchers or by the person themselves). In terms of the analysis of personal narratives, constructs/variables such as coherence have varying names and are operationalized differently across researchers (Fivush et al., 2011). In some cases, there is a need for the field to coalesce on a "common language" (Adler et al., 2016, p. 169).

Measuring Narrative Identity

The measurement of narrative identity is diverse. One method is the life story interview[4] (McAdams, 2008). This interview covers several domains and times in a person's life. For example, asking a person to describe his or her life's high and low points as well as key transitions when life took a significant turn. Timing is also important, and people can be asked about their lives in the past and present (e.g., early memories, emotional memories from different developmental periods, and times when one faced a challenge or learned something important) as well as in the future. Finally, after describing and reflecting about oneself in light of key moments in one's past, present, and future, people can be asked about what take-home messages or conclusions they draw about themselves (McAdams, 2008).

Prompts that encourage people to elaborate on the seasons of their lives and specific important moments include, for example, being asked what happened, when it happened, who was there, and what this experience reflects or shows about you as a person (McAdams, 2008). Other empirical studies of narrative identity examine personal narratives about discrete life experiences (i.e., time-limited or rare experiences; "examples might include religious conversion, the transition to parenthood, or the death of a significant other" Adler et al., 2016, p. 145) and/or narratives that are subjectively important or emotionally clear (positive or negative; e.g., McLean & Fournier, 2008; Pasupathi & Hoyt, 2009).

In terms of typical study procedures, participants can be asked questions in a one-on-one interview with a research assistant and give answers to structured or semi-structured questions verbally in order to assess features and processes related to a personal narrative or life story. The interview would be audio or video recorded and transcribed, and then the text would be coded. Some researchers opt to give the interview in a written format, in which case questions are read, and a written response is given. Some researchers use both interview and written formats in the same study (e.g., Jennings et al., 2014). Other scholars have analyzed biographies of individuals and then applied life story techniques combined with other textual analysis approaches (e.g., Hammack, 2010). An innovative approach is to ask for personal narratives, but the questions are answered in the presence of someone else, such as a stranger, parent, friend, or romantic partner (Jennings et al., 2014; McLean & Pasupathi, 2011). The discussion that ensues from the answers to the interview questions between participants and the other person can then be audio/video recorded, transcribed, and analyzed. Here, the interest is to examine how listeners contribute to the co-construction of narrative identity (Pasupathi & Hoyt, 2009).

The transcript that is generated can then be analyzed by one or more coders for certain theory-based features indicative of narrative identity processes (e.g., meaning-making – "the degree to which one learns something about oneself from reflecting on past events"; McLean & Breen, 2009, p. 702) or aspects of narratives hypothesized to be associated with other outcomes (e.g., emotional tone). The amount of text to be analyzed for each study participant can be considerable, and some scholars recommend that conceptual coding be done by humans instead of computers (which focus more on linguistic text analysis), as meaning-making can be highly nuanced and difficult to assess by machine (Adler et al., 2016), although this is likely to be a main subject of debate in the coming years (machine, human assisted by machine, and human-only coding of narratives; see Acciai et al., 2025 for an illustration of machine coding in a narrative identity research context). In the field, it is common to find narrative identity researchers generating numerical ratings of the emotional tone (e.g., low to high) of a narrative (positive and/or negative); complexity and nuance; themes of agency, communion, redemption, and contamination; and evidence of coherence (including self-event connections), as well as growth goals (Adler et al., 2016). Coders' ratings can then be calibrated for reliability or consistency. Other textual analysis approaches can involve a qualitative coding of personal narratives. See Morgan and Korobov (2012) for an example of a study that used a thematic analysis approach (i.e., a completely qualitative approach), in which personal narratives about romance were discussed in the presence of friends.

Research Findings on Narrative Identity in Adolescence

Normative Trends in Adolescent Narrative Identity[5] Development

Cross-sectional and longitudinal evidence supports the idea that children can easily describe particular events and times in their lives, but it is rare for children to tell an all-encompassing and nuanced life story when asked to do so (e.g., Fivush et al., 2011). Metaphorically speaking, children can be adept reporters of the daily news of their lives but are not as well equipped to be seasoned historians or biographers of their entire life story – just yet. Adolescence tends to be a turning point in which many young people's capabilities (e.g., cognitive, socio-emotional, linguistic, narration, and interpretative skills) and life experiences as well as sociocultural expectations coalesce, and it becomes more common for individuals to engage in autobiographical reasoning. Furthermore, their personal narratives evidence greater coherence (e.g., Köber et al., 2015).

A German longitudinal study (Köber & Habermas, 2017), with participants that ranged in age from children to adults, provided an in-depth example of methods and selected findings within this research area. This study had two parts. The first part spanned eight years and had several occasions when a group of young participants were asked to provide their entire life story (i.e., from the earliest memory to the present) as well as to describe seven key events in their lives (Köber & Habermas, 2017). At the beginning of the study, there were four age-groups – 8, 12, 16, and 20 years of age ($n = 113$; followed over eight years to ages of 16, 20, 24, and 28 years, respectively); the second part of the study added two additional age-groups – 40 and 65 years of age ($n = 58$; followed over four years to the ages of 44 and 69 years), respectively.

Multiple coders read and rated transcripts of the narratives given by all study participants and generated numerical indices that represented stability (i.e., the percentage of narrative segments and events that came up more than once over time), as well as counts of the types of life events described (e.g., normative or nonnormative). Ratings were given on a seven-point scale indicating the degree to which participants had different indicators of coherence evident in their narratives. For example, was there an undefined to very clear and explicit chronological order to what happened (i.e., temporal coherence)? Was there a deep reflection over how one's story connected to changes in one's personality (i.e., causal–motivational coherence)? Was there a deep reflection by participants on how their narrative events related to broader lessons about life, themselves, or metaphors that served as a conceptual link across parts of the narrative (i.e., thematic coherence; Köber & Habermas, 2017)?

Study results were based on the following individuals over time (e.g., within-subjects longitudinal growth curve analyses with three time points for the younger group), as well as analyses that included both the younger and older age-groups (cross-sectional age comparisons with mean difference tests). Highlights of some key results were that by age 16 years and onward, completed life stories evidenced more stability in comparison to asking participants to provide seven key events in their lives (Köber & Habermas, 2017). Results also indicated that narrative identity was in flux from childhood to late adolescence and young adulthood, when a new degree of stability and insight into one's life story emerged. Even greater stability in narrative identity, however, was likely as one moved further into adulthood. Older relative to younger participants' narratives had more stability, with fewer new events added and more normative life events contained in them (e.g., school graduations; Köber & Habermas, 2017).

Other studies with cross-sectional age-related comparisons between younger and older adults are consistent with findings from the Köber and Habermas (2017) longitudinal study; older (middle-aged and onward), relative to younger adults (e.g., in their 20s and 30s) have evidenced more stability and thematic coherence in their narratives (e.g., McLean, 2008; McLean & Fournier, 2008). Regarding adolescents, other cross-sectional studies of North American adolescents' personal narratives have also indicated that older compared to younger adolescents engaged in more meaning-making (e.g., McLean et al., 2010; Soucie et al., 2012).

Recent longitudinal studies have provided further evidence for contextualized variations in the patterns of stability and change in narration (Lilgendahl & McLean, 2020; McLean et al., 2022). For instance, McLean and colleagues (2022) examined how narrative identity develops over time, focusing on autobiographical reasoning. The researchers followed college students and demonstrated that the mean level increased for one of the core aspects of narrative identity (i.e., exploratory processing) in the context of romance and remained stable in the context of academics. Thus, the context or life domain involved, where autobiographical reasoning is taking place, may matter in narrative identity development.

Overall, the studies relevant to understanding age-related trends in narrative identity development from childhood through adulthood show that older people relative to younger people are better at connecting their life experiences to their own personal and psychological development, deriving meaning from those experiences (i.e., are more likely to engage in autobiographical reasoning), as well as showing more stability in their life stories, particularly if one is a midlife adult or older. Person–context interactions and other psychological and social processes are thought to be essential to adolescent narrative identity development, and the next group of studies sheds light on the social construction of narrative identity.

Spill the Tea![6] *The Social Construction of Narrative Identity*

Another main area of research attention in the narrative identity field concerns social interactions. Here, the focus is to capture personal narratives in real time and in the context of conversations typically with important others (Pasupathi & Hoyt, 2009). The narrative prompts in this type of study are not meant to chronicle an entire lifetime but instead are designed to elicit more discrete life events and memories, such as asking participants for a self-defining memory. An example of a self-defining memory would be what I remember about a particularly vivid life event or an experience that was critical to how I became the person that I am today (e.g., McLean, 2008; McLean & Fournier, 2008) or asking participants to tell a friend in a laboratory setting about a previously untold happy or sad life event (e.g., Pasupathi & Hoyt, 2009).

There can be some overlap between life stories and other personal narratives (e.g., important events; Köber & Habermas, 2017). Personal narratives told in conversational settings, which represent a relational/social developmental context, can exert a gradual impact on how people construct their life stories (Pasupathi & Hoyt, 2009). Ways in which this process may occur are by listeners either encouraging or putting a damper on the interpretative and narrative skills of the narrator, as well as through narrators building up a history of expectation with different listeners about what happens in the storytelling moment. This process is an aspect of relational positioning; for example, when important and/or potentially emotionally charged events are disclosed, and the narrator's voice can be either heard and affirmed or dismissed (McLean & Jennings, 2012). Pasupathi and Hoyt cogently stated the following on this issue:

> In the long run, repeated unresponsiveness likely serves to silence a particular aspect of identity within that specific relationship context, and perhaps to silence that aspect of identity more broadly. . . . The extent of the impact will also depend on the individual's motivation and capacity to seek out alternative social relationships within which particular identities can be elaborated, reflected upon, and thus further developed. . . .
>
> (Pasupathi & Hoyt, 2009, p. 570)

The conversational narrative identity research literature includes cross-sectional, descriptive studies that aim to examine the ebb and flow of a conversation and studies in which the intentions and behaviors of narrators and/or listeners are systematically changed as part of an experiment; many of these studies are laboratory-based. The majority of studies in this area have been conducted with young adult North American university students and their romantic partners or friends, and some studies have also been conducted with adolescents and their friends and/or parents.

Descriptive Conversational Studies

There are numerous studies about parents' and their *children's*[7] reminiscences about events and people (e.g., Fivush et al., 2006). General conclusions derived from these studies are that children's narration and interpretative skills are fostered by parents' support (e.g., attentive listening) for their child's storytelling and elaboration and by children being exposed to parents' elaborative and/or introspective storytelling style (Fivush et al., 2006; Fivush & Kellas, 2025; McLean, 2017). The descriptive conversational narrative identity research literature with adolescents is emerging, but study results thus far tend to be similar to the main findings of the parent–child reminiscence research literature, with some caveats regarding adolescents' age and gender.

A cross-sectional descriptive study by McLean and colleagues provided an illustration of how mothers' support or scaffold narrative identity work in their adolescents and how narrative identity may change as youth move toward the end of adolescence (McLean & Jennings, 2012; McLean & Mansfield, 2012). Scaffolding in this study referred to different types of parental engagement, such as affirming, challenging, or reinterpreting, in response to their adolescent's narrative (McLean & Jennings, 2012). In this study, adolescents were asked to provide personal narratives in the presence of a friend and/or their mother (McLean & Jennings, 2012). A sample of 22 adolescents spoke with both a friend and their mother, and study results indicated that more scaffolding by mothers was generally associated with more meaning-making on the part of adolescents; furthermore, mothers scaffolded more often and differently in comparison to friends (McLean & Jennings, 2012).

With a larger and overlapping sample of 63 adolescents (aged 11–18 years, mean = 13 years), an additional study found that meaning-making on the part of adolescents became more nuanced, likely due to a larger sample with a wider age range (McLean & Mansfield, 2012). In this latter study, adolescents discussed personal narratives in the presence of their mothers. Study results showed that early adolescents had mothers who scaffolded more than older adolescents, and that mothers' scaffolding was associated with greater meaning-making by younger but not older adolescents (McLean & Mansfield, 2012). Thus, a general conclusion from McLean and colleagues' studies is that parental scaffolding may be critical to setting the groundwork for narrative identity development from childhood to middle adolescence, but changes may occur that make the importance of parental scaffolding more qualified during late adolescence. It is also possible that a diverse array of listeners (e.g., friends and romantic partners) may play an increasingly important role in the social construction of narrative identity (McLean & Jennings, 2012; McLean & Mansfield, 2012).

Experimental Conversational Studies

Experimental manipulations have also been part of narrative identity studies in social interaction research paradigms. In this case, listeners can be randomly assigned to different study conditions: Different listeners were assigned in some studies, and different levels of listeners' responsiveness were provided in other studies. The takeaway from these studies is that listeners crucially contribute to shaping the development of narrative identity. Different listeners (e.g., mothers, fathers, and friends) tend to shape different narrations in adolescents and emerging adults (e.g., Pasupathi et al., 2021, 2022). One study with adolescents revealed that mothers greatly engaged in and facilitated greater elaboration and emotional resolution of adolescent narration, while close same-sex friends provided a more playful and creative narrative context that reduced adolescent distress more than mothers (Pasupathi et al., 2022). Levels of responsiveness also mattered: the distracted listener, the engaged and responsive listener (what we might wish for in a good friend or a supportive parent), as well as the agreeable listener (who wholeheartedly supports the interpretations and meaning that narrators derive from their stories), or the contradictory listener who challenges and reinterprets the narrators' insights and lessons learned (e.g., Pasupathi & Hoyt, 2009; Pasupathi & Rich, 2005). Notably, these variations could occur within individuals, suggesting narrative variability may reflect a contextual and temporal process rather than a stable trait of the person (Pasupathi et al., 2020).

Descriptive and Experimental Conversational Studies: General Findings

Research findings from conversational studies on narrative identity, both descriptive and experimental, generally showed that more responsive listeners were generally associated with more interpretative work or meaning-making on the part of the narrator (Jennings et al., 2014; McLean & Pasupathi, 2011; Pasupathi & Hoyt, 2009). Also, listeners who challenged the narrator's story along with giving support and providing a reinterpretation have also been linked with more meaning-making on the part of the narrator (e.g., McLean & Pasupathi, 2011; Pasupathi & Hoyt, 2009; Pasupathi et al., 2021, 2022).

Thus, available evidence points to a dynamic engagement on the part of narrators and listeners when personal narratives are told in a conversational setting; the products and experiences of this engagement are hypothesized to provide the material that can support narrative identity development more generally. Moreover, attentive, skillful listeners can make a difference in terms of fostering a narrator's development, creating a forum for developmental change in how individuals see themselves and their life experiences. Engaged listening, which could involve being attentive, supportive, or supportive combined with challenging and offering new interpretations, tends to be associated with more elaboration and meaning-making by narrators in studies with adolescents and young adults. However, both descriptive and experimental conversational narrative identity studies with adolescents are fewer in number than those with young adults, and more research, including longitudinal studies, is needed to further test this conclusion. It is also important to note that for adolescents, there is a new availability of different listeners (e.g., romantic partners). More research is needed on how different listener responses may have different impacts on a life story presented in conversation.

Research Evidence on What Is an Optimal Narrative Identity

Optimal narrative identity involves the interpretive and reflective work that a narrator utilizes to develop a coherent life story. What is thought to be gained in this process is a greater sense of self-coherence across situations and time, as well as more meaning from one's life experiences. Empirically, it appears that interpretative, meaning-making processes and features[8] should remain central to the theoretical conception of optimal narrative identity development; however, certain conditions must be considered for people in different age-groups (Adler et al., 2016). Finally, from an empirical standpoint, motivational (e.g., finding a sense of purpose through agency and/or communion) and some selected emotional aspects of narratives (e.g., increased redemption and decreased contamination themes) appear to merit greater emphasis in theoretical conceptions of optimal narrative identity development (Adler et al., 2015, 2016; Lilgendahl, 2014; McLean et al., 2020).

Going into the research evidence in more detail, Adler and colleagues (2016) conducted a systematic review and identified 30 studies that examined associations between indicators of narrative identity development and well-being. The studies included samples of adolescents and adults from the general as well as unique populations (e.g., adults who had experienced trauma or were undergoing psychotherapy; Adler et al., 2016). The majority of studies had a cross-sectional design, and a few studies were longitudinal (Adler et al., 2016). The authors' qualitative examination of findings across studies indicated that a broad array of well-being indicators was significantly and positively associated with motivational themes in personal narratives.

For example, a person narrated a past, present, or future-oriented striving after attaining a sense of agency (working to shape one's life and life conditions) and/or connecting with other people, and thereby finding purpose in life (Adler et al., 2016). Well-being was also related to integrative themes in personal narratives that were characterized by learning about oneself or life in general from past events. Such learnings might include self-event connections, gaining a sense of resolution or insight, and experiencing psychological growth that can be of an assimilative nature (adding to the current view of oneself) or an accommodative nature (a more dramatic reorganization; Adler et al., 2016). Furthermore, affective themes in personal narratives, particularly those moving from a negative to a positive interpretation of a series of connected life events (i.e., redemption), were associated with an indicator of well-being (Adler et al., 2016).

The importance of motivational and affective themes for well-being has been further supported by a study with young adults (McLean et al., 2020). In this study, researchers identified three factors of life narratives: motivational (agency and communion) and affective themes (e.g., redemption and contamination), autobiographical reasoning (e.g., thematic coherence and interpretations), and structural aspects (contextual and chronological coherence). Results showed that motivational and affective themes were most important to well-being (as indexed by life satisfaction and depression). As Adler and colleagues (2015, p. 493) noted that

> whether the narrative of the agentic fighter is more myth than reality, for example, is not actually the central point when it comes to impacting [well-being]. Instead, the story itself may support and foster [well-being], regardless of the actual circumstances.

While the aforementioned study results represent a promising start (e.g., Adler et al., 2015, 2016; McLean et al., 2020), there is a need for more longitudinal studies in varied cultural contexts that concern relations between narrative identity development and mental health, particularly studies that span adolescence and adulthood.

Current Directions in Narrative Identity Research

Developmental Processes: What Lies Beyond Autobiographical Reasoning?

In addition to autobiographical reasoning, one important advance over the decade in this field is the accumulation of evidence for the interface between the personal narratives that are discussed in everyday conversations and a life story (e.g., Pasupathi et al., 2021, 2022), which was illustrated in the conversational studies section in this chapter. As Pasupathi remarked, ongoing effort has been devoted to understanding "what we learn when we examine the same person's narratives over time, and across different experiences" (Pasupathi, personal communication, August 2, 2025). Moreover, a promising direction in this field lies in the issues about how narrative identity looks in broader settings where people narrate their life experiences and how narrative identity relates to their decisions about issues such as education, career, and values (Pasupathi, personal communication, August 2, 2025).

Research With a Longitudinal Perspective and Global Reach

As is the case with many research areas within psychology, the narrative identity field is also moving to include more longitudinal studies, particularly those that span early adolescence through adulthood; a longitudinal emphasis would also benefit conversational narrative identity studies, which, to date, have largely focused on university students (Lilgendahl & McLean, 2020; McLean et al., 2022). More longitudinal studies including adolescents would allow for more systematic reviews and/or meta-analyses.

While research studies in the narrative identity field have primarily been conducted in North America (some notable exceptions are studies conducted in Germany, New Zealand, Poland, Taiwan, and Sweden), important work is being undertaken in other parts of the globe as well. For example, Turner and colleagues (2024) examined cross-national variation in narrative identity with adult samples from Japan, Denmark, Israel, and the U.S. They collected written narratives of difficult life events (i.e., low points and life challenges) with samples in the respective countries, and studies revealed remarkable differences in the frequency of narrative topics (redemption, contamination, agency, communion, and meaning-making) as well as the relationship to well-being across countries. The level of redemption, which was favored and associated with benefits in the U.S. sample, was lower among Japanese participants (relative to samples in all of the other three countries). Yet redemption was positively related to well-being among participants living in Japan and the U.S. The level of meaning-making was higher in Israeli participants relative to participants living in the other three countries. However, meaning-making had no association with well-being among any of the samples. Interestingly, new narrative topics emerged in three of the four countries (the exception was the sample from the U.S.). For instance, new narrative topics common in the sample from Japan were acceptance (i.e., resisting the idea of making meaning), communal growth in Denmark (i.e., learning how to offer and receive help), and collective responsibility in Israel (i.e., the influence of collective desires on their lives). The study results were complex and nuanced, and they suggested that the cultural differences in some narrative topics may be firmly rooted in ". . . cultural norms and may indicate master narratives in Japan, Israel, and Denmark – highlighting the critical role of qualitative, inductive approaches in exploring cultural differences" (Turner et al., 2024, p. 1282). More research with representative samples from across the globe would clearly advance the field.

Master Narrative Model

As noted in the prior section, master narratives are attracting more research attention (McLean & Syed, 2016; McLean et al., 2018). Master narratives refer to "culturally shared stories that guide thoughts, beliefs, values, and behaviors" (McLean & Syed, 2016, p. 323). Individuals in a culture can consciously or unconsciously utilize, internalize, and even resist such broad culture-specific stories about what life should be like. How we integrate our own personal identity with this wider, culturally rooted story of what is expected in a person's life is recognized as a central process of identity development. Thus, individuals' interactions and negotiations with their culture's shared stories could facilitate, support, or restrict the development of their personal narratives.

Communication with others, especially family members, may be crucial to this process (Fivush & Kellas, 2025). Individuals who are not able to follow or internalize master narratives – especially people who are marginalized by their society (e.g., gender and sexually diverse youth) – may require alternative narratives (i.e., stories about lives created in resistance to a master narrative; McLean et al., 2018). Thus, in a master narrative approach, individuals and cultures are not assessed separately. Rather, individuals and cultures can be studied in the same metric of narratives (McLean & Syed, 2016). This innovation could alleviate the difficulties encountered by psychology when attempting to study people developing in contexts.

As master narratives inherently reflect broader values in a larger cultural context, researchers have increasingly unpacked characteristics of master and/or alternative narratives in some selected cultural contexts (e.g., the U.S., Sweden, and Japan; see Schwab & Stamper, 2024; Wiking et al., 2023; and Yasui et al., 2025, respectively). An illustrative example of one such study was conducted by Yasui and colleagues (2025). These researchers examined the dynamics of identity formation in negotiating social structures among Japanese emerging adults who experienced the tendency of hikikomori (a Japanese term meaning extreme social withdrawal, which deviates from Japanese sociocultural expectations). Yasui and colleagues (2025) collected data using a combination of questionnaires and interviews. The quantitative analyses showed that emerging adults who experienced hikikomori were more likely to elaborate on master narratives than their non-hikikomori counterparts, supporting the theoretical assumption that people tend to be aware of, reflect on, and hence elaborate master narratives when they deviate from them (McLean et al., 2018).

The qualitative analyses illuminated two major master narratives that may be dominant in the Japanese cultural context: communion based on Japanese social structure and a straight life course. For instance, one hikikomori participant stated that parental pressure to follow the culturally expected life course (i.e., going to university, smoothly transitioning from university to work without failing, and obtaining a stable job) restricted her from freely exploring identity options, as reported by Yasui and colleagues:

> After becoming a university student and starting to live on my own, I found myself in a situation where no one was telling me anything. I had to think for myself and figure out what I wanted to do, and for the first time, I realized that freedom wasn't enjoyable. I thought I was the type of person who would get lost without some kind of path laid out for me, so I feel that maybe it was better when people had expectations of me. But on the other hand, I also feel that if people expect too much from someone with a weak sense of self, when they are told "You're free to do whatever you want," they might end up being unable to take any action at all.
> (H, female, 21 years old; Yasui et al., 2025, p. 13)

As illustrated in the above narrative, individuals who experience marginalization in their society may attempt to pursue a life that is highly valued in their culture (e.g., the culturally sanctioned life course in Japan's traditional social system and a master narrative about what is expected of one's life). Yet, by deviating from this path, individuals may perceive themselves as failures in society and experience considerable difficulties in forming their identity. Research on how to diminish the psychological and social barriers those individuals are facing in developing a narrative identity would be valuable and help them find alternative narratives of their own unique identities (McLean et al., 2018; Schwab & Stamper, 2024). In the next section, this issue is discussed further in the context of the future development of identity-related interventions.

Implications for Social Response

Well-designed and implemented interventions and policies that partner with young people to support their own identity development and future life prospects are essential (Ferrer-Wreder et al., 2014; Piotrowski et al., 2025). In the narrative identity model, individuals can construct a coherent sense of self through autobiographical reasoning in which they reflect on their past, make sense of their present selves, and look forward to their future goals (McAdams & McLean, 2013). Indeed, a higher level of agency in adolescents' narratives predicted a stronger increase in exploration and commitment (van Doeselaar et al., 2020). It could be an important task for narrative identity researchers to undertake the following:

> applied narrative identity work . . . [in which researchers] support programs and curriculum developments that take the idea of narrative identity development seriously . . . to create opportunities for students to forge a narrative identity . . . emphasize[ing] reflective work and journaling activities in addition to more traditional academic challenges.
>
> (Pasupathi, personal communication, August 2, 2025)

Currently, there exist only a handful of published research studies that describe interventions designed to expressly promote certain aspects of narrative identity development (e.g., Tseng, 2017) or explicitly examine how narrative identity development may change when other outcomes are altered as part of a prevention and/or treatment intervention (e.g., recovery from mental ill-health – e.g., Adler, 2012; Adler & Hershfield, 2012; See et al., 2021). By and large, these studies highlight the potential for narrative identity processes to be important to the promotion of positive outcomes and the reduction of problems. While there are some initial indications of promise, substantial descriptive and intervention research is needed in order to inform the ways that social institutions can systematically support youth in their narrative identity development.

Interventions designed to promote narrative identity in adolescents will require careful design, given that different types of meaning-making may have different relations to well-being in adolescence. For example, in studies with adults and children (who are supported by their parents in their interpretations of life events), more meaning-making in personal narratives and life stories (even when something negative may have happened) tended to be associated with greater well-being (McLean et al., 2010). However, in a study by McLean and colleagues (2010), some aspects of meaning-making were related to better well-being, namely, change connections (i.e., this is a type of self-event connection in which participants explain how certain life events played a role in changes in themselves). Yet a different indicator of meaning-making called sophistication (i.e., "specific emotional, psychological, or relational insight from the event that applies to broader areas of the reporter's life") in early adolescent participants was associated with poorer well-being (McLean et al., 2010, p. 174).

The study authors suggested that self-event connections (e.g., change connections) may be cognitively and emotionally easier or developmentally appropriate for early adolescents and thereby are associated with better well-being, but that the more interpretative and introspective types of meaning-making may be ill-suited developmentally for early adolescents. Hence, the association with poorer well-being among early but not late adolescents in this sample may account for this result (McLean et al., 2010). This pattern of findings was also evident in a cross-sectional study with adolescents living in New Zealand (Reese et al., 2017).

If this finding is widely replicated in future research, and if there are lingering negative consequences for early adolescents who engage in more sophisticated meaning-making into later adolescence and adulthood, then there would be important implications for the design of narrative identity-oriented interventions with adolescents. More introspective meaning-making narratives could be beneficial to support late but not early adolescents. Or it may be the case, as other scholars have suggested, that this is a temporary, difficult period for these early adolescents "who are doing the hard work of identity exploration early on" and who later turn out to be fine or even better than fine, because they have a head start on other adolescents (Reese et al., 2017, p. 623). Thus, more longitudinal research studies with adolescent cohorts that include narrative identity processes and other outcomes such as well-being and varied indicators of health are vital to providing a sound basis for interventions to support the development of new narrative identity-related interventions for adolescents.

A parallel avenue to pursue along with longitudinal studies would be to include narrative identity development measurement in the outcome evaluation studies of existing identity interventions that have shown benefits in adolescent samples (e.g., Eichas et al., 2017; for a review, see Crocetti et al., 2025). A focus of a study such as this would be to examine what mediating or moderating role narrative identity-related processes may play in intervention-related change for these existing evidence-based identity interventions. These types of interventions have already evidenced benefits in adolescent samples (Eichas et al., 2017). An aim could be to examine what role narrative identity-related processes have in relation to other intervention targets for change and outcomes in identity interventions such as identity exploration.

Summary

Narrative identity involves a person's attempt to answer the following questions: Across time and the events of my life, among a diversity of other people and situations that I find myself in, what defines me? Who am I, and what do I stand for across time? Indeed, the narrative identity perspective places particular value on developing one's own unique sense of unity or continuity over time and settings. One can put narrative identity in a wider three-layer framework of lifespan personality development that consists of traits, motivations/goals, and narrative identity (McAdams, 2019). Current research evidence shows that adolescence tends to be a developmental period in which it becomes increasingly more common for young people to show greater understanding of how their life experiences relate to who they are as a person as well as to tell personal narratives that are characterized by greater coherence and/or meaning-making than are found among children (Fivush & Kellas, 2025); these trends are likely to continue through adulthood (e.g., Köber & Habermas, 2017). Narrative identity research is a relatively young but fast-growing field within psychology, and there are likely to be many future advances in the field related to the acceleration in the number of longitudinal and intervention studies with adolescents.

Notes

1 Köber and colleagues (2015, p. 261) stated in regard to temporal coherence that

> it serves to let the listener know when an event happened in the narrator's life . . . life narratives are expected to begin no later than with birth. Sometimes birth stories or earliest memories are told to foreshadow the global interpretation of life. . . .

The personal narrative that starts off this chapter (i.e., Sara's story) was not collected as part of a scientific study. Sara's story was told to her granddaughter, who is the first author of this book (LFW), and is retold here for illustrative purposes. Sara began her own life story with her parents' story of how they came to live in Cuba. This break from what is typical in a life story can be called an anachrony (Köber et al., 2015) and could be a product of not following a systematic interview procedure, and/or it could highlight the importance of family relationships and history, which were fundamental to who Sara was and her culture (i.e., a master narrative – cf. Hammack, 2008 – of how a life story should be told).

2 McLean (2005, p. 683–684) distinguished gaining insight and lesson learning in the quote below, in that lesson learning is about:

> a specific lesson from an event that could direct future behavior in similar situations. . . . Gaining insight refers to gleaning meaning from an event that applies to greater areas of life than a specific behavior; with insight, there is often some kind of transformation in the understanding of oneself or others. . . .

3 Autobiographical reasoning is multifaceted and concerns how people see life events as formative to psychological changes or stability in themselves and/or connecting lived experiences to wider life lessons and/or insights (Habermas & Köber, 2014).

4 The questions and prompts for the life story interview can be found at the following website: https://cpb-us-e1.wpmucdn.com/sites.northwestern.edu/dist/4/3901/files/2020/11/The-Life-Story-Interview-II-2007.pdf. The description of the life story interview questions and prompts in this book was paraphrased from this source.

5 An examination of existing empirical studies in peer-reviewed journals using a search engine often used in psychology called PsycINFO yielded 1,562 articles in English (excluding dissertations) with the terms "narrative identity" or "autobiographical reasoning" referenced anywhere in the study. The identified empirical studies began to appear in the mid-1990s, and about 34% were published in the last five years.

6 "Spill the tea!" or "what's the 411?" are slang phrases that can be used in an informal conversation to let other people know (these other people should also know the meaning of these phrases) that you would like to hear what they have to say about themselves and their experiences, and it can also be a request to hear about confidential or emotionally significant details about another person (i.e., gossip).

7 *Italics* were added in this sentence to emphasize that the reference here is specifically to children and not adolescents.

8 Coherence and meaning-making are sometimes defined by different scholars in variable ways; in some cases, these terms are clearly distinct, and in other cases, these terms appear to be conceptually merged, which can lead to a lack of clarity in regard to making conclusions about the empirical associations of different narrative constructs (i.e., measured variables in studies) and correlates (i.e., well-being).

References

Acciai, A., Guerrisi, L., Plebe, A., & Suriano, R. (2025). Neural language models as content analysis tools in psychology. *Philosophical Psychology*. Advanced online publication. https://doi.org/10.1080/09515089.2025.2508942

Adler, J. M. (2012). Living into the story: Agency and coherence in a longitudinal study of narrative identity development and mental health over the course of psychotherapy. *Journal of Personality and Social Psychology, 102*(2), 367–389. https://doi.org/10.1037/a0025289

Adler, J. M., & Hershfield, H. E. (2012). Mixed emotional experience is associated with and precedes improvements in psychological well-being. *PLoS ONE, 7*(4), e35633. https://doi.org/10.1371/journal.pone.0035633

Adler, J. M., Lodi-Smith, J., Philippe, F. L., & Houle, I. (2016). The incremental validity of narrative identity in predicting well-being: A review of the field and recommendations for the future. *Personality and Social Psychology Review, 20*(2), 142–175. https://doi.org/10.1177/1088868315585068

Adler, J. M., Turner, A. F., Brookshier, K. M., Monahan, C., Walder-Biesanz, I., Harmeling, L. H., Albaugh, M., McAdams, D. P., & Oltmanns, T. F. (2015). Variation in narrative identity is associated with trajectories of mental health over several years. *Journal of Personality and Social Psychology, 108*(3), 476–496. https://doi.org/10.1037/a0038601

Atherton, O. E., Grijalva, E., Roberts, B. W., & Robins, R. W. (2021). Stability and change in personality traits and major life goals from college to midlife. *Personality and Social Psychology Bulletin, 47*(5), 841–858. https://doi.org/10.1177/0146167220949362

Bleidorn, W., Schwaba, T., Zheng, A., Hopwood, C. J., Sosa, S. S., Roberts, B. W., & Briley, D. A. (2022). Personality stability and change: A meta-analysis of longitudinal studies. *Psychological Bulletin, 148*(7–8), 588–619. https://doi.org/10.1037/bul0000365

Costa, P. T., Jr., & McCrae, R. R. (2017). The NEO inventories as instruments of psychological theory. In T. A. Widiger (Ed.), *The Oxford handbook of the five factor model* (pp. 11–37). Oxford University Press.

Crocetti, E., Pagano, M., De Lise, F., Maratia, F., Bobba, B., Meeus, W., & Bacaro, V. (2025). Promoting adolescents' personal and social identities: A meta-analysis of psychosocial interventions. *Identity: An International Journal of Theory and Research, 25*(2), 167–196. https://doi.org/10.1080/15283488.2024.2394888

de Silveira, C., & Habermas, T. (2011). Narrative means to manage responsibility in life narratives across adolescence. *The Journal of Genetic Psychology: Research and Theory on Human Development, 172*(1), 1–20. https://doi.org/10.1080/00221325.2010.503254

Eichas, K., Montgomery, M. J., Meca, A., & Kurtines, W. M. (2017). Empowering marginalized youth: A self-transformative intervention for promoting positive youth development. *Child Development, 88*(4), 1115–1124. https://doi.org/10.1111/cdev.12866

Ferrer-Wreder, L, Montgomery, M. J., Lorente, C. C., & Habibi, M. (2014). Identify interventions for adolescents: Promoting optimal identity. In T. Gullotta & M. Bloom (Series Eds.), *The encyclopedia of primary prevention and health promotion* (pp. 1278–1287). Springer. https://doi.org/10.1007/978-1-4614-5999-6_183

Fivush, R., Habermas, T., Waters, T. E. A., & Zaman, W. (2011). The making of autobiographical memory: Intersections of culture, narratives and identity. *International Journal of Psychology, 46*(5), 321–345. https://doi.org/10.1080/00207594.2011.596541

Fivush, R., & Kellas, J. K. (2025). Parental and family storytelling across the generations: An interdisciplinary review. *Parenting, 25*(2), 103–126. https://doi.org/10.1080/15295192.2025.2450497

Fivush, R., Reese, E., & Haden, C. A. (2006). Elaborating on elaborations: Role of maternal reminiscing style in cognitive and socioemotional development. *Child Development, 77*(6), 1568–1588. https://doi.org/10.1111/j.1467-8624.2006.00960.x

Groh, A. M., Narayan, A. J., Bakermans-Kranenburg, M. J., Roisman, G. I., Vaughn, B. E., Fearon, R. M. P., & IJzendoorn, M. H. (2017). Attachment and temperament in the early

life course: A meta-analytic review. *Child Development*, *88*(3), 770–795. https://doi.org/10.1111/cdev.12677
Habermas, T., & Köber, C. (2014). Autobiographical reasoning is constitutive for narrative identity: The role of the life story for personal continuity. In K. C. McLean & M. Syed (Eds.), *The Oxford handbook of identity development* [E-reader version] (pp. 149–165). Oxford University Press. https://doi.org10.1093/oxfordhb/9780199936564.013.010
Hammack, P. L. (2008). Narrative and the cultural psychology of identity. *Personality and Social Psychology Review*, *12*(3), 222–247. https://doi.org/10.1177/1088868308316892
Hammack, P. L. (2010). The political psychology of personal narrative: The case of Barack Obama. *Analyses of Social Issues and Public Policy*, *10*(1), 182–206. https://doi.org/10.1111/j.1530-2415.2010.01207.x
Hammack, P. L. (2014). Theoretical foundations of identity. In K. C. McLean & M. Syed (Eds.), *The Oxford handbook of identity development* [E-reader version] (pp. 11–30). Oxford University Press. https://doi.org/10.1093/oxfordhb/9780199936564.013.027
Hesse, H. (1951). *Siddhartha*. New Directions Publishing Corp.
Jennings, L. E., Pasupathi, M., & McLean, K. C. (2014). "Intricate lettings out and lettings in": Listener scaffolding of narrative identity in newly dating romantic partners. *Self and Identity*, *13*(2), 214–230. https://doi.org/10.1080/15298868.2013.786203
Köber, C., & Habermas, T. (2017). How stable is the personal past? Stability of most important autobiographical memories and life narratives across eight years in a lifespan sample. *Journal of Personality and Social Psychology*, *113*(4), 608–626. https://doi.org/10.1037/pspp0000145
Köber, C., Schmiedek, F., & Habermas, T. (2015). Characterizing lifespan development of three aspects of coherence in life narratives: A cohort-sequential study. *Developmental Psychology*, *51*(2), 260–275. https://doi.org/10.1037/a0038668
Lilgendahl, J. P. (2014). The dynamic role of identity processes in personality development: Theories, patterns, and new directions. In K. C. McLean & M. Syed (Eds.), *The Oxford handbook of identity development* [E-reader version] (pp. 490–507). Oxford University Press. https://doi.org/10.1093/oxfordhb/9780199936564.013.026
Lilgendahl, J. P., & McLean, K. C. (2020). Narrative identity processes and patterns of adjustment across the transition to college: A developmentally contextualized approach. *Journal of Personality and Social Psychology*, *119*(4), 960–977. https://doi.org/10.1037/pspp0000277
Lind, M., Henry, R. C., Jonathan, M. A., & McAdams, D. P. (2025). Development and validation of the Narrative Identity Self-Evaluation Scale (NISE). *Journal of Personality Assessment*, *107*(3), 292–305. https://doi.org/10.1080/00223891.2024.2425663
McAdams, D. P. (1996). What this framework can and cannot do. *Psychological Inquiry*, *7*(4), 378–386. https://doi.org/10.1207/s15327965pli0704_17
McAdams, D. P. (2008). *The life story interview – II: The study of lives research group*. https://cpb-us-e1.wpmucdn.com/sites.northwestern.edu/dist/4/3901/files/2020/11/The-Life-Story-Interview-II-2007.pdf
McAdams, D. P. (2015). Three lines of personality development: A conceptual itinerary. *European Psychologist*, *20*(4), 252–264. https://doi.org/10.1027/1016-9040/a000236
McAdams, D. P. (2019). The emergence of personality. In D. P. McAdams, R. L. Shiner, & J. L. Tackett (Eds.), *Handbook of personality development* (pp. 3–19). Guilford.
McAdams, D. P., & Manczak, E. (2015). Personality and the life story. In M. Mikulincer, P. R. Shave, M. L. Cooper, & R. J. Larsen (Eds.), *APA handbook of personality and social psychology* (pp. 425–446). American Psychological Association. https://doi.org/10.1037/14343-019
McAdams, D. P., & Mayukha, A. (2024). Hiding in plain view: An historical perspective on the study of morality in personality psychology. *Journal of Personality*, *92*(3), 666–682. https://doi.org/10.1111/jopy.12808
McAdams, D. P., & McLean, K. C. (2013). Narrative identity. *Current Directions in Psychological Science*, *22*, 233–238. https://doi.org/10.1177/0963721413475622

McAdams, D. P., & Olson, B. D. (2010). Personality development: Continuity and change over the life course. *Annual Review of Psychology*, *61*(1), 517–542. https://doi.org/10.1146/annurev.psych.093008.100507

McAdams, D. P., & Pals, J. L. (2006). A new big five: Fundamental principles for an integrative science of personality. *American Psychologist*, *61*, 204–217. https://doi.org/10.1146/annurev.psych.093008.100507

McAdams, D. P., Trzesniewski, K., Lilgendahl, J., Benet-Martinez, V., & Robins, R. W. (2021). Self and identity in personality psychology. *Personality Science*, *2*(2), 1–20. https://doi.org/10.5964/ps.6035

McLean, K. C. (2005). Late adolescent identity development: Narrative meaning making and memory telling. *Developmental Psychology*, *41*(4), 683–691. https://doi.org/10.1037/0012-1649.41.4.683

McLean, K. C. (2008). Stories of the young and the old: Personal continuity and narrative identity. *Developmental Psychology, 44*(1), 254–264. https://doi.org/10.1037/0012-1649.44.1.254

McLean, K. C. (2017). And the story evolves: The development of personal narratives and narrative identity. In J. Specht (Ed.), *Personality development across the lifespan* (pp. 325–338). Elsevier Academic Press.

McLean, K. C., & Breen, A. V. (2009). Processes and content of narrative identity development in adolescence: Gender and well-being. *Developmental Psychology*, *45*(3), 702–710. https://doi.org/10.1037/a0015207

McLean, K. C., Breen, A. V., & Fournier, M. A. (2010). Constructing the self in early, middle, and late adolescent boys: Narrative identity, individuation, and well-being. *Journal of Research on Adolescence*, *20*(1), 166–187. https://doi.org/10.1111/j.1532-7795.2009.00633.x

McLean, K. C., Dunlap, D., Jennings, S. C., Litvitskiy, N. S., & Lilgendahl, J. P. (2022). Stability and change in autobiographical reasoning: A 4-year longitudinal study of narrative identity development. *Journal of Personality*, *90*(3), 343–356. https://doi.org/10.1111/jopy.12669

McLean, K. C., & Fournier, M. A. (2008). The content and processes of autobiographical reasoning in narrative identity. *Journal of Research in Personality*, *42*(3), 527–545. https://doi.org/10.1016/j.jrp.2007.08.003

McLean, K. C., & Jennings, L. E. (2012). Teens telling tales: How maternal and peer audiences support narrative identity development. *Journal of Adolescence*, *35*(6), 1455–1469. https://doi.org/10.1016/j.adolescence.2011.12.005

McLean, K. C., Lilgendahl, J. P., Fordham, C., Alpert, E., Marsden, E., Szymanowski, K., & McAdams, D. P. (2018). Identity development in cultural context: The role of deviating from master narratives. *Journal of Personality*, *86*(4), 631–651. https://doi.org/10.1111/jopy.12341

McLean, K. C., & Mansfield, C. D. (2012). The co-construction of adolescent narrative identity: Narrative processing as a function of adolescent age, gender, and maternal scaffolding. *Developmental Psychology*, *48*(2), 436–447. https://doi.org/10.1037/a0025563

McLean, K. C., & Pasupathi, M. (2011). Old, new, borrowed, blue? The emergence and retention of personal meaning in autobiographical storytelling. *Journal of Personality*, *79*(1), 135–164. https://doi.org/10.1111/j.1467-6494.2010.00676.x

McLean, K. C., & Pratt, M. W. (2006). Life's little (and big) lessons: Identity statuses and meaning-making in the turning point narratives of emerging adults. *Developmental Psychology*, *42*(4), 714–722. https://doi.org/10.1037/0012-1649.42.4.714

McLean, K. C., & Syed, M. (2014). The field of identity development needs an identity: An introduction to The Oxford handbook of identity development. In K. C. McLean & M. Syed (Eds.), *The Oxford handbook of identity development* [E-reader version] (pp. 1–10). Oxford University Press. https://doi.org/10.1093/oxfordhb/9780199936564.013.023

McLean, K. C., & Syed, M. (2016). Personal, master, and alternative narratives: An integrative framework for understanding identity development in context. *Human Development*, *58*(6), 318–349. https://doi.org/10.1159/000445817

McLean, K. C., Syed, M., Pasupathi, M., Adler, J. M., Dunlop, W. L., Drustrup, D., Fivush, R., Graci, M. E., Lilgendahl, J. P., Lodi-Smith, J., McAdams, D. P., & McCoy, T. P. (2020). The empirical structure of narrative identity: The initial Big Three. *Journal of Personality and Social Psychology, 119*(4), 920–944. https://doi.org/10.1037/pspp0000247

Morgan, E. M., & Korobov, N. (2012). Interpersonal identity formation in conversations with close friends about dating relationships. *Journal of Adolescence, 35*(6), 1471–1483. https://doi.org/10.1016/j.adolescence.2011.09.005

Pasupathi, M. (2014). Autobiographical reasoning and my discontent: Alternative paths from narrative to identity. In K. C. McLean & M. Syed (Eds.), *The Oxford handbook of identity development* [E-reader version] (pp. 1–30). Oxford University Press. https://doi.org/10.1093/oxfordhb/9780199936564.013.002

Pasupathi, M., Fivush, R., Greenhoot, A. F., & McLean, K. C. (2020). Intraindividual variability in narrative identity: Complexities, garden paths, and untapped research potential. *European Journal of Personality, 34*(6), 1138–1150. https://doi.org/10.1002/per.2279

Pasupathi, M., & Hoyt, T. (2009). The development of narrative identity in late adolescence and emergent adulthood: The continued importance of listeners. *Developmental Psychology, 45*(2), 558–574. https://doi.org/10.1037/a0014431

Pasupathi, M., McLean, K. C., Weeks, T. L., & Hynes, W. (2021). Tailoring narration for distinct audiences in emerging adulthood. *Emerging Adulthood, 9*(6), 725–736. https://doi.org/10.1177/2167696819856753

Pasupathi, M., & Rich, B. (2005). Inattentive listening undermines self-verification in personal storytelling. *Journal of Personality, 73*(4), 1051–1086. https://doi.org/10.1111/j.1467-6494.2005.00338.x

Pasupathi, M., Wainryb, C., Bourne, S. V., & Oldroyd, K. (2022). Mothers and friends as listeners for adolescent anger narration: Distinct developmental affordances. *Developmental Psychology, 58*(4), 778. https://doi.org/10.1037/dev0001322

Piotrowski, K., Naudé, L., & Negru-Subtirica, O. (2025). Crafting an identity for identity interventions. *Identity: An International Journal of Theory and Research, 25*(2), 153–166. https://doi.org/10.1080/15283488.2025.2477490

Reese, E., Myftari, E., McAnally, H. M., Chen, Y., Neha, T., Wang, Q., Jack, F., & Robertson, S. (2017). Telling the tale and living well: Adolescent narrative identity, personality traits, and well-being across cultures. *Child Development, 88*(2), 612–628. https://doi.org/10.1111/cdev.12618

Roberts, B. W., Walton, K. E., & Viechtbauer, W. (2006). Patterns of mean-level change in personality traits across the life course: A meta-analysis of longitudinal studies. *Psychological Bulletin, 132*(1), 1–25. https://doi.org/10.1037/0033-2909.132.1.1

Sameroff, A. J., & Haith, M. M. (Eds.). (1996). *The five to seven year shift: The age of reason and responsibility*. University of Chicago Press.

Schwab, J. R., & Stamper, A. J. (2024). Flourishing in a binary world: The creation of transgender alternative narratives. *Sex Roles, 90*(7), 859–874. https://doi.org/10.1007/s11199-024-01475-0

Seaman, J., Sharp, E. H., & Coppens, A. D. (2017). A dialectical approach to theoretical integration in developmental–contextual identity research. *Developmental Psychology, 53*(11), 2023–2035. https://doi.org/10.1037/dev0000383

See, A. Y., Klimstra, T. A., Shiner, R. L., & Denissen, J. J. A. (2021). Linking narrative identity with schizotypal personality disorder features in adolescents. *Personality Disorders: Theory, Research, and Treatment, 12*(2), 182–192. https://doi.org/10.1037/per0000414

Soucie, K. M., Lawford, H., & Pratt, M. W. (2012). Personal stories of empathy in adolescence and emerging adulthood. *Merrill-Palmer Quarterly, 58*(2), 141–158. 10.1353/mpq.2012.0010

Tompkins, V., Montgomery, D. E., Dore, R. A., & Lee, B. K. (2025). Theory of mind and text comprehension across the lifespan: A meta-analysis. *Developmental Psychology, 61*(6), 1112. https://doi.org/10.1037/dev0001869

Tseng, W. (2017). An intervention using Lego Serious Play on fostering narrative identity among economically disadvantaged college students in Taiwan. *Journal of College Student Development*, *58*(2), 264–282. https://doi.org/10.1353/csd.2017.0019

Turner, A. F., Thomsen, D. K., Tuval-Mashiach, R., Sevilla-Liu, A., Cowan, H. R., Sumner, S., & McAdams, D. P. (2024). Narrative identity in context: How adults in Japan, Denmark, Israel, and the United States narrate difficult life events. *Journal of Personality and Social Psychology*, *127*(6), 1263–1287. https://doi.org/10.1037/pspp0000523

van Doeselaar, L., McLean, K. C., Meeus, W., Denissen, J. J. A. A., & Klimstra, T. A. (2020). Adolescents' identity formation: Linking the narrative and the dual-cycle approach. *Journal of Youth and Adolescence*, *49*(4), 818–835. https://doi.org/10.1007/s10964-019-01096-x

Wiking, K., Gyberg, F., Wängqvist, M., & Svensson, Y. (2023). Family identity and deviations from the master narrative in Sweden. *Identity: An International Journal of Theory and Research*, *23*(2), 137–154. https://doi.org/10.1080/15283488.2022.2146694

Yasui, G., Hihara, S., Sugimura, K., & Schwab, J. R. (2025). Master narratives among youth with hikikomori in the Japanese sociocultural context. *Identity: An International Journal of Theory and Research*, 1–19. Advance online publication. https://doi.org/10.1080/15283488.2025.2510263

4 Identity as Rooted in Society and Culture

> I thought about my ethnic identity a lot through high school. In my early teens, I always felt embarrassed by my parents, who emigrated here when I was seven. I didn't think much about it before then, but by my early teens they kept wanting me to follow their [cultural] and family traditions, and it made me feel really uncomfortable around my friends. So I went through a time of just wanting to forget everything about my Somali background and become "all American." But gradually I came to realize that I am Somali and I shouldn't try to deny it. Seeing other African Americans on TV doing important things started to make me feel kind of proud . . . and now I feel good about myself and being a Somali American.
>
> (Charlie, an 18-year-old college freshman)

This passage comes from an interview undertaken by Kroger in 2006 to obtain background material for her subsequent writing on ethnic identity development during adolescence. Charlie's statement gives us a glimpse of what it is like to belong to more than one world. There are many possible components of social identity, also sometimes called collective identity, which could be based on one's generation, gender, sexuality, ethnicity, nationality, and even a person's support of a sports team or other special interest. Social identity deals with the question of "what group do I belong to?" (Worrell, 2014, p. 3) and can be seen from different angles: individuals interacting with groups, groups interacting with each other, and people and groups embedded in sociocultural and historical changes (Spears, 2011).

To provide an illustration, consider a fictional young man with a Roma heritage[1] living in Berlin. This young man may see himself mostly as a cosmopolitan city dweller who spends a good part of his day laughing at the same Internet memes that every other teenager in Germany is laughing at this week. But how does he make sense of himself as a global citizen, as part of his generation, and in relation to the wider German society? How does he relate to other ethnocultural groups in Berlin? Each of these social groups can be a place where a sense of confusion or belonging and meaning can be found. Azmitia (2014) likened the many different possible components of social identity to boxes that we carry around. While juggling different identity boxes, this fictional young man may also be cultivating what is distinctive and meaningful about himself as an individual. In other words, he is also likely working on

DOI: 10.4324/9781003486336-4

just being himself and figuring out who that is – that is, co-constructing his personal identity, which reflects our individuality and one's individual goals, values, and beliefs that guide them in making important life choices (Crocetti et al., 2018).

This chapter addresses the question of how adolescent identity development progresses as young people learn how to be themselves while still navigating and finding a psychological home in different social and cultural worlds. This chapter will focus on the development of ethnic identity as one example of how sociocultural forces are important to identity development during adolescence. In short, ethnic identity involves the intersection of personal and social identity (Cross et al., 2017) and may be more or less salient to a given adolescent depending on the adolescent and the sociocultural context. Ethnic identity also involves a person's psychological and social association with an ethnocultural group. Ethnocultural groups are often defined by a shared geographical and/or genealogical origin as well as elements of a common culture based on the particulars and history of the ethnocultural group in question (Liebkind et al., 2016).

Sociocultural Approaches to Identity

A historic debate that lies underneath relevant theory, measurement, and information about identity concerns the degree to which individuals can exercise agency (e.g., free will and make choices about who they are) in the midst of their identity development (Burkitt, 2011). Ethnic and cultural identity make an encounter with this debate inevitable. Are people indeed exploring identity options or making choices about who they are, or are social groups and wider forces (e.g., social mobility and opportunity structures, and power relations among groups in a particular society) dictating who people even have the possibility to consider becoming? This person-versus-context debate (see Table 4.1) has implications for how identity itself has been conceptualized by different theorists and within varied disciplines (Burkitt, 2011; Seaman et al., 2017; Spears, 2011).

Table 4.1 Dualisms in the Study of Identity Development

The individual shapes identity	*The context (including culture) shapes identity*
Identity is interior or inside the person	Identity as assigned to a person
My thoughts and emotions about myself	A predefined identity is offered that may (or may not) fit me
Personal identity	Social identity
The unique life I live and the person that I am in my own eyes	National, ethnic, gender/occupation, and group intersections
Identity process	Identity content
Exploration and meaning-making	
Change in individuals	Change in groups
The unique life course of the individual person	Intergroup relations and power dynamics (meaning of groups changing in a society across generations)

There is now a clearer recognition of the importance of examining how individuals can shape their identity along with the ways that society and culture work to co-construct a person's identity (e.g., McLean et al., 2018; Seaman et al., 2017). The word "co-construct" implies that there is a bidirectional association and that the individual and context are both essential when one wants to understand human development in any domain of development (Overton, 2013). The context can include social institutions, cultural activities, practices, beliefs, historical times and conditions, and social interactions between people (Bronfenbrenner & Morris, 2006).

The sociocultural tradition within the field of human development offers practical ways out of the person-versus-context debate (Rogoff, 2023; Rogoff et al., 2018). This tradition derives several key ideas from Lev Vygotsky's scholarly work on the development of mental processes (Holland & Lachicotte, 2007). Several of Vygotsky's ideas that continue to have currency as part of the developmentally oriented sociocultural perspective include his views of human development as embedded in a particular sociocultural context and historical moment, development happening when people interact with each other, as well as when they engage in cultural practices (emphasizing how people's use and adaptation of symbols and tools can move development forward; Rogoff et al., 2018). Many present-day sociocultural researchers who have a developmental orientation would likely reject:

> the assumption of a boundary between people and the events in which they engage, a boundary that divides the individual and the context/culture into separate entities . . . Crucially for the study of lived experience, people do not simply participate. They participate IN some event. And while they are doing so they are IN that process, along with their companions, building on ways of life of prior generations of their cultural communities, in the particular contexts in which they engage.
>
> (Rogoff et al., 2018, p. 7)

In addition to Vygotsky, the sociocultural tradition in human development also has clear connections to cultural psychology. This subfield within psychology has championed the discovery and documentation of contextual diversity for its own sake (Shweder, 2011; Valsiner, 2012). Cultural psychology does not discount the idea that universal developmental processes can exist as ways to explain human development (e.g., exploration and commitment as a universal identity process in the Erikson and Marcia traditions). Yet it is also an ideal within cultural psychology that one should also not assume uniformity/universality (i.e., a developmental process), unless it is actually empirically documented in a diversity of cultures found across the globe (Hammack, 2008; Rogoff et al., 2018). Cultural psychology also recognizes the perverseness and complexity of the cultural and social context in relation to human development and advocates a bidirectional relation between the person and culture, and it challenges identity researchers to not assume that culture's importance to identity development can be reduced down into a single variable that is a static characteristic of the person, and the ways that culture is at work in identity development should be captured by more than one research method (Hammack, 2008).

Some scholars have applied lessons learned from the sociocultural tradition in human development to identity, and the result is that there is greater theoretical synergy achieved between a person's identity-related choices and meaning-making (which implies some degree of agency) and consideration of the roles that other people, signs/symbols, and additional aspects of context play in shaping identity development (e.g., Holland & Lachicotte, 2007; Seaman et al., 2017). This fusion of identity and sociocultural ideals is valuable to advancing identity research because it has a clear stance on the importance of the cultural and historical moment and how individual actions in the world come together to make identity formation possible. Sociocultural approaches would challenge identity researchers to have a deep understanding of a person's lived experience as a basis for the development of valid identity measures (Rogoff et al., 2018). A sociocultural approach to identity would also imply more emphasis on examining how people use what they have at hand to foster their identity (Rogoff et al., 2018). For instance, how do adolescents talk about who they are with others in person or on social media? What are the important identity-related cultural rituals for a particular adolescent? What are the everyday institutional policies or practices young people may encounter at home or school that can foster or inhibit their identity development? In sum, there is a great deal to be gained by taking an integrative approach that transcends the historic person-versus-context debate by fusing ideas from developmental science, sociocultural theories, and cultural psychology and then applying them to the study of identity development (McLean, 2021; Seaman et al., 2017).

Adolescent Ethnic Identity Development

Within this broader framework of ideas, we now switch to the integrative model for ethnic and racial identity (ERI) development (Umaña-Taylor et al., 2014) as a focal point that is in keeping with the sociocultural tradition but has its own unique theoretical inspiration and history. The integrative model for ERI development encompasses a selection of allied but historically separate theories, concepts, and operationalizations (Umaña-Taylor et al., 2014). It includes ideas and propositions from prior theories that are developmental (Phinney, 1989, 1990; Phinney & Baldelomar, 2011; Phinney & Ong, 2007). It also draws from other theories that speak to the African American experience in the United States (U.S.), in which there is the possibility of change in the ERI in response to life experiences that could or could not happen (i.e., non-developmental changes). These theories that were originally focused on the African American experience are well attuned to describing what ERI consists of (i.e., what it feels like) and how social identity functions in the midst of a wider society that has power differentials between social groups (e.g., racial identity theory and the multidimensional model of racial identity; see Cross, 1991; Helms, 1990; Sellers et al., 1998).

The integrative model is also based on a more general social psychology theory called social identity theory[2] (Spears, 2011; Tajfel & Turner, 1986), which also emphasizes how intergroup relations and power dynamics between social groups can be formative to a person's identity. The integrative model for ERI development (Umaña-Taylor et al., 2014) incorporates concepts from theories that have already been addressed earlier in this book (e.g., Erikson's lifespan psychosocial theory and Marcia's identity status model as described in Chapter 2 and narrative identity in Chapter 3). Thus, concepts from Eriksonian and narrative identity approaches are brought back into this chapter, but now as seen through the lens of ethnic identity development and sociocultural forces that may contribute to adolescent identity development. Several researchers have provided new ideas and knowledge about the issues of ethnic identity among adolescents, among them, Deborah Rivas-Drake.

Rivas-Drake the Person

Deborah Rivas-Drake, professor of psychology and education at the University of Michigan, is a leading scholar in the ERI field. Rivas-Drake is one of the codevelopers of the integrative model for ERI development and is the coauthor of a popular book titled *Below the surface: Talking with teens about race, ethnicity, and identity* (Rivas-Drake & Umaña-Taylor, 2019). Her book offers a primer on adolescent ERI for adults who care for youth.

Rivas-Drake was born in New York City. In a conversation with her, she remembered a move that she made with her family from her childhood home in Queens, New York, to Hollywood, Florida, during adolescence. She identified this transition as one of the sparks behind her long-standing interest in identity and context. Queens was and remains one of the most culturally diverse counties in the U.S., and Hollywood, Florida, at the time of Rivas-Drake's move (pre-Hurricane Andrew), was a mostly White and non-Latino community. Rivas-Drake's own cultural background is Latina, and she remembered the move to Florida as a teenager because it was

> really a culture shock . . . a moment where I thought about the context and how different it was from where I was before, and how much it affected . . . how I thought of myself and who I am, where I belonged and who I belonged to.
>
> (Rivas-Drake, personal communication, November 21, 2019)

Rivas-Drake returned to New York City, and as a first-generation college student, she completed her undergraduate degree in psychology at Pace University. She then went on to earn a doctoral degree in education and psychology at the University of Michigan and had a National Science Foundation-supported postdoctoral research fellowship at New York University's Center for Research on Culture, Development, and Education. Rivas-Drake had her first faculty appointment at Brown University, and some years later, she returned to her doctoral alma mater for a faculty position at the University of Michigan.

Rivas-Drake's research studies, many of which are highlighted in this chapter, illustrate how present-day researchers are working in diverse ways to shed new light on how adolescent ethnic and/or racial identity development unfolds in person–context interactions. Her focus has been on how ethnic and/or racial identity is "constructed in relationships and in relation to other people, primarily family, school contexts . . . adults in schools, and peers" (Rivas-Drake, personal communication, November 21, 2019). Rivas-Drake's research has explored the ways that ethnic and/or racial identity can be an asset; in other words, how and when can it be a psychological and/or social resource in different settings and in varied moments in everyday life? Based on her research, she learned that:

> [R]eally . . . anything is only ever an asset, if your context is letting it be an asset . . . if you're able to draw on it or if people are . . . allowing you to bring that part of yourself to the context or to the experience in a way that is productive, and positive, and healthy.
>
> (Rivas-Drake, personal communication, November 21, 2019)

In asking Rivas-Drake about what ideas are at the very front edge of identity research and about what research projects she was presently working on, she said the following:

> [T]here has been a move. I think a lot of momentum is around asking about the role of context . . . I am trying to get deeper into what is happening in schools, and actually what are adults doing that send messages, any kind of message, about how much your identity can be an asset there. . . .
>
> (Rivas-Drake, personal communication, November 21, 2019)

She also went on to discuss several innovations such as the use of network analysis of friendships as well as mixed-method research in studies of adolescent ethnic and/or racial identity development. She also described several new studies that she is working on. They were wide-ranging studies but shared a common concern about how to unpack the complexity of contexts that matter for adolescent identity development, such as the adolescents' lives at home or school. In her remarks, Rivas-Drake made clear the challenges incumbent upon researchers who attempt to address identity in terms of person–context interactions:

> [It's] really hard, because you definitely have to go beyond self-reports . . . you definitely have to have a multi-disciplinary view. Because something like a school context – it's multilevel, multilayered, there's pedagogy, there's climate, there's curriculum, there are just so many ways to understand the school context, that if you really want to understand how it informs identity . . . you have to get into all of that. . . .
>
> (Rivas-Drake, personal communication, November 21, 2019)

Looking into the future, Rivas-Drake was focused on continuing programs of research that advance adolescent ERI development and their implications for academic and sociopolitical development, was enthusiastic about mentoring students and early career scholars, and was ambitious in her efforts to have an impact beyond academia to better connect with youth themselves as well as adults who care for young people (e.g., parents and teachers). Rivas-Drake had several key points that she was working on communicating to both academic and general audiences, for example:

> What we are saying about kids' identity is that it can only be facilitated . . . if . . . people are willing to start asking themselves, What do *I* need to know about my own practices and the way that *I* engage with people who are different from me, in order to not put up a barrier to it [ethnic and/or racial identity][3] being something that kids can express and that I can recognize as an asset?
>
> (Rivas-Drake, personal communication, November 21, 2019)

Rivas-Drake's ideas and research are referred to throughout this chapter, but for detailed research examples of her theory and research efforts with colleagues, see later chapter sections titled "The integrative model for ethnic and racial identity development" and "Research findings on ethnic identity development in adolescence."

The Nature of Culture and Cultural Identity

Ideas about culture, ethnicity, nationality, race, and identity are often confounded with one another in ways that obscure rather than illuminate. It is vital to reflect on what these concepts have in common and how they are distinct. The next three chapter sections are dedicated to clarifying key terms and concepts encountered in the psychological study of ethnic identity.

Regarding culture, there are many formulations about what culture consists of and how it is at work in our lives (Azmitia, 2014). Many conceptualizations of culture involve the proposition that it is made up of stories and history as well as values and beliefs that are expressed in daily life through rituals, lifestyle preferences, diet, dress, art, architecture, socialization, and institutional practices (Azmitia, 2014). Culture is also often taken for granted in our language and social interactions (Hammack, 2008). Further, culture can have an intergenerational presence, with some aspects of culture being held dear for generations, while other parts are discarded or reinterpreted as time passes (Azmitia, 2014). Shweder (2011) noted that culture is evident when a group of people has mutual "understandings of what is true, good, and valuable" and a shared vision in terms of "their conceptions of self, society, and nature" (p. 14). Importantly, the culture that individuals share is not experienced in a uniform way, and people in some cases only adopt aspects of a culture that are consistent with their own sensibilities and experiences (Hammack, 2008). Hoare put it well when she stated:

> Culture has long been conceptualized as that which is integral to the way persons construct and perceive their reality . . . The person is embedded in a society that anchors and sponsors identity . . . Different societies and cultures

> forge, within their citizens, a unique way of shaping and sensing reality . . . identity both absorbs and reflects culture.
>
> (Hoare, 1991, p. 45)

Jensen et al. (2011) described cultural identity as deciding on and taking one's place in a cultural community. Cultural identity involves personal and social identity and is broad because it could apply equally well to a wide range of cultural communities (Jensen et al., 2011), such as a particular generation and the zeitgeist that characterizes its spirit (e.g., the gig economy of millennials), or be descriptive of what unites a group of indigenous people together.

The Nature of Ethnic Identity

A way to get one's bearings when encountering the concept of ethnic identity is to get acquainted with different types of acculturating people and societies (Phinney, 1990). Acculturation is an inevitable part of ethnic identity. Acculturation happens when groups of people (including individuals) navigate different social and cultural worlds (Berry & Sam, 2016; Sam, 2024). It occurs at individual, group, and societal levels (Berry & Sam, 2016; Sam, 2024). Acculturation involves a bidirectional interchange (or relation), and there is recognition that change is taking place as a result of face-to-face (and even virtual/remote) contact between people and cultures (Berry & Sam, 2016).

Acculturation psychology (e.g., Berry & Sam, 2016; Ward & Szabó, 2023) offers several lucid concepts that are helpful to better understand ethnic identity. For example, acculturation psychology has a history of examining issues such as ethnic identity from a global rather than a single national standpoint (e.g., Liebkind et al., 2016). Acculturation strategies (e.g., assimilation, integration, separation, and marginalization – these terms are explained later in the chapter) are also salient when considering ethnic identity. It should be noted that acculturation speaks to a broad range of experiences and social connections that not only include but also go beyond ethnic identity.

Indeed, acculturation has an impact on a wide range of people in different life circumstances, including those in the mainstream host or receiving society as well as individuals who are making a new home for many different reasons. For instance, sojourners such as exchange students or temporary workers are newcomers with a more recent arrival in a host or receiving society and will only have a short stay in their new home (e.g., De Lise et al., 2025). Others who experience acculturation include people who voluntarily (i.e., immigrants) or are forced (i.e., refugees/those seeking asylum) to make their home in a new society (Berry & Sam, 2016). Acculturation can also happen for groups that have a long-standing history in a particular society but have been able to retain elements of their own group's cultural distinctiveness (Berry & Sam, 2016). These sedentary or long-standing groups include indigenous people and ethnocultural groups (Berry & Sam, 2016).

At the individual psychological level, people are changing in terms of how they behave, think, and feel (Berry & Sam, 2016). Acculturation strategies involve attitudes and behaviors about how people are responding to the changes around them and include the acculturation strategies of assimilation (i.e., from a ethnocultural group perspective, this situation would be one in which the person's original culture is lost and the new culture is adopted), integration (i.e., a person is able to strike a balance between two or more cultures, and selected aspects of these cultures are kept in a unique, personal blend), separation (i.e., where the original culture is kept, and the new culture is avoided), and marginalization (i.e., not finding one's psychological home in either the original or new culture; Berry & Sam, 2016; Jensen et al., 2011). Acculturation expectations are what the new host/receiving society promotes as a way that newcomers and sedentary groups can exist in that society (e.g., multiculturalism and segregation; Berry & Sam, 2016). Acculturation strategies and expectations have been considered along with cultural and/or ethnic identity in empirical studies and theoretical work (for a recent review, see Ward & Szabó, 2023).

As noted earlier, this chapter focuses primarily on adolescent identity development in relation to ethnocultural groups. Ethnocultural groups usually have as a central feature a shared geographical and/or genealogical origin (Liebkind et al., 2016) as well as other aspects of a common culture that can be specific and defining to a particular ethnocultural group (Worrell, 2014). The origin of an ethnocultural group can be based in fact or in legend (Liebkind et al., 2016). The diaspora(s) that is at the heart of an ethnocultural group's origin can go back millennia, or, by contrast, can be just a single generation or two back in time (Liebkind et al., 2016).

Ethnic identity is therefore rooted in the individual's psychological and social connection to an ethnocultural group. Yet these social groups are themselves dynamic and have a life of their own outside of the individual's perception of them. Stated differently, ethnocultural groups are not static and set forever in time but instead are created by people (i.e., socially and historically constructed and reworked over time; Liebkind et al., 2016). To illustrate the global pervasiveness of ethnocultural groups, consider the following explanation of what ethnocultural groups are:

> peoples who have a long history of settlement are the descendants of earlier waves of immigrants who have settled into recognizable groups, often with a sense of their own cultural heritage. . . . These ethnocultural groups can be found the world over, for example in French- and Spanish-origin communities in the New World, in the groups descended from indentured workers (such as Chinese and Indian communities in the Caribbean), from those who were enslaved (such as African Americans) and in Dutch and British immigrant groups in Southern Africa, Australia and New Zealand.
>
> (Berry & Sam, 2016, p. 19)

Thus, a large part of ethnic identity development for adolescents is about figuring out who one is in relation to an ethnocultural group and coming to terms with how that group affiliation has bearing on one's relations to other social groups in society (Umaña-Taylor, 2015).[4] It should be noted that there is no one completely accepted definition of ethnic identity in the psychological research literature (Umaña-Taylor, 2011). However, the formulation used in this chapter is one that is commonly used by theorists and researchers in the field (e.g., Meca & Schwartz, 2024; Phinney, 1990; Umaña-Taylor et al., 2024). Further elaboration about the nature of ethnic identity and its development is provided in the description of the integrative model for ERI development among adolescents, which appears later in this chapter.

Ethnic Identity in Relation to National Identity

Like ethnic identity, national identity can also be a social identity that holds special importance for a person (Schwartz et al., 2006). National identity would typically involve the question of who I am in relation to a national government or governments (Liebkind et al., 2016). For instance, what does it mean to be me, to be British and/or European, or German but also Turkish or Nigerian? With a national identity, what it means to be part of a nation, in other words, the national consciousness, spirit, and aspects of a shared culture such as values, is dynamic and is also updated as people and events on the ground change. A national identity can bring together groups of people who may not share a similar geographic and/or genealogical origin, and the spirit of some national identities may prioritize multiculturalism (e.g., Ward & Mak, 2016).

National identity can unite, but it can also divide us from one another, even in the same nation. For example, people may have a sense of belonging and connection and have mastered key parts of a national culture but still are treated as foreigners or newcomers. A qualitative study of German adolescents and young adults with an African heritage conducted by Hubbard and Utsey (2015) illustrated some of the different ways that people encounter the intersection of different components of social identity in their daily lives. For example, in the Hubbard and Utsey (2015) study, one study participant stated:

> I like to hear people ask me where I'm from, and when I tell them, one parent is from Finland, one is from Nigeria, but I grew up in Germany, then I feel special. I'm comfortable with that and I'm proud of it.
>
> (Hubbard & Utsey, 2015, pp. 99–100)

As is evident from the statement above, elements of social identity can intersect in unique and meaningful ways.

The intersection between ethnic and national identity is sometimes seen through the prism of majority (dominant/more powerful)-versus-minority (non-dominant/less powerful) group relations (Berry & Sam, 2016), which has also been called "oppositional group processes" (Wainryb & Recchia, 2014, p. 3). While the majority-versus-minority way of conceptualizing national and ethnic identity and intergroup relations may be reflective of the situation in some nations, it is also a central theme in social identity theory (Tajfel & Turner, 1986). It is important to recognize that the numerical size and/or position and power of a social group do not always go hand in hand (Adams & Abubakar, 2016). For example, in some national contexts, having one numerically large majority group is uncommon (e.g., in the nations of Zambia or Namibia and in present-day South Africa; Adams et al., 2018; Adams & Abubakar, 2016). In other situations, the numerical minority group can hold the most social, cultural, and economic power (e.g., "the White group during apartheid South Africa"; Adams & Abubakar, 2016, p. 361). Further, acculturation can also sometimes take place among groups that do not have a substantial power differential (Berry & Sam, 2016).

Intersections between minority/majority group status and ethnic and national identity may not necessarily pattern themselves in the same ways across nations. For researchers, the concept of a minority and majority group can be useful when used to describe study participants' group affiliations, but researchers should also not assume an uncritical use of such terms. Use of the majority and minority distinction by researchers should be informed by a thorough appreciation of the history and current interactions between culture-related social groups in the national context relevant to the study in question (e.g., Adams et al., 2018).

Ethnic Identity in Relation to Racial Identity

A reason to reflect on the construct of racial identity is because of the historical role that it has played in theoretical and measurement approaches to adolescent ethnic identity development (Schwartz et al., 2014). Worrell (2014) noted that race as a biological construct has been abandoned in scientific circles because it does not accurately explain variations in visible physical attributes of humans (i.e., this is called phenotype variation). For instance, variations in visible physical characteristics such as skin color and facial and hair features are wider within than across supposed racial groups (Worrell, 2014). Even if one just focuses on what people appear to look like to others (i.e., phenotypic characteristics) in a group of people in general, there is a litany of problems in the reliability and validity of the measurements of these characteristics (López et al., 2015).

Erikson (1975) described a concept called pseudo-speciation. In this case, Erikson noted "the tendency of humans to ignore the fact that they are a single species" (Kay, 2018, p. 265). Erikson's remarks about pseudo-speciation (or prejudice and discrimination) are also relevant when considering what continued psychological studies on how people perceive the concept of race may mean or yield:

> While man is obviously one species, he appears and continues on earth split up into groups (from tribes to nations, from castes to classes, from religions to ideologies) . . . we recognize here the human propensity to bolster one's own sense of inner mastery by bunching together and prejudging whole classes of people . . . In case you are now already lustily berating your favorite adversary . . . I must warn you that insight demands first of all the recognition of the fact that a human propensity such as has just been described is shared in some more or less form by all of us.
>
> (Erikson, 1975, pp. 175–176)

Given that the concept of race is steeped in ethical problems, it is not scientifically useful as a way to explain why people look differently from each other, and can be a catalyst for prejudice, discrimination, and, in the words of Erikson (1975), pseudo-speciation. Some scholars (e.g., Way & Rogers, 2014; Worrell, 2014) have contended that racial identity can be important to the study of identity development because racism exists all over the world, for all age-groups (cf. Del Carmen Dominguez Espinosa & Dantas, 2016; Umaña-Taylor, 2016). Further, individuals' subjective views of themselves in terms of racial identity can be reflective of existing power differentials between social groups and could be important to understanding the social reality that people encounter in their daily lives (Way & Rogers, 2014). Racial identity would involve a consideration of who one is in connection with a racially defined social group in a given society (Rivas-Drake, Syed et al., 2014). Racial identity would not just involve affiliation or ascription by others of people to a racial group but would also concern individuals' understanding and possibly their engagement in a shared culture that comes along with what it is like to be part of that racial group (Worrell, 2014).

Thus, racial identity has been called "subjective, self-ascribed" (Schwartz et al., 2014, p. 59) and is considered to be psychologically, socially, and historically constructed (Worrell, 2014). Racial identity would also be rooted in how individuals are perceived and treated in racial terms by others (i.e., racialized experiences; Umaña-Taylor et al., 2014). Scholars have also made arguments for the consideration of racial and ethnic identity as a combined construct based on empirical grounds, in that there are some studies that include the measurement of ERI in the same study and/or in a meta-analysis (e.g., Smith & Silva, 2011); stark delineations between these constructs do not appear to be warranted due to high significant positive correlations, and in some situations, both constructs are related to adjustment in similar ways (Rivas-Drake, Seaton et al., 2014). However, such findings have mainly been demonstrated in study samples from the U.S. and may or may not generalize further.

The main focus of this chapter is on adolescent ethnic identity development. However, it is recognized that racial identity may enter into ethnic identity development, depending on the young person's life experiences and social reality. Arguably, young people themselves are the most credible informants as to whether racial and/or ethnic identity (Schwartz et al., 2014) is important or if other components of social identity, such as religious identity, are more salient (Verkuyten, 2016). Studies illustrative of these points are highlighted later in this chapter (e.g., Daha, 2011).

The Integrative Model for Ethnic and Racial Identity Development

Umaña-Taylor et al. (2014, p. 23) defined ERI "as a multidimensional, psychological construct that reflects the beliefs and attitudes that individuals have about their ethnic–racial group memberships, as well as the processes by which these beliefs and attitudes develop over time." ERI development is thought to unfold as part of a normative lifespan developmental process. It is posited that ERI development is particularly salient for those who have more than one ethnic and/or racial background (i.e., bi-ethnic) *or* for individuals who are part of an ethnocultural and/or racial group that has less sociocultural power in society (Umaña-Taylor et al., 2014). In this model, there is a consideration of identity content (e.g., beliefs that have a cognitive developmental and social basis) and change processes (e.g., what my ethnocultural group means to me changes and/or is maintained as I explore, make meaning, and commit/resolve; Umaña-Taylor et al., 2014). The developmental domains of ERI involve the whole person, including affect, behavior, and cognition; ERI development is thought to take shape in an interaction between the developing individuals and their contexts (e.g., at home, in peer groups, in school, and via media; Umaña-Taylor et al., 2014).

As Umaña-Taylor and colleagues (2014) noted, this model is based on prior theories about social and ethnic/racial identity, including cognitive and psychosocial developmental theories (e.g., Piaget and Erikson, with extensions by Marcia and Phinney), as well as the inclusion of concepts from social identity theory (Tajfel & Turner, 1986) and from Cross (1971). In an extension of the integrative model, Cross and colleagues (2017) added more emphasis on content, namely focusing on different kinds of situations in which people enact their ethnicity or other social identity affiliations in everyday life and in relationships. An illustration of an enactment is code switching, which involves changing one's language, accent, and/or behavior in ways that signify to others a person's competence in a particular cultural context (Cross et al., 2017).

The integrative model includes a description of how ERI should normatively change from childhood through young adulthood. In childhood, children might understand concepts such as ethnicity in more concrete terms, which differs from the more nuanced, abstract appreciation of ethnicity they are likely to have in adolescence (Rivas-Drake, Syed et al., 2014), as well as what I and other people begin to call me in terms of my ethnicity (i.e., the self and others' group identifications/labeling; Umaña-Taylor et al., 2014). ERI in childhood may also concern the ethnocultural knowledge based on a child's own experience and through socialization (Umaña-Taylor et al., 2014). The content and processes involved in childhood center on "ethnic categorization, knowledge, and behaviors" (Umaña-Taylor et al., 2014, p. 28).

In adolescence, young people's cognitive and socio-emotional capabilities, such as perspective taking and social comparison, deepen and become more integrated, and adolescents also have a wider range of life experiences and knowledge of their societies (Umaña-Taylor et al., 2014). These growing capacities and experiences combine with normative sociocultural transitions to make it more likely that adolescents will attempt to explore and commit to a personally meaningful vision of what it means for them to be part of an ethnocultural or racial group (i.e., exploration – engaging in reflection and seeking experiences or other people to discuss and possibly try out new possibilities together; commitment/resolution – deciding on a way of living in and relating to the group; Rivas-Drake, Syed et al., 2014).

Identity exploration and commitment are thought to work alongside other developmental change processes such as collective self-verification, which concerns the notion of whether or not the adolescent fits group ideals of what it means to belong or be considered part of the group. Collective self-verification lies at the interface between individuals' subjective perception of group belonging and the reception they get from the social feedback of other group members (Umaña-Taylor et al., 2014). Illustrative of this idea, a participant in an interview study with adolescents and emerging/young adults, who had an indigenous Mapuche heritage and were living in the Chilean cities of Temuco and Santiago, stated, "I **don't** know the pronunciation of words, therefore I'm LIKE **embarrassed** to say that I am (Mapuche). Because, **no**, I **don't** know, I feel **bad** because there are people that do know and I **don't**" (Oteíza & Merino, 2012, p. 307).[5]

Identity content is also of importance. For example, salience (i.e., an event happens to me that makes me think about myself in relation to my group), certainty (i.e., even though my group may have less social power and I have experienced discrimination based on my group affiliation, to what degree do I remain committed to this group?), and private regard or affirmation (i.e., do I feel proud and/or good about my group? Rivas-Drake, Seaton et al., 2014) are all important facets to the content of one's identity. It is also posited that adolescents will develop a deeper understanding of how their group is viewed by others (i.e., public regard), have greater insight into intergroup relations and power dynamics between groups, and have a more accurate sense of the implications of those dynamics for themselves than will younger children (Umaña-Taylor et al., 2014).

From childhood to adolescence, ERI development shifts from understanding how sociocultural categories and labels work and might apply to oneself; ERI also involves adolescents experiencing what it means to be part of their ethnocultural group and putting their capabilities and knowledge to use so they can put their own distinctive signature on ERI. In the integrative model, similar to the acculturation strategy of marginalization, one potential response to the encounter with ERI is to negate it from one's overall identity (i.e., identity self-denial). It is thought that adults encounter the same processes and content that were at work in adolescence but have the additional challenge to infuse their ERI – where it fits, has meaning, and adds richness – into other facets of their identity (Umaña-Taylor et al., 2014). Relative to adolescents, adults should also be better prepared to engage in meaning-making (e.g., searching for coherence across time and situations as part of narrative identity development) in regard to their ethnicity (Umaña-Taylor et al., 2014).

An Optimal Sense of Ethnic Identity

For those adolescents who are connected to an ethnocultural group, a well-developed ethnic identity should be an asset that allows people to successfully navigate, adapt to, and even thrive within the sociocultural worlds that mean the most to them (Rivas-Drake et al., 2022). An interview study with 55 second-generation Iranian American adolescents conducted by Daha (2011) provided several illustrations, in adolescents' own words, about how social identity works for them as a resource. For example, one participant remarked:

> Being an Iranian among all the kids at school shows that I am an individual. [My culture] is related to my authenticity here in America.
>
> (Boy, 16½ years old; Daha, 2011, p. 555)

Another participant stated:

> Culture is very important to me. I feel like it gives a little bit of perspective to me. I view things with 2 angles. I feel like I have sort of a self-identity that is deeper. More layers to it. I think culture has given me that aspect.
>
> (Boy, 18 years old; Daha, 2011, p. 555)

In an ideal situation, adolescents who are part of an ethnocultural group (or a racial or national minority) go through a multifaceted process of learning more about their group and its place in their society, come to a self-defined sense of what that group affiliation means to them, and end with a positive evaluation of their group (Rivas-Drake, Seaton et al., 2014). Adolescents, as they transition into adulthood, should make meaning of what their group signifies in their lives, and they should ideally experience more coherence and unity between personal and social identity as well as across the different components of social identity.

Analysis of the Integrative Model of Ethnic and Racial Identity Development

The integrative model sets the stage for a movement past the fragmentation that has historically characterized research on ethnic and/or racial identity (Rivas-Drake, Seaton et al., 2014). Fragmentation is related to the confusion in terminology and differential conceptualization of key constructs and their measurement and has resulted in an inability to generate insights that encompass the research literature as a whole (Rivas-Drake, Seaton et al., 2014). Although the model has several strengths, some limitations are acknowledged in the model.

One open question about this model concerns the tradition in most theories about ERI, including the integrative model, that takes as a starting point the proposition that culture-related social identity would be of most importance to the development of those in a minority social position (e.g., Phinney, 1990; Umaña-Taylor et al., 2014). However, this is an empirical question that has not yet been thoroughly examined. The model is designed to speak most directly to ethnocultural groups and other minority groups living in the U.S. and is therefore attuned to and reflective of this context. This yields the question of its current generalizability. Different kinds of cultural identity could also be of particular importance to the identity development of those in the sociocultural mainstream or majority in a society. Research on culture-related social identity does exist in majority groups, but much more research on this topic is needed. Such a research direction would be consistent with acculturation theory (e.g., Berry & Sam, 2016), which sees acculturation as relevant and happening to those in the minority and majority groups alike. The model was highlighted in this chapter because it also has the potential to have value beyond the U.S. – not likely in its exact current form but as adapted to better reflect the wide variation in acculturating people and societies (Verkuyten, 2016).

Other catalysts that could guide subsequent iterations of the integrative model could be systematic programs of research aimed at gaining new insights about ethnic identity from participatory action research (PAR) that is culturally grounded and youth-guided with an insider view of a given culture as a foundation for further theory development. A PAR study conducted by Bhabha and colleagues (2017) provided an illustration of this kind of research. The study was conducted with 20 Roma and non-Roma adolescents who worked in pairs along with input from adult researchers to create, implement, and complete a descriptive study about how adolescents and their families as well as policymakers in Serbia viewed youth opportunities and barriers surrounding school and work (Bhabha et al., 2017). The study was impressive in a number of regards; some 300 adolescents, 57 parents, and 40 policy members/other adult youth stakeholders were interviewed as study participants. Results from study participants highlighted the nature of struggles faced by Roma youths, in particular, to participate and succeed in school and work. For youth researchers, the project gave an opportunity for some to engage in identity work in a supportive setting:

> I have always had trouble with my identity. The project provided me with a starting point for thinking about this. Even when I am with somebody I have known since primary school, I still feel the need to declare my nationality. People tell me that they know, but I still feel the need to say explicitly that I am Roma . . . I have never talked about these insecurities and challenges before, and preparing for the interviews was a good starting point for these kinds of conversations. . . .
>
> (Bhabha et al., 2017, p. 208)

Later in this chapter, other studies with adolescents living outside of the U.S. are highlighted in order to showcase innovative studies on ethnic and other forms of collective identity development in different national contexts.

Measuring Ethnic Identity

There are many options if one wants to use a survey to measure ethnic and/or racial identity with a quantitative approach. The Multigroup Ethnic Identity Measure (MEIM) and the Ethnic Identity Survey (EIS) are highlighted in this section because these surveys have been used in many ERI studies and measure parts of the integrative model, namely the identity processes of exploration and commitment/resolution as well as positive group affect (viewed as identity content).

The MEIM has a ubiquitous presence in the ethnic identity research literature (e.g., Yip et al., 2019). This instrument was created and refined by Jean Phinney and colleagues (Phinney, 1989, 1990; Phinney & Ong, 2007) and is based on Phinney's theory of ethnic identity development, which has its roots in Erikson's ideas about identity exploration and commitment as well as the identity status model as developed by Marcia (1966) but is now applied to ethnic identity development. Phinney's theory (1990) and the MEIM are also derived from social identity theory's emphasis on having a positive evaluation of one's social group (Phinney, 1990).

Phinney (1990) proposed that ethnic identity development would become particularly important during adolescence for ethnic minority youth. The developmental process is thought to start with an unexamined ethnic identity, which could mean that ethnic identity is not on the adolescent's radar screen (diffusion) or that the adolescent has uncritically adopted external views about what ethnicity should mean in life (foreclosure) to movement toward a period of exploration of ethnicity (moratorium) to an authentic, self-defined, and internalized sense of one's own ethnicity and how it fits into one's wider identity and society at large (achievement; Phinney, 1990).

Different editions of the MEIM exist and range from six to 20 items (Schwartz et al., 2014). There has been variability in the different editions of the MEIM used across studies and variation among researchers in how they work with the MEIM items to create different scale scores (i.e., to specify what the MEIM is exactly measuring, working to get close correspondence among item content, how people typically interpret and respond to items, and theory; Schwartz et al., 2014). The availability and widespread use of the MEIM have brought the study of ethnic identity development into many adolescent research initiatives that did not have a primary focus on identity development (Umaña-Taylor et al., 2004). Use of the MEIM has, for example, mainstreamed inquiries of ERI development into more general adolescent studies on a wide range of topics. The popularity of the MEIM among researchers could be linked to some of its virtues such as a history of good scale reliability (Umaña-Taylor et al., 2004). The MEIM is also relatively brief, so it is feasible to add this instrument to a larger assessment battery, but it still offers a multidimensional scale that is indicative of the rich concept of ethnic identity rather than just an ethnic label or identification. The MEIM is also not restricted to use with one particular ethnocultural or racial group and therefore could be used in many parts of the world, as was done in the International Comparative Study of Ethno-Cultural Youth (Berry et al., 2006). As more studies with the MEIM were conducted over the years, the variation in how researchers worked with the MEIM has continued (Meca et al., 2023). As studies accumulated, more was learned about the MEIM's factor structure. In some cases, a consistent picture of the factor structure did not emerge, or the dimensions/scales that were identified did not always correspond with Phinney's (1989, 1990) original formulations of the multidimensional structure of ethnic identity development (Meca et al., 2023).

The Ethnic Identity Scale (EIS) represents another main quantitative indicator of ERI. The EIS has several parallels to the MEIM, such as sharing a similar theoretical basis and not being group specific (Douglass & Umaña-Taylor, 2015; Umaña-Taylor et al., 2004). Like the MEIM, the EIS also has different versions ranging from nine to 17 items. The EIS provides scale scores of ethnic identity exploration, resolution (i.e., identity commitment), and affirmation (i.e., positive affect for one's group) with generally good reliability. Evidence for the internal consistency and validity of the EIS has been accumulated (Douglass & Umaña-Taylor, 2015).

Beyond the sole use of surveys to measure ERI development, there are many innovative mixed-method approaches, such as the quantitative analysis of friendship networks in combination with survey-based assessments (e.g., Jugert et al., 2020; Rivas-Drake et al., 2017; for more details of this analysis, see Kornienko & Rivas-Drake, 2022). Registry (e.g., how ethnically diverse is the adolescent's school) and self-reported data about ERI, such as the MEIM (e.g., Douglass & Yip, 2015, p. 214), are additional mixed-methods approaches used to study ERI. Other methods used in ERI studies have included interviews on life story, turning point, or other life event narratives (e.g., Komolova et al., 2020) as well as conversations with friends (e.g., Moffitt & Syed, 2021). Semi-structured interviews that are not rooted in a narrative identity framework have also been used in ERI studies (Bhabha et al., 2017; Way & Rogers, 2014). In addition to these mixed-method approaches, interdisciplinary approaches (e.g., sociological, historical, and neurodevelopmental) are also expected to broaden knowledge of ERI and the range of techniques to assess ERI in diverse contexts (Rogers et al., 2020).

Recently, researchers have increasingly recognized that more attention to negative affect for one's group should be paid when using the EIS (Meca et al., 2022; Umaña-Taylor, 2024). Although the positive dimension of EIS is crucial for promoting individuals' adjustment, individuals belonging to minority groups living in less inclusive contexts may feel negative affect (e.g., self-hatred) for their groups, and this may function as a risk factor for their adjustment (Umaña-Taylor, 2024). Empirical work on ethnic identity affect is building, but this line of enquiry suggests a promising future direction to further understanding the "ecological realities" (Umaña-Taylor, 2024, p. 219) of ethnic identity.

Research Findings on Ethnic Identity Development in Adolescence

The psychological ERI research literature is vibrant and expanding.[6] To get a sense of the present-day importance of ethnic and national identity, consider that, according to a United Nations report, 3.7% of the world's population are international immigrants (United Nations, 2025). This represents a 50% increase in the number of international immigrants since 1990 (United Nations, 2025). International immigrants include people who are fleeing their homes as refugees or as asylum seekers as well as individuals on the move to pursue educational or work opportunities (United Nations, 2025). The first subsection here provides a brief overview of an assortment of research studies with adolescents living in different parts of the world. These studies use different theoretical and research methods. The aim of this subsection is to demonstrate the global relevance of ERI development. The other two subsections that follow address what is known thus far about normative trends in ERI development and what evidence exists about what is optimal ERI development (i.e., the ERI–adaptation connection).

Empirical Illustrations of Ethnic and National Identity's Global Relevance

Several cross-sectional studies concerning ethnic and/or national identity have been conducted with adolescents in many countries (e.g., Aydinli-Karakulak & Dimitrova, 2016; Dimitrova et al., 2018; Dimitrova, Musso, et al., 2017; Dimitrova, Van de Vijver, et al., 2017; Umaña-Taylor et al., 2024; for a recent review, see Ward & Szabó, 2023). An early key study is the International Comparative Study of Ethno-Cultural Youth conducted by Berry and colleagues (2006). This was a large cross-sectional study of 7,977 adolescents. The adolescents included those with a relatively recent immigration history and those without such a history (i.e., mainstream youth) living in 13 countries (e.g., Australia, France, Finland, Norway, Sweden, the U.S., and Portugal: Berry et al., 2006). The study combined ideas from acculturation psychology, such as measurement of acculturation attitudes and behaviors, along with developmental views of ethnic identity (i.e., Phinney, 1990, and the use of the MEIM), as well as measurement of national identity and other intercultural constructs (Berry et al., 2006).

Using cluster analysis, researchers identified four acculturation profiles, the most common of which was an integration profile, which included 36.4% of the immigrant youth in the study and was characterized by engagement in heritage or origin and national cultures, including elevated ethnic and national identity development (Berry et al., 2006). This profile was significantly associated with better psychological and sociocultural adaptation/adjustment (Berry et al., 2006). Girls were more likely than boys to be in the integration profile (Berry et al., 2006). Other acculturation profiles identified were an ethnic (22.5%), diffuse (22.4%), and national profile (18.7%). The diffuse profile was significantly connected with reduced adaptation/adjustment, and boys were more likely than girls to be in this profile (Berry et al., 2006).

A more contemporary multinational, cross-sectional study by Dimitrova, Van de Vijver, and colleagues (2017) also illustrated the benefits of examining ethnic identity across different cultural and national settings. Their study differed from the International Comparative Study of Ethno-Cultural Youth (Berry et al., 2006) in that it was designed to speak to the well-being of adolescents in a settled ethnocultural group within Europe, who have a distinct history, rather than many different groups of immigrant youth acculturating in a wide range of receiving or host societies. The Dimitrova, Van de Vijver, et al. (2017) study involved measuring adolescents' engagement in their ethnic, national, family, and religious identity (e.g., centrality, positive group affect, and involvement in group activities). The sample consisted of 1,221 middle adolescents (52% Roma and 48% mainstream) living in Bulgaria, the Czech Republic, Kosovo, and Romania (Dimitrova, Van de Vijver, et al., 2017).

This study has advantages over previous works, such as the measurement of several components of collective identity, the inclusion of ethnic minority and majority youth, and the measurement of ethnic and national identity in ethnic minority youth. For participants in general, results revealed that being more engaged in family and religious identity was associated with feeling better (i.e., elevated well-being) and that engagement in national identity was not significantly connected to adolescents' well-being (Dimitrova, Van de Vijver, et al., 2017). An important finding was that greater engagement in Roma identity was related to feeling worse (i.e., lower well-being) among Roma adolescents living in Bulgaria and Kosovo (Dimitrova, Van de Vijver, et al., 2017), and ethnic identity engagement by Roma adolescents was not associated with well-being in the Czech Republic and Romania. Researchers suggested that improvements in the life conditions of Roma people in Bulgaria and Kosovo may be particularly neglected relative to the other nations in this study (Dimitrova, Van de Vijver, et al., 2017). This is an important study because the study results for Roma youth depart from the wider research literature that supports a positive association between ERI development and many indicators of adolescent adaptation and thriving. Thus, although there is a general consensus about the positive association between strong ERI and well-being in minority and immigrant groups, this positive association can be affected by factors including national social norms and majority group expectations (Ward & Szabó, 2023).

Normative Trends in Ethnic and Racial Identity Development: Quantitative Longitudinal Studies

This section concerns what can be learned from longitudinal studies of ERI.[7] The studies described here include quantitative measurement of ERI-related processes and/or content and come primarily from the U.S. Even though variability is evident, the general consensus is that different aspects of ERI are likely to grow across adolescence (e.g., Booth et al., 2022; Huang & Stormshak, 2011; Hughes et al., 2017).

A study conducted by Huang and Stormshak (2011) provided a fundamental illustration of a longitudinal study of ERI development in adolescence. This study was conducted in the Pacific Northwest region of the U.S. and included 379 adolescents who self-identified as having an ethnic, racial, or indigenous background (i.e., Latino, African American, Asian, American Indian, or mixed ethnicity; Huang & Stormshak, 2011). Positive group affect, ERI-related exploration and commitment, and ethnic group behaviors were measured annually by way of the MEIM, and ERI indices were combined into a single score (Huang & Stormshak, 2011).

Researchers identified six trajectories as youth moved from 6th to 9th grades (approximately 12–15 years old; trajectories were not moderated by gender; Huang & Stormshak, 2011). Growth in ERI was evidenced by 47.3% of the sample who could be described by trajectories that showed growth in ERI at a moderate or sharp pace (47.3%). Stability was also evident in the 30.1% of adolescents who had a high stable ERI trajectory (i.e., these youth had explored and sorted out ERI issues early on in their adolescence and stayed that way). Researchers attributed this high stability trajectory to the location of the study, which tended toward ethnic homogeneity and may have led some adolescents to an earlier than typical navigation of ERI questions as a minority living in a majority setting. Other less frequently occurring trajectories included a low stable (4.5%) pattern or decline in ERI (18.1%) at a moderate or sharp pace. Some trajectories were more or less common with youth in different minority groups. This study offers a multifaceted picture of ERI development in cultural minority adolescents who lived in a relatively ethnically homogeneous region of the U.S. (Huang & Stormshak, 2011). Results from other longitudinal studies in more recent or ethnically heterogeneous regions of the U.S. (e.g., Booth et al., 2022; Hughes et al., 2017) also support a general normative trend toward growth in aspects of ERI during adolescence.

Research Evidence on Optimal Ethnic and Racial Identity Development

Several studies speak to a diverse array of benefits associated with ERI development in adolescents and adults. For instance, a ten-month longitudinal study with two cohorts of 140 Turkish/German children and adolescents indicated, in the older cohort (13–15 years old), that when ethnic identity exploration was low and commitment was elevated (reminiscent of foreclosure), youth would have fewer cross-ethnic friends (Spiegler et al., 2016). Researchers suggested that supporting national minority youths' identity explorations around their group affiliations could facilitate a greater reaching out and connection between youth with different ethnicities (Spiegler et al., 2016). A longitudinal study of 125 Israeli adolescents who have a recent immigration history from the former Soviet Union also showed that from 8th to 10th grade, group centrality (i.e., how important the national minority group is in your life) and positive group affect were associated prospectively with less peer-rated aggression (Benish-Weisman, 2016). Longitudinal studies conducted in the U.S. also support a positive prospective association between indicators of ERI development and a diverse range of outcomes such as adolescents having a closer connection to their peers, greater school adjustment, and clear beliefs in civic engagement (e.g., Bañales et al., 2020; Hoffman et al., 2019; Medina et al., 2020; Wantchekon et al., 2023). Importantly, ERI can also serve as a source of resilience to racism and xenophobia (Rivas-Drake et al., 2022), implying the potential role of ERI for creating a more inclusive society in this era of division and discrimination.

Turning now to meta-analyses and narrative reviews, Smith and Silva (2011) conducted an important meta-analysis that examined the ERI–adaptation connection, with adaptation measured in terms of well-being, self-esteem, and mental health. Participants were primarily nonclinical samples of people identifying with a minority group living in either the U.S. or Canada (e.g., African American, Asian American, Latino, and Native American: Smith & Silva, 2011). The meta-analysis included 184 studies, including 41,626 adults and youths with an average age of 22.9 years (Smith & Silva, 2011). The studies often used the MEIM as a composite/total score that could include exploration, commitment, and/or affirmation (i.e., positive group affect). Results showed that higher levels of ERI were associated with higher well-being, self-esteem, and less depression and behavior problems. The ERI–adaptation connection was applicable to both males and females; however, associations were stronger for those younger than 40 years old

(Smith & Silva, 2011). This latter result supports the idea that ERI should have particular developmental salience for adolescents and emerging or young adults.

A meta-analysis of 46 studies conducted by Rivas-Drake, Syed et al. (2014) examined the importance of positive ethnic–racial affect (i.e., having a good/proud feeling about one's own ethnic–racial group, operationalized as affirmation, private regard, and pride in varying surveys with different theoretical origins) to adaptation (i.e., as indexed by, for example, academic achievement, mental health and symptoms, social competence, and well-being). Studies of this meta-analysis included children or adolescents from the main ethnic and/or racial groups in the U.S. (i.e., African American, Latino, and Asian American youth; studies with indigenous youth were not included in this meta-analysis). The primary results showed significant associations between positive ethnic–racial affect and different indicators of adaptation (e.g., less depression and greater social competence), as well as reduced health risk (e.g., less substance use). As in the Smith and Silva (2011) meta-analysis, the positive associations between ERI and adaptation held for boys and girls as well as across ethnic/racial groups.

Rivas-Drake, Seaton et al. (2014) also conducted a narrative review of the U.S. ethnic/racial minority and indigenous adolescent ERI research literature, but in this case, they were able to include a wider array of ERI indicators in comparison to the aforementioned meta-analysis on positive affect (Rivas-Drake, Syed et al., 2014); the ERI indicators included identity exploration, commitment (resolution), centrality, positive affect, and public regard. An illustrative finding from this review was that adolescents' ERI development was positively associated with psychosocial functioning and mental health; these associations were found across most of the ethnic/racial groups included in the review (Rivas-Drake, Seaton et al., 2014). The finding that ERI played a key role in mental health was confirmed in a more recent narrative review focusing on African Americans during the period of emerging adulthood and adulthood in the U.S. (Walker et al., 2024).

Another meta-analysis of 51 studies conducted in the U.S. with samples from early adolescence to adulthood provided a more nuanced picture concerning the role of ERI in adjustment outcomes, especially its protective and detrimental effects on discrimination (Yip et al., 2019). A novel finding of this study was that the ERI commitment could be a protective factor, but exploration increased vulnerability to the impact of discrimination (e.g., negative mental health). Moreover, the buffering effect of ERI varied across sample characteristics; for instance, the buffering effect of ERI commitment was stronger in Latinx than Asian-heritage individuals. Such variability informs the need for incorporating context into ERI studies.

In summary, along with a growing number of longitudinal studies on ERI development, the three meta-analyses and two narrative reviews generally provide converging evidence that ERI development can serve as a developmental asset for young people. However, the weight of this evidence is primarily for adolescents in minority groups in North America. Evidence for a positive ERI development–adaptation connection also exists outside of North America (e.g., Berry et al., 2006; Spiegler et al., 2016). However, there may be exceptions to this general conclusion based on the particular ethnocultural or national minority group considered and the context (e.g., Dimitrova, Van de Vijver, et al., 2017; for a review, see Ward & Szabó, 2023).

Current Directions in Ethnic Identity Research and Theory

Empirical knowledge is building that improves our understanding of the ways that context, such as interpersonal and school/neighborhood-level factors, is important to adolescent ethnic identity development (Mims & Williams, 2020). Longitudinal studies have unpacked that a variety of aspects of context, including different people (e.g., parents and peers), settings (e.g., classrooms and schools), and experiences (e.g., discrimination), support or inhibit ERI development. Parents have been viewed as the most crucial agents to promote adolescent ERI (e.g., Constante et al., 2020; Mims & Williams, 2020; Nelson et al., 2018). Yet the role of ethnic socialization in families (e.g., teaching children about the relevant history, culture, and heritage of their ethnicity) in ERI development may not be straightforward. For example, Constante and colleagues (2020) not only reported that high levels of ethnic socialization experiences are related to initial higher levels of ethnic identity commitment (resolution) but also predicted a decline in ethnic identity commitment over time; this finding suggests that adolescents might rely more on people outside the family (e.g., friends and peers) as they get older. Friends or peers are indeed another important resource for adolescent and emerging adult ERI development (e.g., Jugert et al., 2020; Moffitt & Syed, 2021; Nelson et al., 2018; Umaña-Taylor et al., 2020).

A take-home message from these studies is that ERI development happens along converging experiences such as whether or not adolescents' parents were born abroad or not (from the origin ethnic group), whether or not families socialized children about their origin ethnic group, whether or not youths' friends are supportive of their origin ethnic group, as well as interacting with more generic peer processes with friends becoming more similar on ERI development over time. Other important findings are the bidirectional relationships between ERI and discrimination experiences during adolescence (e.g., Cheon & Yip, 2019; Meca et al., 2020). For instance, a longitudinal study with Latino adolescents in the U.S. revealed that greater levels of ethnic identity belonging (resembling commitment) led to greater perceptions of discrimination one year later, and vice versa (Meca et al., 2020). These results highlight the urgent need to develop programs that promote coping strategies against discrimination and positive ERI development in minority adolescents (Cheon & Yip, 2019).

All in all, current studies have advanced knowledge about how ERI development is deeply embedded in interactive sociocultural contexts (Ward & Szabó, 2023). Syed et al. (2018), however, pointed out that the majority of research on ERI development has conceptualized contexts as objective settings in which interactions and activities take place (e.g., peer relations, schooling, and discrimination), as illustrated in this section. Syed and colleagues (2018, p. 216) proposed that contexts can also be conceptualized subjectively, as "the same 'context' is perceived differently for individuals who are a part of it." Including subjective measures, such as asking about how adolescents define and describe their ethnic group or daily interactions with other ethnic peers (Syed et al., 2018), could help to improve the measurement and theoretical incorporation of context into ERI studies.

While longitudinal ethnic identity development studies are increasing, more studies with direct measurement of context outside of the U.S. are important to these efforts. Studies about the ERI development–adaptation connection in different ethnocultural, indigenous, and national minority groups could also focus on what surviving, doing well, and/or thriving means for youth in their ecology and how social identity relates to this adaptation. This approach would be in keeping with the idea of adaptive culture (Perez-Brena et al., 2018), which challenges researchers to seek out a close understanding of the young person's social reality and also allows for the possibility that youth can take diverse pathways to arrive at adaptation and thriving.

Implications for Social Response

Several courses of action can be taken from the ERI research literature. On the basis of descriptive research findings, it has been recommended that national governments and other stakeholders in the welfare of youth find ways to encourage immigrant youth to retain and explore their culture of origin and to provide abundant opportunities for these youth to be meaningfully involved in the national society/culture (Berry et al., 2006). However, it should be noted that a recent meta-analysis that examined findings from cross-sectional and longitudinal studies indicated that immigrant individuals' acculturation strategies (i.e., integration or biculturalism) had a limited role to play in adjustment (Bierwiaczonek & Kunst, 2021). In contemporary societies in which adolescents are more deeply engaged in globalization, migration, and digitalization than in previous historical eras, researchers need to pay more attention to contextual factors (e.g., age, immigration, generational status, and discrimination) that possibly nuance the relationship among acculturation, ERI development, and adjustment (Sam, 2024).

Then, what, in particular, appears to be promising as a way to support youth in their ERI development? Interventions specifically designed to support ERI development offer several practical techniques and insights. In a recent meta-analysis of a wide diversity of ethnic identity interventions, Crocetti and colleagues (2025) found across 17 studies with adolescent samples that most of the reviewed studies were designed for adolescents in specific minority groups. For instance, Sisters of Nia (Belgrave et al., 2004) and Young Empowered Sisters (Thomas et al., 2008) were programs for adolescent African American girls with intervention activities aimed at reducing risk and promoting ethnic identity. Conversation Club was a group mentoring intervention designed for newcomer adolescents in Canada (Pryce et al., 2019). Conversely, the Identity Project was designed as a universal school-based intervention program for both ethnic minority and majority adolescents (Umaña-Taylor, 2023). According to Crocetti and colleagues' (2025) meta-analysis, frequently occurring actions/activities across relevant interventions included the creation of time and the opportunity to discuss identity, culture, and ethnicity in personal terms in a supportive context with peers and an engaged adult. Other common intervention activities included a chance to learn about the ethnic and/or racial group's (or groups') culture and history and take part in cultural activities as well as different types of exercises and discussions aimed at helping adolescents personalize and make meaning of how their group relates to them and to make sense of intergroup relations. Such interventions typically lasted for a few months and had a small group format and a trained adult intervention leader or mentor (Crocetti et al., 2025).

In regard to the effectiveness of the interventions in Crocetti and colleagues' (2025) meta-analysis, it was concluded that intervention effects on targeted outcomes showed a small yet significant effect. These effects were consistent and less affected by factors such as the gender balance, percentage of minorities, and the mean age of participants. Limitations of this generally beneficial finding for these interventions are that the evidence bases for these interventions are derived from studies mostly conducted in North America and only two studies from a European context. Thus, more intervention studies conducted with adolescents outside North America are high on the agenda in this era of migration around the world.

The aforementioned meta-analysis paints a broad picture. Therefore, it is useful to go into some detail about one of the more rigorous and larger-scale intervention trials of a specific ERI intervention: the Identity Project conducted by Umaña-Taylor and colleagues (Umaña-Taylor, Douglass, et al., 2018; Umaña-Taylor, Kornienko, et al., 2018). These researchers developed and tested the Identity Project in a randomized controlled trial with pre-, post-, and a one-year follow-up. The Identity Project is conducted with 218 middle adolescents self-identifying as African American, Black, Latino, Asian American, American Indian or Native American, and White. The intervention was given as part of an elective course in schools, and the control condition was an active control that concerned learning more about post-high school educational and job possibilities. It consisted of activities that promoted greater knowledge about what ERI is and how it develops, awareness raising about different cultural traditions and symbols, group histories and intergroup relations, and a reflection on one's own family history, as well as photovoice activities with a storyboard and group discussion (Umaña-Taylor, Douglass, et al., 2018). Intervention-related benefits included pretest to posttest change in ERI-related exploration, which was associated with a later increase in ERI-related resolution and then changes up to one year later in overall identity coherence, improved grades, more academic engagement and self-esteem, and reduced depressive symptoms (Umaña-Taylor, Kornienko, et al., 2018).

The Identity Project has also been implemented and tested with adolescents living in diverse cultural contexts in Europe (i.e., Germany, Greece, Italy, Norway, and Sweden: Juang et al., 2023; Juang & Hwang, 2024). In these trials of the Identity Project, researchers applied the basic framework of the Identity Project with some modifications according to different histories of immigration, school climate, and cultural heritages across countries (e.g., Juang et al., 2024; Schachner et al., 2024). For teachers, the researchers have provided training that included seminars about culturally responsive teaching, activities to promote students' ethnic–cultural identities, theoretical knowledge relevant to ethnic–cultural identities (e.g., stereotypes), and group discussions (e.g., Abdullahi et al., 2024; Pevec-Zimmer et al., 2024). Overall, intervention research in ERI is underway, and the results of the Identity Project in several European countries suggest a better understanding of how intervention-related effects may differ across diverse cultural contexts.

Summary

Sociocultural approaches to adolescent identity development generally emphasize the role that social and/or cultural group memberships play in the identity formation process of adolescence. Ethnic identity development lies at the intersection of personal and social identity, and it has been offered as an illustration of how social and cultural forces can be at work in the person–context interactions that are at the heart of identity development for many adolescents. Much more research is needed on adolescent ethnic identity development in various parts of the world. Yet what can be concluded thus far is that across the developmental period of adolescence, individuals are likely to explore who they are in relation to the cultures and social groups that mean the most to them. For many youths, engagement in questions around ERI is associated with better adaptation and well-being. There are also several types of activities and settings that offer promising ways to support young people as they address this challenge/opportunity.

Notes

1 Roma are a diverse ethnocultural group that has many subgroups that go by different names such as Roma, Stinti, and Kale, as well as other names (Flecha & Soler, 2013). Roma people live all over the world but have their largest numerical concentrations in Europe and Eastern Europe in particular (e.g., Romania and Bulgaria; Dimitrova et al., 2021). Roma people have their genealogical origins in Northern India but have, in many cases, a centuries-long history and a distinct sociocultural presence in many of the countries in which they live (i.e., a sedentary ethnocultural group for generations in several nations). Roma people, including youth, have many substantial strengths and evidence of thriving, yet Roma people have also been historically subjected to severe discrimination and persecution by the majority and other minority groups in the countries in which they live (Dimitrova et al., 2021).

2 Social identity theory (Tajfel & Turner, 1986) posits that people can form a social group on even the most trivial or minimal of grounds as part of an experiment, but also in our daily experience, more consequential social groups that we affiliate with will have an impact on our own identity as we strive to keep a positive view of ourselves and our group even in the midst of devaluation by other social groups (Spears, 2011).

3 In this quote, the text in *[brackets and italics]* was added by Laura Ferrer-Wreder.

4 Illustrating the concept of ethnic identity further, one could ask, what does belonging to a particular ethnic group mean to me in terms of the totality of who I am as a person at a particular moment in my life (as an adolescent or as an adult, as a parent or as a child; Umaña-Taylor et al., 2014)? How do I fit in and/or depart from all that comes with being part of this group? If I am part of this group, what does that mean for how I will relate to other groups that I come into contact with?

5 The formatting in this quote was preserved and appears as it does in the original article. The quote appears in the article in Spanish and in a translated English edition made by the study authors.

6 For instance, a non-systematic search of the PsycINFO database can provide a broad view of the field. A search that required that the words "ethnic identity" or "racial identity" be in the title of the document would show that in the 1950s and the 1960s, only a handful of scholarly documents were published in each decade (i.e., books, journal articles, and dissertations). This was followed by substantial, successive increases in the number of documents published per decade from the 1970s up through the 1990s, and from the 2000s to the present, there have been approximately 3,381 scholarly documents published thus far.

7 At the time of writing this chapter, a cursory search of the PsycINFO database identified 139 records when the search required that the words "ethnic identity" or "racial identity" or "ethnic–racial identity" be in the document title and that the study in question had to be longitudinal with children and/or adolescents in the study sample and the document should be peer reviewed.

References

Abdullahi, A. K., Berne, S., Juang, L. P., & Frisén, A. (2024). Framing ethnicity in initial teacher education: A focus group study with Student teachers. *Identity: An International Journal of Theory and Research, 24*(4), 269–287. https://doi.org/10.1080/15283488.2024.2366905

Adams, B., & Abubakar, A. (2016). Acculturation in Sub-Saharan Africa. In D. Sam & J. Berry (Eds.), *The Cambridge handbook of acculturation psychology* (pp. 355–374). Cambridge University Press.

Adams, B. G., Naudé, L., Nel, J. A., Van de Vijver, F. J. R., Laher, S., Louw, J., & Tadi, F. (2018). When there are only minorities: Identity and in-group/out-group orientations of emerging adults in four South African ethnocultural groups. *Emerging Adulthood, 6*(1), 7–16. https://doi.org/10.1177/2167696817752755

Aydinli-Karakulak, A., & Dimitrova, R. (2016). Brief report: When does identity lead to negative affective experiences? A comparison of Turkish–Bulgarian and Turkish–German adolescents. *Journal of Adolescence, 47*(1), 125–130. https://doi.org/10.1016/j.adolescence.2015.09.010

Azmitia, M. (2014). Reflections on the cultural lenses of identity development. In K. C. McLean & M. Syed (Eds.), *The Oxford handbook of identity development* [E-reader version] (pp. 1–20). Oxford University Press. https://doi.org/10.1093/oxfordhb/9780199936564.013.033

Bañales, J., Hoffman, A. J., Rivas-Drake, D., & Jagers, R. J. (2020). The development of ethnic-racial identity process and its relation to civic beliefs among Latinx and Black American adolescents. *Journal of Youth and Adolescence, 49*(12), 2495–2508. https://doi.org/10.1007/s10964-020-01254-6

Belgrave, F. Z., Reed, M. C., Plybon, L. E., Butler, D. S., Allison, K. W., & Davis, T. (2004). An evaluation of sisters of Nia: A cultural program for African American girls. *Journal of Black Psychology, 30*(3), 329–343. https://doi.org/10.1007/s10964-020-01254-6

Benish-Weisman, M. (2016). Brief report: Ethnic identity and aggression in adolescence: A longitudinal perspective. *Journal of Adolescence, 47*(1), 131–134. https://doi.org/10.1016/j.adolescence.2015.05.015

Berry, J., & Sam, D. (2016). Introduction. In D. Sam & J. Berry (Eds.), *The Cambridge handbook of acculturation psychology* (pp. 1–8). Cambridge University Press.

Berry, J. W., Phinney, J. S., Sam, D. L., & Vedder, P. (2006). Immigrant youth: Acculturation, identity, and adaptation. *Applied Psychology: An International Review, 55*(3), 303–332. https://doi.org/10.1111/j.1464-0597.2006.00256.x

Bhabha, J., Fuller, A., Matache, M. Vranješević, J., Chernoff, M. C., Spasić, B., & Ivanis, J. (2017). Reclaiming adolescence: A Roma youth perspective. *Harvard Educational Review, 87*(2), 186–224. https://doi.org/10.17763/1943-5045-87.2.186

Bierwiaczonek, K., & Kunst, J. R. (2021). Revisiting the integration hypothesis: Correlational and longitudinal meta-analyses demonstrate the limited role of acculturation

for cross-cultural adaptation. *Psychological Science*, *32*(9), 1476–1493. https://doi.org/10.1177/09567976211006432
Booth, M. Z., Gerard, J. M., Deom, G. M., & Frey, C. J. (2022). Deconstructing adolescent ethnicity: A longitudinal analysis of ethnic-racial identity development and self-categorization. *Journal of Adolescence*, *94*(3), 366–379. https://doi.org/10.1002/jad.12028
Bronfenbrenner, U., & Morris, P. A. (2006). The bioecological model of human development. In R. M. Lerner & W. Damon (Eds.), *Handbook of child psychology: Theoretical models of human development* (pp. 793–828). John Wiley & Sons.
Burkitt, I. (2011). Identity construction in sociohistorical context. In S. J. Schwartz, K. Luyckx, & V. L. Vignoles (Eds.), *Handbook of identity theory and research* (pp. 267–283). Springer Science + Business Media.
Cheon, Y. M., & Yip, T. (2019). Longitudinal associations between ethnic/racial identity and discrimination among Asian and Latinx adolescents. *Journal of Youth and Adolescence*, *48*(9), 1736–1753. https://doi.org/10.1007/s10964-019-01055-6
Constante, K., Cross, F. L., Medina, M., & Rivas-Drake, D. (2020). Ethnic socialization, family cohesion, and ethnic identity development over time among Latinx adolescents. *Journal of Youth and Adolescence*, *49*(4), 895–906. https://doi.org/10.1007/s10964-019-01139-3
Crocetti, E., Pagano, M., De Lise, F., Maratia, F., Bobba, B., Meeus, W., & Bacaro, V. (2025). Promoting adolescents' personal and social identities: A meta-analysis of psychosocial interventions. *Identity: An International Journal of Theory and Research*, *25*(2), 167–196. https://doi.org/10.1080/15283488.2024.2394888
Crocetti, E., Prati, F., & Rubini, M. (2018). The interplay of personal and social identity. *European Psychologist*, *23*(4), 300–310. https://doi.org/10.1027/1016-9040/a000336
Cross, W. E., Jr. (1971). The Negro-to-Black conversion experience. *Black World*, *20*(9), 13–27.
Cross, W. E., Jr. (1991). *Shades of black: Diversity in African American identity*. Temple University Press.
Cross, W. E., Jr., Seaton, E., Yip, T., Lee, R. M., Rivas, D., Gee, G. C., Roth, W., & Ngo, B. (2017). Identity work: Enactment of racial-ethnic identity in everyday life. *Identity: An International Journal of Theory and Research*, *17*(1), 1–12. https://doi.org/10.1080/15283488.2016.1268535
Daha, M. (2011). Contextual factors contributing to ethnic identity development of second-generation Iranian American adolescents. *Journal of Adolescent Research*, *26*(5), 543–569. https://doi.org/10.1177/0743558411402335
Del Carmen Dominguez Espinosa, A., & Dantas, S. (2016). Acculturation in Central and South America. In D. Sam & J. Berry (Eds.), *The Cambridge handbook of acculturation psychology* (pp. 227–247). Cambridge University Press.
De Lise, F., Klimstra, T. A., Johnson, S. K., & Crocetti, E. (2025). Going out of the comfort zone: A longitudinal mixed-methods analysis of adolescents' identity development around study abroad experiences. *Identity: An International Journal of Theory and Research*, 1–24. Advance online publication. https://doi.org/10.1080/15283488.2025.2479817
Dimitrova, R., Buzea, C., Taušová, J., Uka, F., Zakaj, S., & Crocetti, E. (2018). Relationships between identity domains and life satisfaction in minority and majority youth in Albania, Bulgaria, Czech Republic, Kosovo, and Romania. *European Journal of Developmental Psychology*, *15*(1), 61–82. https://doi.org/10.1080/17405629.2017.1336997
Dimitrova, R., Musso, P., Naudé, L., Zahaj, S., Solcova, I. P., Stefenel, D., Uka, F., Jordanov, V., Jordanov, E., & Tavel, P. (2017). National collective identity in transitional societies: Salience and relations to life satisfaction for youth in South Africa, Albania, Bulgaria, the Czech Republic, Kosovo and Romania. *Journal of Psychology in Africa*, *27*(2), 150–158. https://doi.org/10.1080/14330237.2017.1301722
Dimitrova, R., Sam, D., & Ferrer-Wreder, L. (Eds.). (2021). *Roma minority in a global context: Taking a positive approach to research, policy, and practice*. Oxford University Press. https://doi.org/10.1093/oso/9780190654061.001.0001

Dimitrova, R., Van de Vijver, F. J. R., Taušová, J., Chasiotis, A., Bender, M., Buzea, C., Uka, F., & Tair, E. (2017). Ethnic, familial, and religious identity of Roma adolescents in Bulgaria, Czech Republic, Kosovo, and Romania in relation to their level of well-being. *Child Development*, *88*(3), 693–709. https://doi.org/10.1111/cdev.12786

Douglass, S., & Umaña-Taylor, A. J. (2015). A brief form of the ethnic identity scale: Development and empirical validation. *Identity: An International Journal of Theory and Research*, *15*(1), 48–65. https://doi.org/10.1080/15283488.2014.989442

Douglass, S., & Yip, T. (2015). Adolescent ethnic identity in context: Integrating daily diaries, biannual surveys, and school-level data. In C. E. Santos & A. J. Umaña-Taylor (Eds.), *Studying ethnic identity: Methodological and conceptual approaches across disciplines* (pp. 203–233). American Psychological Association.

Erikson, E. H. (1975). *Life history and the historical moment*. W. W. Norton & Company.

Flecha, R., & Soler, M. (2013). Turning difficulties into possibilities: Engaging Roma families and students in school though dialogic learning. *Cambridge Journal of Education*, *43*(4), 451–465. https://doi.org/10.1080/0305764X.2013.819068

Hammack, P. L. (2008). Narrative and the cultural psychology of identity. *Personality and Social Psychology Review*, *12*(3), 222–247. https://doi.org/10.1177/1088868308316892

Helms, J. E. (1990). *Black and White racial identity: Theory, research, and practice*. Greenwood Press.

Hoare, C. H. (1991). Psychosocial identity development and cultural others. *Journal of Counseling & Development*, *70*(1), 45–53. https://doi.org/10.1002/j.1556-6676.1991.tb01560.x

Hoffman, A. J., Agi, A. C., Rivas-Drake, D., & Jagers, R. J. (2019). Peer support development among Black American and Latinx Adolescents: The role of ethnic–racial centrality. *Developmental Psychology*, *55*(12), 2637–2648. https://doi.org/10.1037/dev0000829

Holland, D., & Lachicotte, W., Jr. (2007). Vygotsky, Mead, and the new sociocultural studies of identity. In H. Daniels, M. Cole, & J. Wertsch (Eds.), *The Cambridge companion to Vygotsky* (pp. 101–135). Cambridge University Press.

Huang, C. Y., & Stormshak, E. A. (2011). A longitudinal examination of early adolescence ethnic identity trajectories. *Cultural Diversity and Ethnic Minority Psychology*, *17*(3), 261–270. https://doi.org/10.1037/a0023882

Hubbard, R. R., & Utsey, S. O. (2015). A qualitative study of biracial identity among Afro-Germans living in Germany. *Identity: An International Journal of Theory and Research*, *15*(2), 89–112. https://doi.org/10.1080/15283488.2015.1023438

Hughes, D. L., Del Toro, J., & Way, N. (2017). Interrelations among dimensions of ethnic-racial identity during adolescence. *Developmental Psychology*, *53*(11), 2139–2153. https://doi.org/10.1037/dev0000401

Jensen, L. A., Arnett, J. J., & McKenzie, J. (2011). Globalization and cultural identity. In S. J. Schwartz, K. Luyckx, & V. L. Vignoles (Eds.), *Handbook of identity theory and research* (pp. 285–301). Springer Science + Business Media.

Juang, L. P., & Hwang, C. P. (2024). The importance of ethnic-racialized identities to becoming and being culturally responsive and equity minded educators. *Identity*, *24*(4), 257–268. https://doi.org/10.1080/15283488.2024.2388248

Juang, L. P., Schachner, M. K., Aral, T., Schwarzenthal, M., Kunyu, D., & Löhmannsröben, H. (2024). Effects of a brief self-affirmation writing intervention among 7th graders in Germany: Testing for variations by heritage group, discrimination experiences and classroom diversity climate. *Social Psychology of Education*, *27*(3), 651–685. https://doi.org/10.1007/s11218-023-09789-9

Juang, L. P., Umaña-Taylor, A. J., Schachner, M. K., Frisén, A., Hwang, C. P., Moscardino, U., Motti-Stefanidi, F., Oppedal, B., Pavlopoulos, V., Abdullahi, A. K., Barahona, R., Berne, S., Ceccon, C., Gharaei, N., Moffitt, U., Ntalachanis, A., Pevec, S. Sandberg, D. J., Zacharia, A., & Syed, M. (2023). Ethnic-racial identity in Europe: Adapting the identity project intervention in five countries. *European Journal of Developmental Psychology*, *20*(6), 978–1006. https://doi.org/10.1080/17405629.2022.2131520

Jugert, P., Leszczensky, L., & Pink, S. (2020). Differential influence of same- and cross-ethnic friends on ethnic-racial identity development in early adolescence. *Child Development, 91*(3), 949–963. https://doi.org/10.1111/cdev.13240

Kay, A. (2018). Erikson online: Identity and pseudospeciation in the internet age. *Identity: An International Journal of Theory and Research, 18*(4), 264–273. https://doi.org/10.1080/15283488.2018.1523732

Komolova, M., Pasupathi, M., & Wainryb, C. (2020). "Things like that happen when you come to a new country": Bosnian refugee experiences with discrimination. *Qualitative Psychology, 7*(1), 93–113. https://doi.org/10.1037/qup0000127

Kornienko, O., & Rivas-Drake, D. (2022). Adolescent intergroup connections and their developmental benefits: Exploring contributions from social network analysis. *Social Development, 31*(1), 9–26. https://doi.org/10.1111/sode.12572

Liebkind, K., Mähönen, T., Varjonen, S., & Jasinskaja-Lahti, I. (2016). Acculturation and identity. In D. Sam & J. Berry (Eds.), *The Cambridge handbook of acculturation psychology* (pp. 30–49). Cambridge University Press.

López, I., Walker, L. H. M, & Spinel, M. Y. (2015). Understanding the association between phenotype and ethnic identity. In C. E. Santos & A. J. Umaña-Taylor (Eds.), *Studying ethnic identity: Methodological and conceptual approaches across disciplines* (pp. 119–148). American Psychological Association.

Marcia, J. E. (1966). Development and validation of ego-identity status. *Journal of Personality and Social Psychology, 3*(5), 551–558. https://doi.org/10.1037/h0023281

McLean, K. C. (Ed.) (2021). *Cultural methods in psychology: Describing and transforming cultures*. Oxford University Press. https://doi.org/10.1093/oso/9780190095949.001.0001

McLean, K. C., Lilgendahl, J. P., Fordham, C., Alpert, E., Marsden, E., Szymanowski, K., & McAdams, D. P. (2018). Identity development in cultural context: The role of deviating from master narratives. *Journal of Personality, 86*(4), 631–651. https://doi.org/10.1111/jopy.12341

Meca, A., Allison, K., Cruz, B., Wright, A., Gonzales-Backen, M., & Scury, M. (2023). Cultural identity development among ethnic-racial minorities: An examination of ethnic-racial identity, national identity, and biculturalism. In B. Halpern-Felsher (Ed.), *Encyclopedia of child and adolescent health* (pp. 79–92). Elsevier. https://doi.org/10.1016/B978-0-12-818872-9.00178-3

Meca, A., Gonzales-Backen, M., Davis, R., Rodil, J., Soto, D., & Unger, J. B. (2020). Discrimination and ethnic identity: Establishing directionality among Latino/a youth. *Developmental Psychology, 56*(5), 982–992. https://doi.org/10.1037/dev0000908

Meca, A., Gonzales-Backen, M., Rodil, J. C., Cowan, I., Sharma, S., Webb, T. N., & Hayes, T. (2022). The ethnic identity scale: Affirmation, really? *Cultural Diversity & Ethnic Minority Psychology, 28*(4), 493–502. https://doi.org/10.1037/cdp0000485

Meca, A., & Schwartz, S. J. (2024). Cultural stress theory: An overview. *Cultural Diversity and Ethnic Minority Psychology, 30*(4), 603–612. https://doi.org/10.1037/cdp0000704

Medina, M. A., Rivas-Drake, D., Jagers, R. J., & Rowley, S. J. (2020). Friends matter: Ethnic-racial identity and school adjustment among African American and Latino early adolescents. *Applied Developmental Science, 24*(4), 376–391. https://doi.org/10.1080/10888691.2018.1524712

Mims, L. C., & Williams, J. L. (2020). "They told me what I was before I could tell them what I was": Black girls' ethnic-racial identity development within multiple worlds. *Journal of Adolescent Research, 35*(6), 754–779. https://doi.org/10.1177/0743558420913483

Moffitt, U., & Syed, M. (2021). Ethnic-racial identity in action: Structure and content of friends' conversations about ethnicity and race. *Identity: An International Journal of Theory and Research, 21*(1), 67–88. https://doi.org/10.1080/15283488.2020.1838804

Nelson, S. C., Syed, M., Tran, A. G. T. T., Hu, A. W., & Lee, R. M. (2018). Pathways to ethnic-racial identity development and psychological adjustment: The differential associations of cultural socialization by parents and peers. *Developmental Psychology, 54*(11), 2166–2180. https://doi.org/10.1037/dev0000597

Oteíza, T., & Merino, M. E. (2012). Am I a genuine Mapuche? Tensions and contradictions in the construction of ethnic identity in Mapuche adolescents from Temuco and Santiago. *Discourse & Society*, *23*(3), 297–317. https://doi.org/10.1177/0957926511433455

Overton, W. F. (2013). A new paradigm for developmental science: Relationism and relational-developmental systems. *Applied Developmental Science*, *17*(2), 94–107. https://doi.org/10.1080/10888691.2013.778717

Perez-Brena, N., Rivas-Drake, D., Toomey, R. B., & Umaña-Taylor, A. J. (2018). Contributions of the integrative model for the study of developmental competencies in minority children: What have we learned about adaptive culture? *American Psychologist*, *73*(6), 713–726. https://doi.org/10.1037/amp0000292

Pevec-Zimmer, S., Juang, L. P., & Schachner, M. K. (2024). Promoting awareness and self-efficacy for culturally responsive teaching of pre-service teachers through the *Identity Project* – a mixed methods study. *Identity: An International Journal of Theory and research*, *24*(4), 288–306. https://doi.org/10.1080/15283488.2024.2344086

Phinney, J. S. (1989). Stages of ethnic identity development in minority group adolescents. *Journal of Early Adolescence*, *9*(1–2), 34–49. https://doi.org/10.1177/0272431689091004

Phinney, J. S. (1990). Ethnic identity in adolescents and adults: Review of research. *Psychological Bulletin*, *108*(3), 499–514. https://doi.org/10.1037/0033-2909.108.3.499

Phinney, J. S., & Baldelomar, O. A. (2011). Identity development in multiple cultural contexts. In L. A. Jensen (Ed.), *Bridging cultural and developmental approaches to psychology: New syntheses in theory, research, and policy* (pp. 161–186). Oxford University Press.

Phinney, J. S., & Ong, A. D. (2007). Conceptualization and measurement of ethnic identity: Current status and future directions. *Journal of Counseling Psychology*, *54*(3), 271–281. https://doi.org/10.1037/0022-0167.54.3.271

Pryce, J. M., Kelly, M. S., & Lawinger, M. (2019). Conversation club: A group mentoring model for immigrant Youth. *Youth & Society*, *51*(7), 879–899. https://doi.org/10.1177/0044118X18780526

Rivas-Drake, D., Pinetta, B. J., Juang, L. P., & Agi, A. (2022). Ethnic-racial identity as a source of resilience and resistance in the context of racism and xenophobia. *Review of General Psychology*, *26*(3), 317–326. https://doi.org/10.1177/10892680211056318

Rivas-Drake, D., Seaton, E. K., Markstrom, C., Quintana, S., Syed, M., Lee, R. M., Schwartz, S. J., Umaña-Taylor, A. J., French, S., & Yip, T. (2014). Ethnic and racial identity in adolescence: Implications for psychosocial, academic, and health outcomes. *Child Development*, *85*(1), 40–57. https://doi.org/10.1111/cdev.12200

Rivas-Drake, D., Syed, M., Umaña-Taylor, A., Markstrom, C., French, S., Schwartz, S. J., & Lee, R. (2014). Feeling good, happy, and proud: A meta-analysis of positive ethnic–racial affect and adjustment. *Child Development*, *85*(1), 77–102. https://doi.org/10.1111/cdev.12175

Rivas-Drake, D., & Umaña-Taylor, A. J. (2019). *Below the surface: Talking with teens about race, ethnicity, and identity*. Princeton University Press.

Rivas-Drake, D., Umaña-Taylor, A. J., Schaefer, D. R., & Medina, M. (2017). Ethnic-racial identity and friendships in early adolescence. *Child Development*, *88*(3), 710–724. https://doi.org/10.1111/cdev.12790

Rogers, L. O., Kiang, L., White, L., Calzada, E. J., Umaña-Taylor, A. J., Byrd, C., Williams, C., D., Marks, A., & Whitesell, N. (2020). Persistent concerns: Questions for research on ethnic-racial identity development. *Research in Human Development*, *17*(2–3), 130–153. https://doi.org/10.1080/15427609.2020.1831881

Rogoff, B. (2023). Mutually constituting, fractal: Individual and cultural aspects of holistic process. *Review of Research in Education*, *47*(1), 60–83. https://doi.org/10.3102/0091732X231224666

Rogoff, B., Dahl, A., & Callanan, M. (2018). The importance of understanding children's lived experience. *Developmental Review*, *50*(Part A), 5–15. https://doi.org/10.1016/j.dr.2018.05.006

Sam, D. L. (2024). 50+ years of psychological acculturation research: Progress and challenges. *International Journal of Intercultural Relations*, *103*(April), Article 102076. https://doi.org/10.1016/j.ijintrel.2024.102076

Schachner, M. K., Hölscher, S., Moscardino, U., Ceccon, C., Juang, L., & Pastore, M. (2024). Adolescent cultural identity development in context: The dynamic interplay of the identity project with classroom cultural diversity climate in Italy and Germany. *Journal of Youth and Adolescence*, *53*(11), 2480–2498. https://doi.org/10.1007/s10964-024-02031-5

Schwartz, S. J., Montgomery, M. J., & Briones, E. (2006). Toward an interdisciplinary study of acculturation, identity, and culture. *Human Development*, *49*(1), 42–43. https://doi.org/10.1159/000090303

Schwartz, S. J., Syed, M., Yip, T., Knight, G. P., Umaña-Taylor, A. J., Rivas-Drake, D., & Lee, R. M. (2014). Methodological issues in ethnic and racial identity research with ethnic minority populations: Theoretical precision, measurement issues, and research designs. *Child Development*, *85*(1), 58–76. https://doi.org/10.1111/cdev.12201

Seaman, J., Sharp, E. H., & Coppens, A. D. (2017). A dialectical approach to theoretical integration in developmental–contextual identity research. *Developmental Psychology*, *53*(11), 2023–2035. https://doi.org/10.1037/dev0000383

Sellers, R. M., Smith, M. A., Shelton, J. N., Rowley, S. A. J., & Chavous, T. M. (1998). Multidimensional model of racial identity: A reconceptualization of African American racial identity. *Personality and Social Psychology Review*, *2*(1), 18–39. https://doi.org/10.1207/s15327957pspr0201_2

Shweder, R. A. (2011). Commentary: Ontogenetic cultural psychology. In L. A. Jensen (Ed.), *Bridging cultural and developmental approaches to psychology: New syntheses in theory, research, and policy* (pp. 303–310). Oxford University Press.

Smith, T. B., & Silva, L. (2011). Ethnic identity and personal well-being of people of color: A meta-analysis. *Journal of Counseling Psychology*, *58*(1), 42–60. https://doi.org/10.1037/a0021528

Spears, R. (2011). Group identities: The social identity perspective. In S. J. Schwartz, K. Luyckx, & V. L. Vignoles (Eds.), *Handbook of identity theory and research* (pp. 201–224). Springer Science + Business Media.

Spiegler, O., Verkuyten, M., Thijs, J., & Leyendecker, B. (2016). Low ethnic identity exploration undermines positive interethnic relations: A study among Turkish immigrant-origin youth. *Cultural Diversity and Ethnic Minority Psychology*, *22*(4), 495–503. https://doi.org/10.1037/cdp0000090

Syed, M., Juang, L. P., & Svensson, Y. (2018). Toward a new understanding of ethnic-racial settings for ethnic-racial identity development. *Journal of Research on Adolescence*, *28*(2), 262–276. https://doi.org/10.1111/jora.12387

Tajfel, H., & Turner, J. (1986). The social identity theory of intergroup behavior. In W. Austin & S. Worchel (Eds.), *Psychology of intergroup relations* (pp. 7–24). Nelson-Hall.

Thomas, O., Davidson, W., & McAdoo, H. (2008). An evaluation study of the Young Empowered Sisters (YES!) program: Promoting cultural assets among African American adolescent girls through a culturally relevant school-based intervention. *Journal of Black Psychology*, *34*(3), 281–308. https://doi.org/10.1177/0095798408314136

Umaña-Taylor, A. J. (2011). Ethnic identity. In S. J. Schwartz, K. Luyckx, & V. L. Vignoles (Eds.), *Handbook of identity theory and research* (pp. 791–801). Springer Science + Business Media.

Umaña-Taylor, A. J. (2015). Ethnic identity research: How far have we come? In C. E. Santos & A. J. Umaña-Taylor (Eds.), *Studying ethnic identity: Methodological and conceptual approaches across disciplines* (pp. 11–26). American Psychological Association.

Umaña-Taylor, A. J. (2016). A post-racial society in which ethnic-racial discrimination still exists and has significant consequences for youths' adjustment. *Current Directions in Psychological Science*, *25*(2), 111–118. https://doi.org/10.1177/0963721415627858

Umaña-Taylor, A. J. (2023). Promoting adolescent adjustment by intervening in ethnic-racial identity development: Opportunities for developmental prevention science and considerations for a global theory of change. *International Journal of Behavioral Development, 47*(4), 352–365. https://doi.org/10.1177/01650254231162614

Umaña-Taylor, A. J. (2024). Revisiting the conceptualization and measurement of ethnic-racial identity affect: Recommendations for future directions. *Child Development Perspectives, 18*(4), 215–220. https://doi.org/10.1111/cdep.12517

Umaña-Taylor, A. J., Douglass, S., Updegraff, K. A., & Marsiglia, F. F. (2018). A small-scale randomized efficacy trial of the identity project: Promoting adolescents' ethnic–racial identity exploration and resolution. *Child Development, 89*(3), 862–870. https://doi.org/10.1111/cdev.12755

Umaña-Taylor, A. J., Kornienko, O., Douglass Bayless, S., & Updegraff, K. A. (2018). A universal intervention program increases ethnic-racial identity exploration and resolution to predict adolescent psychosocial functioning one year later. *Journal of Youth and Adolescence, 47*(1), 1–15. https://doi.org/10.1007/s10964-017-0766-5

Umaña-Taylor, A. J., Kornienko, O., McDermott, E. R., & Motti-Stefanidi, F. (2020). National identity development and friendship network dynamics among immigrant and non-immigrant youth. *Journal of Youth and Adolescence, 49*(3), 706–723. https://doi.org/10.1007/s10964-019-01181-1

Umaña-Taylor, A. J., Quintana, S. M., Lee, R. M., Cross, W. E., Rivas-Drake, D., Schwartz, S. J., Syed, M., Yip, T., & Seaton, E. (2014). Ethnic and racial identity during adolescence and into young adulthood: An integrated conceptualization. *Child Development, 85*(1), 21–39. https://doi.org/10.1111/cdev.12196

Umaña-Taylor, A. J., Sladek, M. R., Safa, M. D., Uribe Tirado, L. M., & Vega, L. M. T. (2024). Examining ethnic-racial identity development and adjustment among Colombian adolescents. *Journal of Applied Developmental Psychology, 93*, Article 101672. https://doi.org/10.1016/j.appdev.2024.101672

Umaña-Taylor, A. J., Yazedjian, A., & Bámaca-Gómez, M. (2004). Developing the ethnic identity scale using Eriksonian and social identity perspectives. *Identity: An International Journal of Theory and Research, 4*(1), 9–38. https://doi.org/10.1207/S1532706XID0401_2

United Nations (2025). *International migrant stock* 2024: *Key facts and figures*. UNDESA/POP/2024/DC/NO. 13. Retrieved August 12, 2025, from https://www.un.org/development/desa/pd/sites/www.un.org.development.desa.pd/files/undesa_pd_2025_intlmigstock_2024_key_facts_and_figures_advance-unedited.pdf

Valsiner, J. (2012). Psychology courting culture: Future directions and their implications. In J. Valsiner (Ed.), *The Oxford handbook of culture and psychology* (pp. 1092–1104). Oxford University Press.

Verkuyten, M. (2016). Further conceptualizing ethnic and racial identity research: The social identity approach and its dynamic model. *Child Development, 87*(6), 1796–1812. https://doi.org/10.1111/cdev.12555

Wainryb, C., & Recchia, H. (2014). Youths' constructions of meanings about experiences with political conflict: Implications for processes of identity development. In K. C. McLean & M. Syed (Eds.), *The Oxford handbook of identity development* [E-reader version] (pp. 369–386). Oxford University Press. https://doi.org/10.1093/oxfordhb/9780199936564.013.008

Walker, C. J., Williams, C. D., Hood, K. B., & Lozada, F. T. (2024). Narrative review: Examining the associations between ethnic-racial identity and mental health outcomes among African American emerging adults and adults. *Identity: An International Journal of Theory and Research, 24*(3), 173–193. https://doi.org/10.1080/15283488.2024.2320431

Wantchekon, K. A., McDermott, E. R., Jones, S. M., Satterthwaite-Freiman, M., Baldeh, M., Rivas-Drake, D., & Umaña-Taylor, A. J. (2023). The role of ethnic-racial identity and self-esteem in intergroup contact attitudes. *Journal of Youth and Adolescence, 52*(11), 2243–2260. https://doi.org/10.1007/s10964-023-01819-1

Ward, C., & Mak, A. (2016). Acculturation theory and research in New Zealand and Australia. In D. Sam & J. Berry (Eds.), *The Cambridge handbook of acculturation psychology* (pp. 314–336). Cambridge University Press.

Ward, C., & Szabó, Á. (2023). Acculturation, cultural identity and well-being. *Nature Reviews Psychology*, *2*(5), 267–282. https://doi.org/10.1038/s44159-023-00171-2

Way, N., & Rogers, O. (2014). "They say black men won't make it, but I know I'm gonna make it": Ethnic and racial identity development in the context of cultural stereotypes. In K. C. McLean & M. Syed (Eds.), *The Oxford handbook of identity development* [E-reader version] (pp. 269–285). Oxford University Press. https://doi.org/10.1093/oxfordhb/9780199936564.013.032

Worrell, F. C. (2014). Culture as race/ethnicity. In K. C. McLean & M. Syed (Eds.), *The Oxford handbook of identity development* [E-reader version] (pp. 249–268). Oxford University Press. https://doi.org/10.1093/oxfordhb/9780199936564.013.029

Yip, T., Wang, Y., Mootoo, C., & Mirpuri, S. (2019). Moderating the association between discrimination and adjustment: A meta-analysis of ethnic/racial identity. *Developmental Psychology*, *55*(6), 1274–1298. https://doi.org/10.1037/dev0000708

5 Bicultural Identity Development

> I remember when I was younger, I wanted to be Swedish. Who is American in Sweden? There are not many of us. Now that I'm older, a new thing for me is when I meet new people, I say my name is Richard [English pronunciation]. Before, when I was younger, I would just say I'm Rikard [Swedish pronunciation]. Because, I didn't want to answer the questions. Now, I like the questions, like 'Richard, where does that come from?'
>
> (Richard, a 19-year-old student)[1]

This chapter begins a new format. In this and the subsequent chapters of this volume, there is an exploration of novel extensions and a mapping of where the edges of our knowledge are in selected areas of identity theory, research, and practice.[2] In this chapter, the focus is on bicultural identity, meaning a person who has personal and social connections to more than one cultural community (Benet-Martínez et al., 2021). Bicultural identity places attention on the intersection of multiple cultures and the developing person. In other words, how do people navigate the intersection of different facets of their cultural identity (Benet-Martínez et al., 2021)? Schwartz and colleagues (2006, p. 6) noted, "Cultural identity refers to a sense of solidarity with the ideals of a given cultural group and to the attitudes, beliefs, and behaviors manifested toward one's own (and other) cultural groups as a result of this solidarity."

In the next chapter, Chapter 6, there is a similar simultaneous consideration of how adolescents make sense of who they are in light of the blending or confluence of different facets of their identity, but in this case, the exploration involves the intersection of sexual and gender identity. Shared underlying themes in this and the next chapter (Chapters 5 and 6) include the value of intersectional research approaches[3] and the pursuit and attainment of a sense of continuity and wholeness in one's identity across contexts and time (i.e., identity integration[4]: Mitchell et al., 2021; Syed & McLean, 2016). Intersectionality and identity integration are described in detail in Chapter 6, and concise explanations of these ideas are in the endnotes to this chapter.

This chapter is organized with a first section that sets a wider contextual and conceptual groundwork for understanding bicultural identity. Bridging contexts and

DOI: 10.4324/9781003486336-5

ideas begin the chapter; some contexts are novel, such as globalization and global population trends in immigration, while other bridging ideas were first described in Chapter 4, such as the sociocultural tradition in the field of human development, culture, and acculturation psychology. In the case of acculturation, in this chapter, there is a substantial expansion of the treatment of this area due to the central role it has played in the bicultural identity field. The next chapter section describes a specific theory about bicultural identity, called the bicultural identity integration (BII) framework (Benet-Martínez et al., 2021). A summary of BII's evidence base is included in that section. The chapter then turns to a description of two research exemplars. These empirical examples give a concrete illustration of themes and/or research practices consistent with exciting, new directions for research on bicultural identity development and their implications. Finally, the chapter ends with a summary.

Bridging Contexts and Ideas

Globalization

Globalization is fueled by intercultural contact, and it reaches us through commerce, tourism, and short-term exchanges (Jensen, 2022). Globalization also happens through the blending of heritage and receiving cultures across generations. Turner and colleagues (2010, p. 51) stated that

> . . . globalization is a multidimensional process of change that involves increased connectivity across economies and societies, creating a greater awareness of the globe as a common point of reference. It is a process that makes the world a single place. . . .

Globalization is not new; however, globalization's pace and pervasiveness are (Jensen, 2022; Turner et al., 2010). For example, learning about other cultures, even if from a distance, is commonplace among many of today's adolescents and emerging adults (Jensen, 2022). Globalization is pushed along by changes in technology use, movements of people, and how wider socioeconomic opportunities present themselves (Turner et al., 2010).

The direction of globalization's messages, such as values that embrace individual autonomy and gender equality, regularly emanates from and spreads across developed nations with ripples and impacts reaching those who live in developing nations (Jensen, 2022). Further, youth who live in cities are more likely to be involved in the global youth culture, relative to youth who live in the countryside, and such an urban/rural divide is especially evident in developing nations (Jensen, 2022; Katzarska-Miller & Faucher, 2022). Arguably, digital mediums, like social networking and video games, are major accelerants for globalization (see Chapter 7 for more on digital life and identity). Adolescents' and emerging adults' developmental openness to identity work and their "locked in"[5] relationship with digital mediums make globalization vital to consider when thinking about present-day adolescents' and emerging adults' identity development.

Revisiting the Sociocultural Perspective and Culture

The sociocultural perspective (Rogoff, 2023) and culture were first described in Chapter 4. Here, in this chapter, these ideas provide a wider basis for understanding adolescents' bicultural identity development. Rogoff (2023), a pioneering scholar of the sociocultural perspective, explained the following:

- The sociocultural perspective is a metatheory about human development. In other words, it is a theory for how developmental theories should work.
- According to the sociocultural perspective, development happens when people act in the world, and development is inseparable from the cultural–historical moment.
- In Rogoff's (2023, p. 61) own words, ". . . people transform their participation in sociocultural activities with both individual and cultural contributions mutually constituting one holistic process flowing across generations."

Also, culture is a critical theme throughout this chapter and in several other parts of this volume. For example, it helps us to understand fields and ideas like cultural psychology, cultural identity, and bicultural identity. Below is a summary of what the term "culture" can mean, given that there are many ways to describe what culture is and how humans use it. Matsumoto and Hwang (2021) described culture as having several key elements as follows:

- Culture involves group-based values, attitudes, beliefs, and actions/behaviors that help us to adapt across the life course and in diverse contexts. Culture offers us a limited range of solutions to life's challenges and opportunities, so people do not have to reinvent the wheel or start from scratch each generation.
- Culture is passed on and reinterpreted by each generation in ways that are cumulative yet in keeping with the demands of the time.
- Culture is represented in the "meaning and information systems" that humans create (Matsumoto & Hwang, 2021, p. 59).

Acculturation Revisited and Expanded

Ways to bring sociocultural and psychological perspectives to bear on our understanding of how identity development takes place in light of globalization and immigration experiences involve seeing the intercultural contacts that take place between people and societies through the lens of acculturation psychology (Sam, 2024). Globalization implies that some measure of psychological (at the individual, person level) and social (at the group and societal levels) acculturation is taking place. Immigration experiences can also spur changes in cultural identity through the person's engagement in acculturation tasks and experiences (Schwartz et al., 2006). Further, acculturation research has been a main venue for research into biculturalism and bicultural identification, which is a foundation for the study of bicultural identity (Benet-Martínez et al., 2021; Meca et al., 2023). Thus, returning to the field of acculturation psychology is vital for any consideration of bicultural identity. See the list below for a reminder about acculturation and its fundamental features.

Ward and Szabó (2023) laid out acculturation's elements as described below.

- Acculturation happens when people enter a new sociocultural world, also called proximal or direct acculturation, and/or can take place remotely via globalization.
- The acculturating person is changing in "beliefs, attitudes, values, behaviours and identities," and members of the majority culture are also changing due to contact (Ward & Szabó, 2023, p. 268). Importantly, identity, with a focus on ethnic, national, and religious identity, is often included in the conceptualization and measurement of the psychological process of acculturation that happens at the level of the individual person.
- Acculturation happens at the individual level by way of acculturation strategies.

In this volume, acculturation and acculturation strategies were first introduced in Chapter 4. The list below provides a recap of acculturation strategies. Sam (2024) as well as Ward and Szabó (2023) described acculturation strategies as having the following elements.

- Acculturation strategies involve attitudes, behaviors, and facets of identity surrounding how to navigate one's heritage culture along with a new culture. Acculturation can happen proximally/directly and/or remotely.
- For the assimilation acculturation strategy, the origin is culture lost, and the new culture is taken on.
- The separation acculturation strategy involves the origin culture being retained and the new culture being largely kept at a distance.
- For the integration acculturation strategy, there is a balancing or fusion of the origin and the new culture.
- The marginalization acculturation strategy consists of the origin and new culture being kept at a distance and not integrated into individuals' lives and who they are.

Currently, there is a recognition that acculturation strategies can be employed in a specific way across contexts/life domains and may or may not be indicative of any overall approach that is applied uniformly to all aspects of life (Karataş, 2025). A domain-specific conceptualization of acculturation strategies differs from widely used acculturation psychology research practices that lean toward a more uniform, generalized (merging across life domains) measurement of acculturation strategies.

For example, an adolescent could use an assimilation acculturation strategy in a private domain such as being at home with other family members, and this strategy could vary depending on parents' own acculturation and the young person's ethnic/heritage socialization within the family (Karataş, 2025). The same adolescent could use an integration acculturation strategy in a public domain such as at school, depending on the school's policies and practices around cultural diversity and intergroup contact as well as the prevalence of intercultural friendships and peers at school (Karataş, 2025). As Karataş (2025, p. 319) stated, ". . . exploring acculturation in separate life domains and considering conditions specific to each may help better address the associations between acculturation and adjustment during adolescence . . ." A life domain-specific approach to acculturation is where the current state of the science in acculturation psychology is moving (e.g., Karataş, 2025; Sam, 2024).

Acculturation Among Minority Groups and Social Identity

Acculturation has been studied systematically by social scientists for at least 50 years, and the predominant research focus has been on proximal/direct and enduring intercultural contact and the psychological acculturation of individuals who are in minority groups within a wider society (Sam, 2024). Minority groups who have been the subject of research attention have ranged from those immigrating firsthand themselves, referred to as immigrants or first generation, as well as subsequent generations of individuals, who are the children (second generation), grandchildren, and great-great-grandchildren of immigrants with one or more parents being immigrants (Sam 2024). Studied minority groups have also included those who are indigenous people or other settled minority groups/diasporas that are differently defined depending on the national context's history and present-day society (e.g., Roma people; Sam, 2024). Belonging to a minority group or groups can provide a basis for social identity. See Tables 5.1a and 5.1b for a description of different facets of social identity, particularly relevant to bicultural identity; some of these facets of social identity are first described in Chapter 4.

When considering social identity, it is useful to reflect on what personal identity has generally meant, involving an individual's answers to some of the following questions: Who and what are distinctively me? What are my goals, values, and beliefs, and my life history as it relates to my utterly unique sense of who I am? Indeed, there is only one of us. Social and personal identity can be infused with

Table 5.1a Facets of Social Identity Relevant to Bicultural Identity

Facet	*Explanation*
Social identity	A sense of belonging to a social group, which is affective and has psychological and behavioral consequences (Schwartz et al., 2006). Social identity also includes a consideration of ascribed identity, intergroup relations, and the minority group's standing in society. Processes of change from social identity theory (Tajfel & Turner, 1986) include "self-categorization, social identification, and social comparison" (Ward & Szabó, 2023, p. 268).
Cultural identity	A sense of belonging, cognitively and emotionally, to a cultural community or communities (Jensen, 2022). Multicultural identity "incorporates attachments and loyalties toward two or more cultures" (Benet-Martínez et al., 2021, p. 246).

Table 5.1b Facets of Social Identity Relevant to Bicultural Identity

Facet	*Explanation*
Ethnic identity	A personal, subjective, and social sense of belonging to an ethnocultural group, with this group defined by a shared place and/or intergenerational origin and culture (Phinney et al., 2001; Umaña-Taylor et al., 2014).
National identity	A psychological and social connection to a national government. "... while national cultures certainly exist, cultural groups also exist within nations" (Matsumoto & Hwang, 2021, p. 70). Depending on the national context considered, there can be a single or many majority groups that make up the mainstream society (Ward & Szabó, 2023).
Religious identity*	A psychosocial sense of one's self as part of a religion and/or religious community, with markers of religious identity consisting of the individual's exploration and commitment to religious beliefs and values and/or involvement with religious practices or religiosity (de Bruin-Wassinkmaat et al., 2019).

Note

* de Bruin-Wassinkmaat and colleagues (2019) noted that religious identity can be considered to be unique relative to other social identity domains because it involves a person's connection to the divine.

one another – coinciding and informing one another – and yet other personally held aspects of our identity can be absolutely idiosyncratic to ourselves and our life experiences. Social identity often involves others and concerns a person's answers to questions like: Am I part of this group? Do I think, feel, and act like I belong? Do others put me in this group when they see or talk to me, an ascribed identity? How can being in this group connect to me psychologically in terms of adding meaning to my life and helping me make sense of it? How does the wider society see this group, and what does this mean for me?

Schwartz and colleagues (2006, p. 11), in their conceptual review of acculturation and identity, put forward the contention that "... the person's personal identity – one's most fundamental goals, values, and beliefs and the coherence among these ideals – has the potential to stabilize the individual during the transition to a new society." These scholars went on to develop a theoretical proposition that identity development and the experience of acculturation are connected through changes in cultural identity, and coherence in one's personal identity should act as a compass that guides acculturating individuals through their encounters with new ideas and people, as well as the opportunities and challenges in a receiving society (Schwartz et al., 2006). Indeed, these scholars noted, "Particularly when it is self-chosen, personal identity can help shield the individual from external pressures by specifying exactly what is within the person's 'realm of possibility' and what is not" (Schwartz et al., 2006, p. 23).

Immigration Experiences and Proximal Acculturation

As noted, acculturation can happen in direct and enduring ways, sometimes called proximal or direct acculturation, and acculturation can also take place remotely and on an intermittent, time-limited basis (Ferguson et al., 2020). Direct and enduring intercultural contact occurs, for example, when young people move to a new home by immigrating across national borders or migrate to a new region within their birth nation.

To have a sense of the scale and numbers involved in the movement of immigrating people globally in recent years, consider that the number of individuals in the global population who are living in a country other than where they were born was just less than three percent in the 1990s through early 2000s (1990–2005), which is about 153 million people, of which 24 million were children (UNICEF, 2021). In 2020, the global immigrant population was 3.6 percent (of the global population), which amounted to 281 million people, of which 36 million were children (UNICEF, 2021). Differently expressed, in 2020, one out of every 66 children worldwide had immigrated to another country (UNICEF, 2021).

Other global population trends showed that in the year 2022, several million people were displaced around the world (i.e., 117 million people; McAuliffe & Oucho, 2024). Displaced persons are, for example, people who are refugees, people who are seeking asylum, and people who are internally displaced due to conflicts and/or disasters, human-made and/or natural (McAuliffe & Oucho, 2024). Further, there was a 30% increase across a two-year period (2020–2022) of those seeking asylum, which equates to 5.4 million people (McAuliffe & Oucho, 2024).

Global population trends show that if individuals immigrate across national borders, the receiving society will likely be in the same global region in which the person was born (UNICEF, 2021). For instance, if children born in an Asian country were to immigrate, they would likely immigrate to another Asian country, and the new receiving society would probably have relatively better economic conditions than the child's origin/birth society (UNICEF, 2021). Globally, it is also the case that migration within national borders, for example, moving from the countryside to the city or from one city to another, is more common than crossing national borders (McAuliffe & Oucho, 2024; UNICEF, 2021).

In summary, international immigration from 1970 to 2020 increased from a share of 2.3% to 3.6% of the global population, with the vast majority of the global population remaining in their native countries (McAuliffe & Oucho, 2024). But, if people do immigrate, they are likely to go to a nation within their global region (UNICEF, 2021). In recent years, the share of displaced people across national borders and within their native countries due to violence, conflict, and/or disasters has increased annually, and the international response to resettle and/or support refugees and other displaced persons remains variable across receiving nations (McAuliffe & Oucho, 2024). Children and young people are an important part of the overall global population of migrating people across and within national borders (UNICEF, 2021).

Children and young people who have immigration experiences are increasingly being considered in scientific research studies from a strengths-based perspective (Marks et al., 2020; Motti-Stefanidi, 2018). For example, what do youth and families with an immigration background contribute to a receiving society and themselves? What are their potentials, skills, and relational assets? What is their progress in developmental tasks, like bicultural identity development? What is their progress in acculturative tasks?

How is their well-being and movement through sociocultural transitions? Having a greater scientific focus on positive adaptation does not mean that the long-standing challenges faced by youth with an immigration background are disregarded, but rather, that they are not the sole focus of research attention. When problems are the only focal point, we are left with an incomplete understanding of the young person (e.g., Marks et al., 2020). This chapter contributes, with its focus on the potential strengths gained through bicultural identity development, to this wider scientific work that seeks to have a more balanced focus on understanding the development of young people who have immigration experiences.

Remote and Direct Acculturation in a Globalized World

To provide a realistic view of bicultural identity development, it is important to recognize that direct and remote acculturation are co-occurring in many parts of the world. Remote acculturation has been defined as ". . . acculturation resulting from indirect and/or intermittent exposure to a specific non-native culture(s) via globalization avenues" (Ferguson et al., 2023, p. 385). This type of acculturation involves the cross-national and sometimes global spread of different trends and ideas, such as physical fitness cultures, beauty standards and practices, activities and interests, diets, and food/drinks (Gillespie et al., 2022).

An innovative focus group study by Ferguson and colleagues (2020) provides a case in point on how youth navigate direct and remote acculturation. In this study, Latinx heritage adolescents living in the United States (U.S.) were asked about biculturalism in a direct acculturation context, and Jamaican adolescents living in Jamaica were also asked about biculturalism, but in this case, questions were focused on biculturalism in relation to their experiences with remote acculturation experiences with the mainstream culture of the U.S. (Ferguson et al., 2020). Below are some selected illustrative quotes from participants in Ferguson and colleagues' (2020) study. Paulina, who was 16 years old, born in Mexico, and living in the U.S., stated:

> Well, I'm American culture and Colombian culture. Because I have a boyfriend that, he's Colombian, so I feel a part of their culture. You know, since I'm always talking to them, always with them, I feel like a part of their culture. It's not like I was born in their culture, but I feel part of it.
>
> (Ferguson et al., 2020, p. 442)

Thirteen-year-old Naresh, born and living in Jamaica, stated:

> Well, for me, sometimes a feel American when I'm around certain friends . . . sometimes I feel Jumiekan . . . when I'm at [school], I'm a Jamaican but when I'm elsewhere, in a {inaudible}, a feel like . . . cuz me and my, me and my friends, ahn I mean FRIENDS, when we go out, we don't behave like Jumiekans [Jamaicans] cuz we don't speak patwa [Jamaican Patois] for one . . . I don't speak patwa . . . so . . . sometime – I'll act,

> sometimes the way my [American/-ized] friends speak, I will sometimes adapt to their accent. . . .
>
> (Ferguson et al., 2020, p. 444)

Fourteen-year-old Richie, born and living in Jamaica, remarked:

> Tings a si people do . . . si, somebody di deh America ahn style Miss ahn you pick it up yu feel American now, cuz yu doing it. [Things I see other people do . . . I see somebody who was visiting America and is now fashionable, you pick it up, you feel American now because you are doing it.]
>
> (Ferguson et al., 2020, p. 444)

These responses from adolescent participants represent a glimpse into how encounters with globalization and navigating multiple cultures are part of the daily life of many adolescents, even those without an experience or history of immigration to a new country.[6] These statements also show how adolescents make sense of themselves and relate to an increasingly globalized world, in which it is not uncommon to develop an identity that involves the blending of heritage and non-heritage cultures.

Bicultural Identity Integration (BII) and Its Evidence Base

Several theories and research fields are dedicated to explaining how individuals navigate their sense of belonging to more than one cultural community (Ward & Szabó, 2023). The developmental identity theories described in Chapters 2–4 are also relevant to this question and are reflected in this chapter's research exemplars. Considering the theoretical and disciplinary diversity that exists surrounding bicultural identity (e.g., Ward & Szabó, 2023), it is important to sketch out some of the main focal points of scholarly attention in this area. Bicultural identity research concerns itself with documenting the range of identity solutions that people use to answer the question of how belonging to multiple cultural communities relates to who they are (Benet-Martínez et al., 2021). As an illustration of this point, consider the comments from a participant in Lilgendahl and colleagues' study, who was elevated on BII and had a positive emotional ending to a memory written down in a narrative identity prompt.

> . . . Without little events and memories such as this one. I would be very confused as to who I am culturally, ethnicity-wise, and relationship-wise. I am extremely proud of my heritage, and I believe it has made me a more unique, interesting person today.
>
> (Lilgendahl et al., 2018, p. 1610)

Another main research concern revolves around the question of how different identity solutions, in the context of having a bicultural identity, connect to the young person's well-being, life satisfaction, and adaptation (e.g., Baumert et al.,

2025). The next chapter section addresses both of these concerns from the standpoint of Benet-Martínez and colleagues' (2021) framework for BII. See Ward and Szabó (2023) for a description and analysis of other theories and research about bicultural identity.

From an individual differences perspective,[7] Benet-Martínez and colleagues (2002, 2021) posited that for people who belong to more than one cultural community, bicultural identity is a relatively enduring psychological aspect of the person that will vary across individuals. Put differently, people will solve the question of how belonging to more than one cultural community connects with who they are in a variety of ways, differing in salience and strength of the question to the person, as well as in the quality of the solution. BII has been measured across two dimensions, namely harmony versus conflict and blendedness versus dissociation (Benet-Martínez et al., 2021). The bicultural identity integration scale is a self-reported survey consisting of 17 items, with items rated on a five-point scale ranging from strongly agree to strongly disagree (Huynh et al., 2018). Important elements across the harmony/conflict dimension involve how people feel about their bicultural experiences and how these affective appraisals are characteristic of who they are as bicultural individuals (Benet-Martínez et al., 2021; Szabó et al., 2020). An example item given by Szabó and colleagues (2020, p. 707) for the harmony/conflict dimension on the BIIS-2 was "I feel torn between the Hispanic and American cultures." The blendedness/dissociation dimension involves how bicultural people think about how well the two cultures that they belong to coexist with each other (i.e., blend or are integrated with each other; Schwartz et al., 2019). A sample item designed to measure blendedness given by Szabó et al. (2020, p. 707) was "I cannot ignore the Hispanic or American side of me." Items about dissociation reflect an identity solution that is compartmentalized with facets of cultural identity kept separate in different life domains (i.e., "I keep the Hispanic and American cultures separate" Szabó et al., 2020, p. 1). In other words, for this dimension, there is a focus on a cognitive appraisal of the two cultures' coexistence in the person's life and sense of identity (Szabó et al., 2020). See the earlier description in this chapter from Karataş (2025) about a life domain-specific approach to acculturation research for a possible conceptual connection to BII's dissociation dimension.

Benet-Martínez et al. (2021), Meca et al. (2023), and Ward and Szabó (2023) provided narrative reviews of BII's evidence base. Descriptions of research with BII follow in the lists below, with studies involving samples of adolescents and/or adults who have immigration experiences or who are members of a minority group. In a narrative review of the bicultural identity research literature, Ward and Szabó (2023) noted that studies had found generally positive associations between blendedness and harmony with:

- more time living in a receiving nation
- more use of the receiving nation's language
- more identification with both the heritage/origin and the receiving nation's cultures

Ward and Szabó (2023) also noted that existing BII studies showed a negative association between blendedness and harmony with acculturation attitudes related to assimilation, separation, and marginalization.

Ward and Szabó (2023) concluded that for blendedness, there was evidence for positive associations with:

- an integration attitude toward acculturation
- more experiences with multiple cultures and languages early in life

Ward and Szabó (2023) and Meca et al. (2023) also concluded that existing research studies supported a positive association between harmony and well-being, as well as a negative association between harmony and indicators of stress and mental ill-health. Benet-Martínez and colleagues' (2021) framework for bicultural identity is noteworthy in that it has been heuristic in terms of measurement development and a building body of research for over two decades that compares and contrasts this view of bicultural identity with other allied perspectives.

In Benet-Martínez and colleagues' (2021) conceptualization of bicultural identity, there are many additional strengths, such as a focus on the affective and cognitive aspects of cultural identity (Schwartz et al., 2019) and highlighting how important the subjective view of one's identity is, which is also consistent with formulations of ethnic identity (e.g., Phinney et al., 2001). This framework also directly hones in on what it is like for people to navigate multiple cultural communities in a way that does not consider cultural identity as simply additive or inherently oppositional or does not view the heritage and new cultural communities as necessarily independent facets of sociocultural identity. In BII, there is less emphasis on the individuals' strength of identification with different cultural communities and their level of engagement in cultural practices/behaviors (Benet-Martínez et al., 2021). Group identification and cultural behaviors/practices are elements of bicultural identity that are emphasized in social identity theory, acculturation theory, and theories about ethnic identity development (Benet-Martínez et al., 2021).

Some have argued that BII works best as a description of the content of bicultural identity or the characteristics of bicultural persons, rather than a process explanation for how BII develops over time or is maintained (e.g., Szabó et al., 2020; Ward & Szabó, 2023). The abundance of cross-sectional studies and the scarcity of longitudinal research with the BII were limitations recognized by Benet-Martínez and colleagues (2021), and this feature of the existing BII research literature limits insight into developmental change and causality. Important questions for this field include seeking answers to how bicultural identity develops and is managed within families as well as how bicultural identity development is expressed across cultural contexts that differ in the support available for a bicultural identity, such as in receiving contexts that vary in policy and practices surrounding resettlement and multiculturalism (Benet-Martínez et al., 2021; Meca et al., 2023; Ward & Szabó, 2023).

Research Exemplars

The research exemplars provided here focus specifically on the intersection of heritage and national cultural identity, ". . . identity duality . . ." (Lilgendahl et al., 2018, p. 1599), among young people with immigration experiences (see Tables 5.2a and 5.2b). It should be noted that, like any single research study, the results of these exemplar studies are preliminary, and future research is needed to replicate or qualify and extend these individual research findings.[8]

Schwartz et al. (2019): A Theoretically Diverse Diary Study

Schwartz and colleagues (2019) conducted an innovative 12-day diary study that sought to answer several research questions, such as how do different theoretical explanations for bicultural identity relate to each other at the beginning of this study and over time? Other research questions these scholars sought to answer were, in what ways do bicultural identity elements change on a day-to-day basis (i.e., daily variability)? And, finally, are day-to-day changes in bicultural identity elements important to how study participants felt at the end of a 12-day study period? (Schwartz et al., 2019). This investigation was a quantitative study that

Table 5.2a Overview of Selected Features of the Schwartz et al. (2019) Research Exemplar With Bicultural Identity Measured as an Integrated Construct

Study measures	*Study design*	*Study sample*
Self-report surveys on bicultural identity indices: blendedness (compartmentalization), harmony (conflict), hybridizing, alternating, and outcome indices were well-being, depressive, and anxiety symptoms	Short-term longitudinal 12-day diary study	873 Hispanic university students in the U.S. (average age: 21)

Note. Two different theories about bicultural identity are examined in this study.

Table 5.2b Overview of Selected Features of the Lilgendahl et al. (2018) Research Exemplar With Bicultural Identity Measured as an Integrated Construct

Study measures	*Study design*	*Study sample*
Surveys on heritage culture identification, BII-2: bicultural harmony (conflict), blendedness (distance) composite score used, and positive and negative affect. Narrative prompts about memories of being bicultural (a first memory, an emotionally significant memory). Participants wrote narratives for the two prompts. Coded for valence and exploratory processing	Narrative identity approach and cross-sectional	77 university students in the U.S. (average age: 20)

Note. See Chapter 3 for more about narrative identity.

relied on self-report survey responses, and the sample was a group of Hispanic university students living in Miami, Florida, in the U.S. (Schwartz et al., 2019). Participants self-defined their heritage as Cuban (41%), Colombian (13.2%), Nicaraguan (7.5%), Venezuelan (7.2%), Dominican (6.5%), and other (24.6%; Schwartz et al., 2019).

A diary study provides unique insight into how changes from day to day (i.e., variability) in some area of experience or functioning can be important to another outcome, like how people feel at a later time point, with a consideration of how people felt when they started the study (i.e., a mini-longitudinal study). On day 2 through day 11 of this 12-day diary study, participants rated two different conceptualizations of bicultural identity as measured by a subset of items each day, which gave an index of day-to-day change or stability in elements of bicultural identity (Schwartz et al., 2019).

For bicultural identity, one framework that was used was Benet-Martínez and colleagues' (2021) blendedness versus compartmentalization and harmony versus conflict, as measured by the bicultural identity integration scale (Huynh et al., 2018). The other theory about bicultural identity was developed by Ward and colleagues, which focuses on cultural identity styles (see Ward & Szabó, 2023, for an overview). Ward and Szabó (2023) described the cultural identity style perspective as being about how more than one cultural identity is maintained in practice; put differently, what strategies are open to the person to meet this challenge? Ward and Szabó (2023, p. 271) stated, "The hybrid identity style involves combining elements from two or more cultures in a novel way. The alternating identity style refers to changing cultural identities based on the circumstances."

The Multicultural Identity Styles Scale (MISS; Ward et al., 2018) is a self-report survey of 14 items that provides an index of hybridizing and alternating. Sample items of hybridizing given by Schwartz et al. (2019, p. 30) were "I see myself as a culturally unique mix of Hispanic and American," and an alternating sample item was as follows: "I alternate on being Hispanic and American depending on the circumstances." The uniqueness and overlap of BII-2 and MISS have been examined in another psychometric study with Hispanic young adults living in the U.S. (Szabó et al., 2020), and the findings of this research exemplar study by Schwartz et al. (2019) provide further insight into these respective frameworks for bicultural identity.

In summary, in regard to measurement and study procedure, on day two through day 11, elements of bicultural identity were measured from the BII and cultural identity style perspective (Schwartz et al., 2019). On days 1 and 12, the full assessment battery was completed by study participants, including the aforementioned bicultural identity elements, as well as measures of well-being and internalizing (depressive and anxiety) symptoms (Schwartz et al., 2019). See Table 5.2a.

Selected study results from the Schwartz and colleagues (2019) diary study found that the BII constructs of blendedness and harmony were positively associated with each other as well as the cultural identity style of hybridizing at the beginning of this 12-day study. Further, blendedness and harmony predicted a later positive change in hybridizing (Schwartz et al., 2019). Other results showed that the specific identity elements of blendedness, harmony, and hybridizing appeared to vary along with one another over time, from the daily diary results (Schwartz et al., 2019). Thus, if one of the noted identity elements were to change, then the other elements were also likely to change in the same direction (going up or down over time on a daily basis during the study). Finally, study results showed that daily variability in hybridizing was related to a subsequent decrease in well-being and that daily variability in blendedness was prospectively associated with more internalizing symptoms (Schwartz et al., 2019).

Some highlights from this innovative study are that BII and cultural identity styles are related conceptualizations of bicultural identity but that these constructs have distinctions, consistent with other studies that have compared these constructs (e.g., Szabó et al., 2020). Schwartz and colleagues (2019) singled out the importance of BII's blendedness and harmony as potential intervention targets, given these bicultural identity elements' roles in predicting subsequent hybridizing and in turn being connected in a beneficial way to well-being and mental health. Other key points made by these scholars included the lack of detrimental associations with daily variations in the alternating identity style with well-being and mental health in this sample (Schwartz et al., 2019).

Lilgendahl et al. (2018) Study: The Importance of a Happy Ending?

Lilgendahl and colleagues (2018) conducted a theoretically and methodologically innovative study that was cross-sectional and involved 77 university students who were 18–22 years old living on the East Coast of the U.S. Participants reported diverse ethnic, racial, and national backgrounds, with 82% of the sample born outside of the U.S. or having a parent who was born outside of the U.S. (Lilgendahl et al., 2018). The study procedure involved participants writing a response to two narrative prompts about memories concerning being bicultural (Lilgendahl et al., 2018).

Participants' written responses were analyzed by two coders for the emotional tone of the memory as a whole and how the memory ended (i.e., was the ending of the narrative growth oriented or not), as well as exploratory processing (Lilgendahl et al., 2018). Exploratory processing was defined as interpretative processing that is intentional, reflective, and elaborate in regard to how the events in the memory relate to individuals' sense of themselves (Lilgendahl et al., 2018). The self-report survey part of this study involved participants rating their heritage culture identification, as well as harmony/conflict and blendedness/distance as measured by the BII-2. The scoring of the BII-2 differed in the Lilgendahl et al. (2018) study from the Schwartz et al. (2019) study, in that a single BII-2 composite score was used in the Lilgendahl et al. (2018) study, with higher scores indicative of more harmony and blendedness (combined). Other quantitative measures in the Lilgendahl et al. (2018) study focused on participants' positive and negative affect. See Table 5.2b.

Study results showed that most memories had an overall emotionality to them that was somewhat negative, and yet positively charged memories were also generated by study participants (Lilgendahl et al., 2018). Some results showed that a positive ending valence of the narrative was associated with more blendedness and harmony (Lilgendahl et al., 2018). Narrative explorative processing was only associated with blendedness and harmony in a correlation analysis for memory 2 and not 1, and this significant association did not remain in the regression analysis that controlled for the presence of other study constructs. Lilgendahl and colleagues interpreted the meaning of this finding as follows:

> . . . both negative and positive memories may be important for healthy narrative identity development, but in different ways and requiring different types of processing . . . Indeed, positive bicultural memories may affirm identity in an uncomplicated way, whereas negative bicultural memories may require some reflection and processing for positive meaning to emerge that supports developing feelings of bicultural identity harmony and blendedness.
>
> (Lilgendahl et al., 2018, p. 1611)

In summary, the two research exemplars chosen for this chapter had innovative study designs, were theoretically diverse, and, most importantly, were in keeping with the central theme of this chapter, specifically examining the identity implications of the intersection of belonging to more than one cultural community.[9] The central limitation of these research exemplar studies concerns study generalizability, in that these study samples were not nationally representative samples of university students living in the U.S., clearly nonrepresentative of the global population of young people. Further, the samples were in the late adolescent to young adult age range, further limiting generalizability to early and middle adolescents and late adolescents in high school or out of work, study, or training. Given that there are key limitations, these exemplar studies remain creative and forward-looking.

Summary

Take-home messages from this chapter are that bicultural identity has high societal importance in light of globalization through the global movement of ideas and people. Further, bicultural identity is a long-standing subject of inquiry across different psychological fields, such as developmental, social and personality, cultural, and acculturation psychology. These fields would benefit from more scholarly interchange, and there have been calls for more conceptual bridging ideas and cross-subfield research efforts (e.g., Motti-Stefanidi, 2018; Phinney et al., 2001; Sam, 2024; Schwartz et al., 2006; Ward & Szabó, 2023). The research exemplars in this chapter illustrate some of the potential value added by this type of bridging research.

In research aimed at understanding the strengths of young people who are part of a minority group and/or have immigration experiences, including identity development, it is important to be prepared to expect diversity within any given minority group and to conceptualize what it means to adapt and thrive in relation to that group's context (e.g., Marks et al., 2020). Researchers in this area have also stressed the importance of using culturally and situationally relevant intersectional research approaches and theory (e.g., Cunningham et al., 2023; Spencer, 2021). Research and theory development on bicultural identity would benefit from a greater incorporation of intersectional research approaches conducted in a variety of global contexts. Other advances may also be gained by greater inclusion of diverse identity and acculturation concepts, such as comparing and contrasting in the same study the connections and distinctions between bicultural identity elements and identity integration (Mitchell et al., 2021) in research designs that are well-suited to document developmental change and be reflective of the ways that culture is infused throughout adolescents' and emerging adults' identity work (e.g., Rogoff, 2023).

Notes

1 This passage comes from pilot interviews undertaken by Laura Ferrer-Wreder in 2025 to obtain background information about bicultural identity development; a pseudonym was used in this quote.

2 Theories and research conclusions of Chapters 2 through 4 are revisited when fitting and useful to advancing what we know about identity in the selected areas addressed in Chapters 5–8.

3 Intersectionality involves the use of certain guiding principles as a basis for scientific research; such principles include the recognition of complexity and how social power is important to human development. Specifically, some guiding principles are that groups are diverse, and this diversity should not be ignored in a scientific study, and science should seek to understand social power dynamics as it relates to groups and the individual (Cole, 2009; Crenshaw, 1991). Further, the subject of research attention in some intersectional research perspectives on identity is what it means to be part of more than one group, or in other words, what a person's total identity package is (Azmitia, 2014; Moffitt et al., 2023), and how this is navigated by the individual in particular sociocultural and historical life contexts (e.g., Bowleg et al., 2023). See Moffitt and colleagues' (2023) review of the identity literature and Chapter 6 of this book for more about intersectionality and identity.

4 Mitchell and colleagues (2021) described identity integration as a sense of continuity in one's identity. The identity process of change/development posited to foster identity integration includes identity commitment work, meaning-making, and a growth-oriented explorative process (Mitchell et al., 2021). Identity integration was further described by Mitchell and colleagues (2021) by breaking the concept down into four distinct but potentially intersecting elements, namely, contextual, temporal, ego, and person–society integration, with further description as follows:

- Contextual integration involves harmony across different life domains.
- Temporal integration consists of making meaning out of who one is across one's lifetime and projecting it into the future.
- Ego integration is characterized by a person who has a sense of harmony across life domains and across their lifetime/life course.
- Person–society integration is reflected by how who one is fits with societal and cultural expectations as told through master and alternative narratives.

See Chapter 6 for more on identity integration.

5 The phrase "locked in" is U.S.-based slang used by some adolescents, and it can mean that one is fully committed to or concentrating on something. It can also mean that one is committing or recommitting oneself to a goal. In this chapter, it is the first meaning that is used.

6 Whether or not remote acculturation is beneficial or harmful has been the subject of some research attention, particularly as it relates to health (Jensen, 2022), with some evidence of increased risk for youth in terms of increases in unhealthy diet and smoking associated with a heightened U.S. orientation (Ferguson et al., 2023). However, there has also been evidence for benefits in other areas of health such as physical activity. Take, for example, a cross-sectional study of Jamaican adolescents and their mothers (330 dyads); results showed that for early adolescent participants, the youths' mothers' orientation to a remote culture (the U.S.) was associated with greater physical activity in youth, but that for middle adolescent participants, the adolescents' own orientation to the U.S. culture was connected to greater youth physical activity, and this was interpreted to be related to the greater autonomy of middle relative to early adolescents in this cultural setting (Gillespie et al., 2022). Remote acculturation is less frequently examined than direct acculturation; however, remote acculturation represents an emerging area for identity research. It includes one's globalized identity, or the experiencing of oneself as part of a global human community.

7 Individual differences come out of a tradition of inquiry within psychology called differential psychology, and illustrations of these relatively stable but still malleable psychological differences across people could include intelligence or personality traits.

8 See Chapter 4's section called "Empirical Illustrations of Ethnic and National Identity's Global Relevance" for additional empirical study examples that have implications for understanding bicultural identity.

9 There are other empirically rigorous longitudinal studies that examine adolescents' heritage and national identity over time. See Baumert et al. (2025), Quan et al. (2022), and Schwartz et al. (2016) for examples of these studies.

References

Azmitia, M. (2014). Reflections on the cultural lenses of identity development. In K. C. McLean & M. Syed (Eds.), *The Oxford handbook of identity development* [E-reader version] (pp. 1–20). Oxford University Press. https://doi.org/10.1093/oxfordhb/9780199936564.013.033

Baumert, J., Becker, M., Jansen, M., Nagy, G., & Köller, O. (2025). Development of life satisfaction in immigrant youth: The role of transition decisions and cultural identification. *Journal of Personality and Social Psychology*, *129*(3), 576–601. https://doi.org/10.1037/pspp0000566

Benet-Martínez, V., Lee, F., & Cheng, C. (2021). Bicultural identity integration: Components, psychosocial antecedents, and outcomes. In M. J. Gelfand, C. Chiu, & Y. Hong (Eds.), *Handbook of advances in culture and psychology* (pp. 244–284). Oxford University Press. https://doi.org/10.1093/oso/9780190079741.003.0006

Benet-Martínez, V., Leu, J., Lee, F., & Morris, M. W. (2002). Negotiating biculturalism: Cultural frame switching in biculturals with oppositional versus compatible cultural identities. *Journal of Cross-Cultural Psychology*, *33*(5), 492–516. https://doi.org/10.1177/0022022102033005005

Bowleg, L., Malekzadeh, A. N., AuBuchon, K. E., Ghabrial, M. A., & Bauer, G. R. (2023). Rare exemplars and missed opportunities: Intersectionality within current sexual and gender diversity research and scholarship in psychology. *Current Opinion in Psychology*, *49*, Article 101511. https://doi.org/10.1016/j.copsyc.2022.101511

Cole, E. R. (2009). Intersectionality and research in psychology. *American Psychologist*, *64*(3), 170–180. https://doi.org/10.1037/a0014564

Crenshaw, K. (1991). Mapping the margins: Intersectionality, identity politics, and violence against women of color. *Stanford Law Review*, *43*(6), 1241–1299. https://doi.org/10.2307/1229039

Cunningham, M., Swanson, D. P., Youngblood, J., II, Seaton, E. K., Francois, S., & Ashford, C. (2023). Spencer's Phenomenological Variant of Ecological Systems Theory

(PVEST): Charting its origin and impact. *American Psychologist*, *78*(4), 524–534. https://doi.org/10.1037/amp0001051

de Bruin-Wassinkmaat, A., de Kock, J., Visser-Vogel, E., Bakker, C., & Barnard, M. (2019). Being young and strictly religious: A review of the literature on the religious identity development of strictly religious adolescents. *Identity: An International Journal of Theory and Research*, *19*(1), 62–79. https://doi.org/10.1080/15283488.2019.1566067

Ferguson, G. M., Causadias, J. M., & Simenec, T. S. (2023). Acculturation and psychopathology. *Annual Review of Clinical Psychology*, *19*, 381–411. https://doi.org/10.1146/annurev-clinpsy-080921-080622

Ferguson, G. M., Iturbide, M. I., & Raffaelli, M. (2020). Proximal and remote acculturation: Adolescents' perspectives of biculturalism in two contexts. *Journal of Adolescent Research*, *35*(4), 431–460. https://doi.org/10.1177/0743558419868221

Gillespie, S., Eales, L., Simpson, D. D., & Ferguson, G. M. (2022). Remote acculturation and physical activity among adolescent-mother dyads in Jamaica: A developmental dyadic moderation. *Journal of Cross-Cultural Psychology*, *53*(6), 643–658. https://doi.org/10.1177/00220221221101172

Huynh, Q.-L., Benet-Martínez, V., & Nguyen, A.-M. D. (2018). Measuring variations in bicultural identity across U.S. ethnic and generational groups: Development and validation of the Bicultural Identity Integration Scale – Version 2 (BIIS-2). *Psychological Assessment*, *30*(12), 1581–1596. https://doi.org/10.1037/pas0000606

Jensen, L. A. (2022). Globalization: Human development in a new cultural context. In J. Y. Chiao, S. Li, R. Turner, S. Y. Lee-Tauler, & B. A. Pringle (Eds.), *The Oxford handbook of cultural neuroscience and global mental health* (pp. 464–484). Oxford University Press. https://doi.org/10.1093/oxfordhb/9780190057695.013.24

Karataş, S. (2025). Zooming in on proximal life domains: A literature review on family, peer, and school dynamics in adolescents' acculturation and psychosocial adjustment. *European Journal of Developmental Psychology*, *22*(3), 317–339. https://doi.org/10.1080/17405629.2024.2433754

Katzarska-Miller, I., & Faucher, M. (2022). Changes in conceptualization of self and identity as a function of globalization. In I. Katzarska-Miller & S. Reysen (Eds.), *Globalized identities: The impact of globalization on self and identity* (pp. 19–51). Palgrave Macmillan/Springer Nature. https://doi.org/10.1007/978-3-031-04644-5_2

Lilgendahl, J. P., Benet-Martinez, V., Bishop, M., Gilson, K., Festa, L., Levenson, C., & Rosenblum, R. (2018). "So now, I wonder, what am I?": A narrative approach to bicultural identity integration. *Journal of Cross-Cultural Psychology*, *49*(10), 1596–1624. https://doi.org/10.1177/0022022118801555

Marks, A. K., Woolverton, G. A., & Coll, C. G. (2020). Risk and resilience in minority youth populations. *Annual Review of Clinical Psychology*, *16*, 151–163. https://doi.org/10.1146/annurev-clinpsy-071119-115839

Matsumoto, D., & Hwang, H. C. (2021). Culture and psychology. In J. Y. Chiao, S. Li, R. Turner, S. Y. Lee-Tauler, & B. A. Pringle (Eds.), *The Oxford handbook of cultural neuroscience and global mental health* (pp. 57–74). Oxford University Press. https://doi.org/10.1093/oxfordhb/9780190057695.001.0001

McAuliffe, M., & Oucho, L. A. (Eds.). (2024). *World migration report 2024*. International Organization for Migration (IOM), Geneva. https://publications.iom.int/books/world-migration-report-2024

Meca, A., Allison, K., Cruz, B., Wright, A., Gonzales-Backen, M., & Scury, M. (2023). Cultural identity development among ethnic-racial minorities: An examination of ethnic-racial identity, national identity, and biculturalism. In B. Halpern-Felsher (Ed.), *Encyclopedia of child and adolescent health* (1st ed., pp. 79–92). Elsevier. https://doi.org/10.1016/B978-0-12-818872-9.00178-3

Mitchell, L. L., Adler, J. M., Carlsson, J., Eriksson, P. L., & Syed, M. (2021). A conceptual review of identity integration across adulthood. *Developmental Psychology, 57*(11), 1981–1990. https://doi.org/10.1037/dev0001246
Moffitt, U., Katsiaficas, D., Ghavami, N., Minor, I., Padilla, D., & Rogers, L. O. (2023). Intersectionality and identity: A systematic review and qualitative analysis of U.S. research in psychological science. *Identity: An International Journal of Theory and Research, 23*(4), 288–313. https://doi.org/10.1080/15283488.2023.2223647
Motti-Stefanidi, F. (2018). Resilience among immigrant youth: The role of culture, development and acculturation. *Developmental Review, 50*, Part A, 99–109. https://doi.org/10.1016/j.dr.2018.04.002
Phinney, J. S., Horenczyk, G., Liebkind, K., & Vedder, P. (2001). Ethnic identity, immigration, and well-being: An interactional perspective. *Journal of Social Issues, 57*(3), 493–510. https://doi.org/10.1111/0022-4537.00225
Quan, C., Costigan, C. L., & Kobayashi, K. M. (2022). Ethnic and national identity development processes: The role of cultural behaviors and gender. *Cultural Diversity & Ethnic Minority Psychology, 28*(1), 1–12. https://doi.org/10.1037/cdp0000475
Rogoff, B. (2023). Mutually constituting, fractal: Individual and cultural aspects of holistic process. *Review of Research in Education, 47*(1), 60–83. https://doi.org/10.3102/0091732X231224666
Sam, D. L. (2024). 50+ years of psychological acculturation research: Progress and challenges. *International Journal of Intercultural Relations, 103*, Article: 102076, 1–13. https://doi.org/10.1016/j.ijintrel.2024.102076
Schwartz, S. J., Meca, A., Ward, C., Szabó, Á., Benet-Martínez, V., Lorenzo-Blanco, E., Sznitman, G. A., Cobb, C. L., Szapocznik, J., Unger, J. B., Cano, M. Á., Stuart, J., & Zamboanga, B. L. (2019). Biculturalism dynamics: A daily diary study of bicultural identity and psychosocial functioning. *Journal of Applied Developmental Psychology, 62*, 26–37. https://doi.org/10.1016/j.appdev.2018.12.007
Schwartz, S. J., Montgomery, M. J., & Briones, E. (2006). The role of identity in acculturation among immigrant people: Theoretical propositions, empirical questions, and applied recommendations. *Human Development, 49*(1), 1–30. https://doi.org/10.1159/000090300
Schwartz, S. J., Unger, J. B., Baezconde-Garbanati, L., Zamboanga, B. L., Córdova, D., Lorenzo-Blanco, E. I., Huang, S., Des Rosiers, S. E., Soto, D. W., Lizzi, K. M., Villamar, J. A., Pattarroyo, M., & Szapocznik, J. (2016). Testing the parent–adolescent acculturation discrepancy hypothesis: A five-wave longitudinal study. *Journal of Research on Adolescence, 26*(3), 567–586. https://doi.org/10.1111/jora.12214
Spencer, M. B. (2021). Acknowledging bias and pursuing protections to support anti-racist developmental science: Critical contributions of phenomenological variant of ecological systems theory. *Journal of Adolescent Research, 36*(6), 569–583. https://doi.org/10.1177/07435584211045129
Syed, M., & McLean, K. C. (2016). Understanding identity integration: Theoretical, methodological, and applied issues. *Journal of Adolescence, 47*(1), 109–118. https://doi.org/10.1016/j.adolescence.2015.09.005
Szabó, Á., Ward, C., Meca, A., & Schwartz, S. J. (2020). Testing the construct validity and empirical distinctiveness of the Multicultural Identity Styles Scale (MISS) and the Bicultural Identity Integration Scale (BIIS-2) [Supplementary material, p. 1–2]. *Psychological Assessment, 32*(7), 705–712. https://doi.org/10.1037/pas0000825
Tajfel, H., & Turner, J. (1986). The social identity theory of intergroup behavior. In W. Austin & S. Worchel (Eds.), *Psychology of intergroup relations* (pp. 7–24). Nelson-Hall.
Turner, B. S., Khondker, H. H., & Robertson, R. (2010). *Globalization east and west.* Sage Publications. https://doi.org/10.4135/9781446251089
Umaña-Taylor, A. J., Quintana, S. M., Lee, R. M., Cross, W. E., Rivas-Drake, D., Schwartz, S. J., Syed, M., Yip, T., & Seaton, E. (2014). Ethnic and racial identity during

adolescence and into young adulthood: An integrated conceptualization. *Child Development, 85*(1), 21–39. https://doi.org/10.1111/cdev.12196
UNICEF – United Nations Children's Fund (2021, April). *Migration.* UNICEF. https://data.unicef.org/topic/child-migration-and-displacement/migration/
Ward, C., Ng Tseung-Wong, C., Szabo, A., Qumseya, T., & Bhowon, U. (2018). Hybrid and alternating identity styles as strategies for managing multicultural identities. *Journal of Cross-Cultural Psychology, 49*(9), 1402–1439. https://doi.org/10.1177/0022022118782641
Ward, C., & Szabó, Á. (2023). Acculturation, cultural identity and well-being. *Nature Reviews: Psychology, 2*(5), 267–282. https://doi.org/10.1038/s44159-023-00171-2

6 Intersectionality and the Confluence of Gender and Sexual Identity

> Last week I went in to take the written test for my driver's license. The form said I had to check whether I was male or female. I always hate that kind of question – like there are only those two gender options! For me, it's kind of a fluid sort of thing – whether I feel male or female, or maybe nothing at all . . . it's all kind of uncertain for me right now. . . .
>
> (Sam, 17-year-old high school student)

Intersectionality and identity integration are approaches that scientists can use in order to avoid disaggregating, isolating, or statistically controlling away the nuance described in the quote above. Like the previous chapter, this and the subsequent chapters (i.e., Chapters 5, 6, 7, and 8) are unique in focus and organization. They are dedicated to describing novel extensions and mapping where the edges of our knowledge are in selected identity areas. This chapter explores how intersectionality and identity integration can deepen what we know about adolescent gender and sexual identity development.

Briefly, intersectionality is a framework that can guide research (Bowleg et al., 2023). It encourages researchers to attend to how people live within social and power structures while also considering a person's total identity package across salient life domains (Moffitt et al., 2023). Identity integration is based on Eriksonian psychosocial theory and focuses on individuals' sense of continuity and/or wholeness in their identity across contexts and time (Mitchell et al., 2021; Syed & McLean, 2016).

In this chapter, the first section is an overview of intersectionality and identity integration. Then, there is an explanation of other ideas important to understanding psychological research about adolescent gender and sexual identity. To give further life to these concepts, they are seen in light of a selected theory about gender or sexual identity. Although there are growing synergies, historically, theories and the psychological research literature on gender and sexual identity have developed in parallel (Quintana & Pfaus, 2024). This second chapter section reflects this division, in that key concepts connected to gender identity are addressed first, followed by concepts relevant to sexual identity. In these sections, there is also a critical reflection on the past and current meanings of these concepts. This segment is

DOI: 10.4324/9781003486336-6

followed by a chapter section in which two key research examples are discussed in detail in order to provide a concrete illustration of themes and/or research practices consistent with intersectionality and/or identity integration. A summary concludes the chapter.

Bridging Ideas

Intersectionality

Intersectionality has transdisciplinary importance. The approach has been used in psychology, sociology, social work, human–computer interaction, and developmental science, as well as literature, legal, feminist, critical race, and women's studies (Bowleg et al., 2023; Hammack & Manago, 2025), and has been important to the ongoing struggles for civil rights movements for many groups (Crenshaw, 1991; Russell et al., 2023). Intersectionality is not a psychological theory that explains how identity development takes place but rather a framework for scientific research. Aspects of Erikson's (1968) lifespan psychosocial theory and the concept of identity integration (Syed & McLean, 2016) can be applied in ways that are consistent with an intersectional approach and pick up where intersectionality leaves off.

Parent and colleagues (2013, p. 640), in reference to conclusions reached by Stewart and McDermott (2004), concisely summed up several of the core ideas of intersectionality as focusing on "nonhomogeneity of groups, location of persons within power structures and acknowledgement of the relations between those structures, and the unique effects of identifying within more than one group." "Nonhomogeneity of groups" (Parent et al., 2013, p. 640) refers to people who see themselves as part of a social group, for example, women, who will have similarities but will also come to that group with important individual and subgroup differences.

From the perspective of intersectionality and the effects of identifying with more than one subgroup, one facet of identity does not take precedence over another. It is the total package of how people put together their identity in combination with what individuals and society deem as important (in regard to identity), and these intersections are the subjects of scientific inquiry (Bowleg et al., 2023). By using the tenets of intersectionality, many studies have provided new insights into the experience and implications of what it is like for a person to belong to more than one world and/or cultural community (e.g., Hammack & Wignall, 2023; Russell et al., 2023). For example, is the confluence of gender, social class, immigration experience, and where the person is in the lifespan most important for understanding this person's identity, as well as their health, well-being, and life chances?

From a scientific perspective, Cole (2009, p. 176) challenged researchers to ask themselves, "Who is included within this category?" For example, if researchers intend to learn more about adolescent girls as part of a study, where does the sample of adolescent girls come from, what historical time period is the study conducted in, what country and what regions are the samples recruited from, and are they recruited from a school, a recreation group, or online? What are these adolescent girls' life conditions, and can these conditions be measured as part of the study?

Scholars working with an intersectional approach would also argue that finding answers to the aforementioned questions has value because the unique content of individuals' total identity package can be essential to gaining insight into people's subjective experiences of themselves. Put differently, what is it like from an individual's perspective to have to navigate multiple identity classifications, some of which do not provide a good identity fit? A statement made by a participant (Marina) in Hammack and colleagues' study illustrates this point well when she stated:

> I don't really think of it as gender. I think of it as more of a feeling. If I look at [a form] where I have to fill out a gender. I'm not like. "I should've picked male. I should've picked female." I feel genderqueer, but I don't wanna change my name and stuff like that. It's just different for anyone. I don't talk about it a lot, because I just don't wanna have to explain myself.
>
> (Hammack et al., 2022, p. 192)

By using an intersectional approach, researchers plan their studies so that they can learn about the complexity and distinctiveness of a person's identity as a whole.

Cole (2009) also encouraged researchers to be aware of intersectional considerations from the beginning of a study, when hypotheses and research questions are formulated, and when a sample is recruited. An intersectional approach would also be important to the later steps of a study when findings are considered in light of what happened in the study and how the study results fit into the wider research literature. This approach would mean that study findings are not overgeneralized and interpretations are not just about individuals being fundamentally different from one another but also that studies consider how differences in psychological outcomes may be due to specific differences in life circumstances (Cole, 2009).

Finally, regarding what Parent and colleagues (2013, p. 640) called the ". . . location of persons within power structures and acknowledgement of the relations between those structures," intersectional research takes into consideration the importance of power and appreciating where people find themselves in a social hierarchy due to their identity (Cole, 2009). If a particular combination of social identity components comes along with social privileges and/or discrimination, then it is vital to understand that unique confluence of benefits and barriers and to recognize that these identity pluses and minuses will not simply be additive or segregated; in other words, the impact on a person is not on a "single axis (e.g., 'race *or* gender')" but are conflated with one another (Bowleg et al., 2023, p. 1). In terms of research practice, structural inequality between people based on their identity is given due consideration when researchers attempt to explain the "why" behind their study results (Cole, 2009).

As intersectionality has gained more visibility and use, concerns have been raised about how individual studies can drift from the approach's original aims. In response, Rosette and colleagues (2025) proposed an expanded way of conceptualizing intersectional research so that when a departure happens from what they termed “primary intersectionality” (i.e., the research focus is about Black women and social inequality), it is clear and recognized. As they explained, “We suggest dividing intersectionality based upon where they fall along two primary dimensions: (1) social inequity focus (present, absent) and (2) demographic content (Black women, subordinate groups, assorted groups)” (Rosette et al., 2025, p. 2). The utility of expansive visions for intersectional research is yet to be determined. However, this kind of conceptual work is needed as intersectional research is conducted with greater frequency outside of its origins in the U.S.

Identity Integration

Identity integration, as described by Syed and McLean (2016) and later applied to the study of adulthood by Mitchell and colleagues (2021), is rooted in Erikson’s (1968) descriptions of the role of continuity in identity development across context and time. In Syed and McLean’s (2016) view of identity integration, four types of identity integration are important: contextual, temporal, ego, and person–society. Contextual integration concerns the ways in which people bring harmony or make peace out of who they are across different areas or domains of their lives. Temporal integration is often captured as part of narrative identity studies, in which people reflect on and describe how they make sense of who they are across their past, present, and expected future. Ego integration is viewed as the combination of both contextual and temporal integration. In other words, how do people come to a workable coexistence between personally and socially important facets of their identity over the course of their lives? Person–society integration refers to the degree of fit that one’s identity has with what is expected within an individual’s society and culture as reflected by master narratives, as well as the expectations of important others (Syed & McLean, 2016).

Identity integration seeks to explain how people can pull different parts of their identities together across context and time into authentic and meaningful infusions that are uniquely their own, as well as acknowledge the role that other people and wider sociocultural factors play in inhibiting or fostering such integration. Processes thought to be important to developing a sense of integration include active and ongoing identity commitment work (i.e., reevaluation and reaffirmation of commitments) and meaning-making, as well as engagement in explorative processes dedicated to personal growth (Mitchell et al., 2021).

Key Concepts and Reflections About Gender Identity

Physiological Sex, Gender, Gender Identity, and Bussey’s Theory

Conceptualizations of physiological sex (also called natal sex) and gender are undergoing reconsideration (Quintana & Pfaus, 2024). Diamond and colleagues provided a clear formulation of physiological sex when they stated that:

> Sex is most often used to describe one’s status as male or female . . . determined biologically via sex chromosomes and assessed at birth by the

> appearance of external genitalia (which generally suffices, except for rare disorders of sexual differentiation in which there may be disjunctures between chromosomal sex and genital morphology).
>
> (Diamond et al., 2011, p. 25)

At birth, physiological sex can be assigned (as male, female, or intersex, based on multidimensional criteria), and aspects of physiological sex can be part of a person's embodied experience (Diamond, 2020). Gender is an expansive concept and is widely considered to be the product of interacting psychological and sociocultural/historical processes. For example, Quintana and Pfaus noted that:

> . . . gender is a socially-constructed entity that defines modes of expression (e.g., play, dress, appearance, attitude) as feminine, masculine, both (e.g., Two-Spirited), or as the multitude of degrees/types of agendered or genderqueer expressions. People may define their gender as binary (masculine or feminine), or along a continuum between the two.
>
> (Quintana & Pfaus, 2024, p. 2969)

By extension, gender identity development involves the processes (e.g., exploration, commitment, meaning-making, and interaction with master narratives) by which people come to see themselves through a gendered lens as well as the ways in which people resist gender as central to the vision of who they are and what matters in their lives.

Some scholars have advocated for a conception of physiological sex and gender that considers these entities as distinct but interrelated (e.g., Quintana & Pfaus, 2024). Other scholars have argued that physiological sex and gender are both sociocultural and historical constructions created by people (e.g., Magnusson & Marecek, 2018). A constructed view of sex and gender has been advocated as a way to include people who do not see their sex and gender as binary (i.e., male or female), as well as in light of observed physiological variation in humans – in criteria sometimes used to determine physiological sex (e.g., sex chromosomes and external genitalia; van Anders, 2015). A constructed view has also been advocated based on how sex and gender have historically been formulated by cultures in various parts of the world. Indeed, some cultures have long had more than two categories for physiological sex and/or have more contingent or context-/role-specific designations to determine a person's sex (Magnusson & Marecek, 2018). Morgenroth proposed a reboot for gender and by implication its relation to physiological sex by stating:

> . . . rather than abandoning the idea of a "true" gender, I argue that we should redefine what "true gender" means, acknowledging that for some people gender does feel innate and static, while others experience it as changing over time and in response to social processes and pressures. Both experiences can be "true," and the former should not be seen as the only way to have a "true" gender identity. . . .
>
> (Morgenroth, 2025, p. 500)

This proposal fits well with an authenticity master narrative (Hammack & Manago, 2025) that emphasizes the importance of living and narrating about one's inner and outer life in ways that are true to one's own life experiences.

Gender plays a substantial role in everyday life and is a defining consideration in the distribution of social power within many societies (Ghavami et al., 2016). Research studies concur that people come to understand gender as a social category and will eventually attempt to see themselves in relation to how gender is conceptualized in their culture and come to adopt a gender identity that is in line with, diverges from, or rejects societal expectations (Baams & Kaufman, 2023; Diamond et al., 2011). Identity issues and questions regarding gender can remain relevant throughout a person's life and can also be significantly reevaluated across development as the place and value of gender itself change in a given society (Diamond, 2023).

There are many disciplines, frameworks, and more specific theories relevant to the study of gender and/or sexual identity development, such as feminist psychology (Magnusson & Marecek, 2018), queer theory (van Anders et al., 2025), dynamical systems models (Diamond, 2018; Diamond et al., 2011), gender schema theory, differential developmental trajectories (Savin-Williams, 2011), social identity theory, social cognitive theory, the identity status model, narrative identity combined with life course approaches (Hammack & Cohler, 2011), and sexual configurations theory (van Anders, 2015). Several of these perspectives would agree that gender identity and sexual identity are multidimensional, multi-determined, and open to change over time, but precisely how physiological sex, gender, and sexuality relate to one another; what dimensions of gender and sexuality are emphasized/measured; and the particulars of how and when change takes place can be points of difference.

One can take Bussey's (2011) theory and its update by Jackson and Bussey (2023) as illustrative of a model in which developmental processes involving gender identity take center stage. This model is an extension of Bandura's social cognitive model. Bussey (2011) proposed that certain factors interact to cocreate gender identity and are instrumental to change in gender identity over time. These factors include aspects of people at the individual level, as well as behavioral and environmental levels. Individual factors include how people understand their physiological sex and gender, self-regulation, agency, and other socio-cognitive processes such as self-efficacy. Behavioral factors include what people do – how gender is signified by individuals' behaviors by doing or enacting gender in everyday life – people select environments. Environmental factors include social, cultural, historical, and structural – how other people react to a person's gender identity as well as how others might model gender, how groups can come together to actualize change as it regards the welfare of gender-related groups, and the social benefits and disadvantages related to gender in a society.

These three multidimensional factors – the person, behavior, and environment – are thought to combine and mutually influence one another, with an emphasis on social factors (e.g., learning through one's own experience and learning through observation) as being a driver of developmental change, particularly early on in development, and individual factors take on greater explanatory weight as children develop their identity (Jackson & Bussey, 2023). In this model, developmental change in gender identity is considered to be ongoing and connected to how gender is learned and navigated by individuals in a given social context (Jackson & Bussey, 2023).[1]

Gender Diversity: Beyond Either/Or Conceptualizations

A mutually exclusive (i.e., one or the other – only female or male), two-category approach to conceptualizing physiological sex and gender has been challenged for a number of reasons (e.g., van Anders, 2015). The two-gender-only way of seeing the physical sex and gender of a person does not encompass the bodies and life experiences of all people (Diamond et al., 2011; Hammack & Manago, 2025; Russell et al., 2023). For instance, people who are gender diverse encompass the many ways in which people make sense of who they are in terms of their bodies and gender, including individuals who have a sense of their gender as different from their birth sex assignment, in other words, transgender, which may or may not involve physical changes to a person's body (Diamond et al., 2011).

Other gender-diverse people may identify with a nonbinary gender identity and may reject gender as self-defining to varying extents and/or may identify somewhere in between or above gender with a unique combination of elements of gender expression put together by the person in a relatively permanent or in a more fluid way (i.e., self-descriptions that people use in these cases have included genderqueer, gender fluid, agender, and/or gender expansive; Russell et al., 2023). Across the lifespan, people whose birth sex assignment and gender identity match (i.e., cisgender) as well as people who have a gender-diverse identity are both likely to engage in exploration and questioning about what gender means in their lives (Baams & Kaufman, 2023; Diamond et al., 2011). As with identity development in general, adolescence and emerging adulthood are prime times to engage in identity work in these areas.

Key Concepts About Sexual Identity and Reflections on the Intersection of Sexual and Gender Identity

Sexuality, Sexual Identity, and Dillon and Colleagues' Theory

Relative to the past, sexuality and sexual identity are viewed in a more multidimensional, diverse (i.e., plural), and changeable light (Diamond, 2023; Hammack & Manago, 2025). Sexual identity is a wide construct that encompasses a number of facets and developmental processes (Savin-Williams, 2011). An important part of sexual identity is sexuality itself, which involves "sexual needs, sexual values, modes of sexual expression, preferred characteristics of sexual partners, preferred sexual activities and behaviors" (Dillon et al., 2011, p. 27). Other dimensions of sexual identity include sexual orientation and sexual orientation identity (Dillon et al., 2011). According to Savin-Williams (2011, p. 672), "sexual orientation is a deeply rooted predisposition toward erotic or sexual fantasies, thoughts, affiliations, affection or bonding with members of one's sex, the other sex, both sexes, or, perhaps, neither sex (asexuality)." Diamond (2023) likened human sexual orientation, which she called sexual patterning, to weighted dice, and the weighted part indicates a proclivity for the dice to land on a certain number, but the actual number that appears on the dice will in fact vary depending on the surface they are rolled on. The loaded dice metaphor reflects a complex interplay between biopsychosocial and contextual interactions that take place in a person's life. More precisely, she noted:

> Environmentally-contingent neural plasticity-specifically plasticity in response to social environments – is the human master adaptation, the advance from which all other advances flow. Although human sexual patterning undoubtedly starts with some deep prenatal roots – "loaded dice" as it were – the surface they land on (grass? wood? wet ice?) affects what shows up.
>
> (Diamond, 2023, p. 2989)

Sexual orientation identity involves a self-recognition of one's sexual orientation as part of one's identity (Dillon et al., 2011). In psychological studies, sexual orientation has been defined and measured in many ways (Baams & Kaufman, 2023). In such studies, people have been asked to self-identify into a category such as heterosexual, homosexual, or bisexual (Baams & Kaufman, 2023). Other identifications that have become more prominent in public discourse and scientific studies include plural (e.g., pansexual, queer) identifications as well as asexual, gray, and demisexual (ace spectrum – can include not experiencing sexual attraction, experiencing sexual attraction less frequently, or only in certain circumstances) and open-ended responses that allow for greater specificity and unique combinations of the confluence of gender/sexuality (Hammack & Manago, 2025). Sexual orientation categories/labels on a gradient have also been used in psychological studies, such as "mostly heterosexual" and "mostly homosexual," reflecting an approach pioneered early on in the study of sexuality (i.e., the Kinsey scale; Diamond, 2023). Although self-categorization into a label or social category can open up possibilities for essential support from a chosen community and can signal to others an openness for new experiences, self-categorization remains but one facet of gender and sexual identity (Baams & Kaufman, 2023; Russell et al., 2023).

The model of sexual identity development described next, as an illustrative theory by Dillon and colleagues (2011), relies in part on ideas from Erik Erikson and James Marcia's identity status model. Dillon and colleagues' (2011) theory consists of concepts such as personal and social identity, exploration and commitment, and identity status. The patterns of change in Dillon's model are relatively cyclical, as they are in Marcia's model of identity development through adulthood, but the starting points in the two models differ (a foreclosure-like status for Dillon and a diffusion status for Marcia as the respective model starting points). Yet there are many similarities between these models, such as the value placed on the individual's search and co-construction of identity, the importance of the context for identity development, and optimal identity development involving a sense of coherence and authenticity.

In Dillon and colleagues' (2011) model, sexual identity is viewed as multidimensional. At the individual personal identity level (i.e., at an intrapsychic level), sexual identity includes a person's sexuality, sexual orientation, and sexual orientation identity. In terms of social identity, individuals can have an open or tacit identification and sense of belonging to a sexual identity-related social group(s) as well as hold beliefs/attitudes about such groups, including an awareness of social power differentials between groups (Dillon et al., 2011). Individual and social identity come together to make up a person's sexual identity, and change happens in the model through identity exploration and commitment, similar to how it is conceptualized by Erikson and Marcia's identity status model (Dillon et al., 2011).

It should be noted that in Dillon and colleagues' (2011) model, there are identity statuses, and individuals' progress in their sexual identity development through these statuses is viewed in relatively malleable ways, in which:

> . . . there are opportunities for circularity and revisiting of statuses throughout the lifespan for a given individual. Thus, points in the model should be thought of as non-linear, flexible, and fluid descriptions of statuses through which people may pass as they develop their sexual identity over the lifespan.
> (Dillon et al., 2011, p. 658)

In this model, people begin their first encounters with their sexual identity with an uncritical adoption of whatever is considered expected in terms of sexuality in their culture (Dillon et al., 2011). Sexual identity (and its interaction with gender identity) is a unique domain of identity development in that sociocultural pressures to conform to particular norms may be highly potent (Diamond, 2023). Dillon and colleagues (2011) proposed that adoption of this unexamined default sexual identity (i.e., like the foreclosed status in Marcia's identity status model) is also likely to involve an uncritical acceptance of the status quo around social advantage and disadvantage for sexual identity-related groups, with the likely privileging of heterosexuality in many cultures. This starting point in sexual identity development is called compulsory heterosexuality by Dillon and colleagues (2011).

According to this model, a moratorium-like period of active identity exploration can move a person out of compulsory heterosexuality and would involve trying out different ideas, behaviors, and preferences related to sexuality (Dillon et al., 2011). Active exploration is intentional and can include behaviors and thought. It is also possible that a person can transition out of compulsory heterosexuality by adopting a type of diffusion orientation in which there is little attention and care paid to exploring or settling on a sexual identity. People can also move directly out of compulsory heterosexuality into a period of deepening commitment in relation to their sexual identity, where the sexual identity is solidified and incorporated into a person's identity (Dillon et al., 2011).

An optimal point in sexual identity development is characterized by the status called synthesis, in which the personal and social aspects of sexual identity are in harmony with each other, and sexual identity is clear, authentic, and self-accepting (Dillon et al., 2011). Synthesis in terms of sexual identity development should be associated with a sense of integration between other aspects of identity that are relevant to sexuality (e.g., gender, religion). Synthesis is not considered to be a permanent end state, and, as noted earlier, this model has the possibility for movement back through the various statuses as the person goes through life and as societal conditions surrounding sexuality change. This model is change-focused and aims to encompass a diversity of experiences.[2] Such models are important given that research studies indicate that some individuals are likely to change, and yet still others will show stability in aspects of sexuality (e.g., sexual attractions and behaviors) and sexual identity from adolescence into emerging adulthood (Baams & Kaufman, 2023; Bishop et al., 2024; Diamond, 2023; Morgan, 2013).

Diversity in Sexual and Gender Identity: Beyond Either/Or Conceptualizations

Research efforts are now focused on understanding adolescent gender and sexual identity with a consideration of diversity and intersections in development. What are a few of the lessons learned so far?[3] Baams and Kaufman (2023, p. 1004) conducted a narrative literature review of published larger-scale population-based studies conducted from 2000 to 2022 with adolescents who are gender and/or sexually diverse (i.e., SOGIE), which they defined as "adolescents who are minoritized and marginalized for their sexual orientation and gender/identity expression (SOGIE)." Examples of gender-diverse people would include those who reported gender as transgender, genderqueer, or gender fluid, or reported a mismatch between sex assigned at birth and gender. Examples of sexual diversity would include lesbian, gay, bisexual, questioning, pansexual, queer, and not sure.

The Baams and Kaufman (2023) review showed that studies had variable measurement practices in regard to asking adolescents about their sexuality and gender identity. For example, many studies would only ask about one facet of sexuality, like attraction or sexual experience or self-identified sexual identity, and this could then impact the percentage of youth who end up in a group or subgroup (based on their experience levels). These scholars also found that it was more common to ask about attraction rather than sexual identity and noted cases where there was a lack of preparation in measurement practices so that bisexual, pansexual, and queer adolescents, as well as transgender and nonbinary adolescents, could identify themselves (Baams & Kaufman, 2023). In other research (e.g., Feinstein et al., 2023), patterns of exposure to discrimination varied by adolescents who identified as bisexual, pansexual, or queer and those adolescents who used multiple sexual identity labels. Thus, as Baams and Kaufman noted:

> . . . our understanding of these concepts and the health and wellbeing of sexually and gender diverse adolescents is limited by the questions we ask, how flexible we allow our surveys and interviews to be, and whether we enable adolescents to report on how they experience sexuality and gender.
>
> (Baams & Kaufman, 2023, p. 1014)

Other lessons learned are that relative to older generations, younger generations may be more likely to self-identify as sexually diverse earlier but that first attractions (10–11 years old) and sexual behaviors (14–15 years old) of sexually diverse youth were similar across cohorts (Bishop et al., 2024). Another line of important research has to do with gender and sexually diverse youth and their health and well-being in the proximal developmental context of schools. Large-scale studies have shown that gender and sexually diverse adolescents benefit from positivc, inclusive school policies (Ioverno et al., 2025; Real et al., 2024) and informed, inclusive school personnel attitudes/behavior (Ioverno et al., 2025; McCauley et al., 2025). In short, intersectionality research approaches are being used more often in the study of adolescent gender and sexual diversity, and this line of inquiry is resulting in a more comprehensive and holistic view of adolescent identity development. Unfortunately, research on adolescent sexuality as a part of human development is not well studied in many parts of the world, and this problem remains a critical limitation in our understanding of adolescence (Baams & Kaufman, 2023).

Research Exemplars

New frontiers for identity research involve realizing, in everyday research practice, all that is implied by bridging ideas like intersectionality and identity integration. As noted in the prior section, scholars have explored and documented how identity intersections are working across a variety of domains and with a diversity of methods (e.g., Baams & Kaufman, 2023; Hammack et al., 2022). As a case in point, in a systematic review of U.S.-based intersectional identity studies, Moffitt and colleagues (2023) found that 149 studies had research findings about the intersection of gender and sexual identity (with adult and adolescent samples, notably using a different literature search approach than the aforementioned Bamms and Kaufman 2023 review). In this chapter section, we focus on two research studies that specifically concern the intersection between adolescent gender and sexual identity. These research exemplars, in different ways, illustrate themes consistent with intersectionality (Cole, 2009) and/or identity integration (Syed & McLean, 2016).

Watson and Colleagues' (2020) Study

The first research exemplar does not directly address identity development. However, this study is important because it was conducted with a sample of contemporary adolescents, and the study results illustrated some of the potential shifts that may be happening around the language used by some youth to describe their gender and sexual identity in the U.S.

The study included 17,112 adolescents, and study recruitment was through community organizations and via social media. Study selection criteria were that youth were 13–17 years old, English speaking, identified as LGBTQ, and lived in the United States (U.S.) during the study participation period (Watson et al., 2020). Youth were asked to self-identify their ethnoracial identity, sex assigned at birth, gender identity, and sexual orientation. Gender identity was measured first by a set of categories (e.g., female, male, and other options) and a "something else" option. If the "something else" option was endorsed, then an open-ended response was made available (this was an adaptive online survey). The gender identity response along with a question of sex assigned at birth allowed for a degree of breadth and depth in the measurement of gender identity. For sexual orientation, a set of options was given, and if "something else" was endorsed, then another set of options was provided, and if "something else" was endorsed again, this was then followed by an open-ended response. The forced-choice categories resulted in 12 gender and 14 sexual orientation identities.

Study results showed that youth commonly used traditional combinations of gender and sexual identity labels (Watson et al., 2020). Most of the sample (67%) identified as cisgender boys or girls and 33% as other genders (e.g., transgender boy, transgender girl, nonbinary transmasculine, or nonbinary transfeminine). A majority of adolescents (73%) also identified as gay, lesbian, bisexual, or heterosexual, and 24% identified as other sexualities (i.e., pansexual, queer, asexual, or questioning). There was a great deal of variation among the write-in labels. For sexual identity, write-in labels included (based on a thematic analysis) "sexually ambiguous, andro sexuality . . ., asexual and queer . . ., sexual identity with caveats, flexible, no label, objectum sexual, focused on dating status, meta sexual, omnisexual, romantic-focused identity, polysexual" (Watson et al., 2020, p. 438).

Other findings in Watson et al. (2020) concerned patterns in the data across constructs and subgroup variation. As noted, emerging sexual identity labels were not in the majority but also were not uncommon. Other analyses showed that cisgender girls who identified with more than one ethnicity/race were more likely to find emerging sexual identity labels as self-descriptive (i.e., pansexual, queer, asexual, or questioning). Other results also showed that cisgender youth were more likely to endorse traditional sexual identity categories like gay, lesbian, bisexual, or heterosexual.

The Watson et al. (2020) study and others (e.g., Feinstein et al., 2023; Garrett-Walker & Montagno, 2023; Srivastava et al., 2024; White et al., 2018) are good examples of how research practices consistent with an intersectional framework are going further in advancing knowledge about adolescent, emerging, and young adult identity. Often in these studies, recruitment of participants is aimed at including underrepresented groups and is open to finding diversity within a wider group; the measurement typically allows for input by participants, and the analysis approaches can handle potentially complex intersections between gender and sexual identity (having both breadth and depth and considering types and gradients; Watson et al., 2020). Many of these studies are not aimed at multidimensional measurement of identity and do not speak to identity development in terms of how adolescents see the contextual or temporal integration of their gender and sexual identity. Yet, in a relatively straightforward manner, the Watson et al. (2020) study and several other studies (e.g., Garrett-Walker & Montagno, 2023; Srivastava et al., 2024; White et al., 2018) are demonstrating how youth are navigating existing sociocultural expectations for gender and sexual identity. Such an understanding is important to efforts that can support adolescent health and well-being (e.g., Feinstein et al., 2023).

The Diamond (2005, 2008) and Diamond and Butterworth (2008) Studies

The second research exemplar is a seminal study conducted by Diamond (2005, 2008). This was a ten-year longitudinal study (with five assessment time points) with 89 late adolescents/emerging adults who, at the time of the study launch/start, were an average age of 19 years and self-identified as women and either had rejected or were questioning a heterosexual sexual orientation (ten participants were not located for continued study participation; Diamond, 2008). Participants were recruited from a number of different organizations and settings, some of which were connected with sexual minorities (Diamond, 2005). Interviews were used to ask participants several questions about how they labeled and thought about their sexual identity as well as sexual attraction and behavior (Diamond, 2008). Study results indicated some variability in sexual attraction and behavior over time (Diamond, 2008). For example, one participant reported that her sexual attraction to women declined from 100% to 50% across four time points, and she stated in an interview the following:

> After I graduated from college . . . I found myself, not necessarily only attracted to both sexes, but also slightly more open-minded to the notion that maybe . . . maybe I can find something in just a person, that I don't necessarily have to be attracted to one sex verses the other . . . since then I've been in, let's see, a couple of different long-term relationships with women and I've had lots of sex with men and currently I'm in a long-term relationship with a man that I find very, very, very enjoyable and, um, fulfilling so it's hard for me to identify so therefore I kind of prefer to not identify or just kind of . . . kind of joke about it and say, "I am not bisexual or homosexual, I'm just sexual."
>
> (Diamond, 2005, p. 126)

Other study results showed that participants evidenced consistency with a homosexual, heterosexual, or bisexual orientation label/identity over the majority of time study points, and some individuals were moving between sexual orientation labels/identities over time, from bisexual to unsure. But a general conclusion was that results did not support the idea that bisexuality represented a transition between heterosexual and homosexual orientations but was relatively stable and viewed as a sexual orientation in its own right (Diamond, 2008).

Relevant to the intersection of gender and sexual identity, in particular, are findings reported by Diamond and Butterworth (2008) concerning four participants, who were part of this wider ten-year longitudinal study (i.e., Diamond, 2005, 2008). These four participants reported changes in both gender and sexual identity development. This subgroup and the wider study findings regarding the documentation of different trajectories in sexual identity development (Diamond, 2008) illustrated several ideas important to intersectionality, such as the non-homogeneity of groups. Diamond (2008) recognized that this study sample was likely to be diverse and was open to identifying similarities as well as differences across the sample. There was also clarity and transparency about the study procedure and about how recruitment into the study was conducted, what that meant for the interpretation of study findings, and what the limits were on the generalizability of study findings (Diamond, 2008).

The subgroup results themselves (Diamond & Butterworth, 2008) also illustrated several substantive issues of importance. For participants in this subgroup, questioning and exploration around sexual attractions, behaviors, and sexual identity were associated with questioning and exploration around one's physical body/appearance and gender identity. Engaging in exploration in these areas would, in turn, later help to clarify participants' sexual attractions and behaviors as well as sexual identity. These subgroup findings also provided insight into the subjective experience of what it was like for participants to have gone from a birth sex assignment of female and heteronormativity to co-create a personally authentic combination of gender and sexual identity for themselves. These subgroup findings were also illustrative of how society and other people often push back against efforts to co-construct a meaningful and authentic gender and sexual identity, which is consistent with the idea of social location and power in the intersectionality framework and the notion of how people navigate person–society integration as described by Syed and McLean (2016). A comment from a participant named Mark provides an example of how Mark experienced the reoccurring pushback of society against having a more intermediate, rather than binary (i.e., female or male, heterosexual or homosexual) gender and sexual identity. Mark noted in an interview that:

> I'm not even going to tackle the pronoun thing because that's too confusing. And I find that "none of the above" pretty much is how I tend to label myself, only because I hate boxes. Hate them. Hate them. And I hate this whole like dichotomy paradigm that our society tends to revolve around. It's black – it's white/it's male – it's female/it's straight – it's gay/whatever. None of those fit.
>
> (Diamond & Butterworth, 2008, p. 374)

Other researchers who have conducted studies with adolescents and emerging adults in this topic area have also noted instances in which some youth are questioning and rejecting a societal status quo surrounding gender and/or sexual identity (i.e., rejecting heteronormativity, as well as gender and sexual binaries) as part of their own identity development (e.g., Hammack & Cohler, 2011; Hammack et al., 2022; Savin-Williams, 2011).

Future identity research with the current generation of youth should take the implications of intersectionality for research practice to heart, as well as conduct more research on identity integration, particularly in regard to gender and sexual identity development in different parts of the world, where norms and social practices surrounding gender, sexuality, ethnicity/culture, and religion vary (Baams &

Kaufman, 2023). The challenges for the future also include the need for more longitudinal empirical examples that have diverse, multidimensional, and mixed-method measurements of gender and sexual identity in the same study (Russell et al., 2023). This type of research will allow for a better understanding of the conditions under which changes and stability in gender and sexual identity are likely and for whom over time (Diamond, 2023). Such research would also keep a focus on better ensuring the creation of safe and resource-rich contexts for all youth.

Summary

Intersectionality and identity integration focus our attention on where important aspects of identity meet and are yet another reflection of the balance between self and others. Intersectionality as a wider framework calls for recognition of how society works to offer opportunities or curtail life chances based on a person's identity and offers several important guidelines for research practice (Cole, 2009). The chapter uses the example of the intersection of gender and sexual identity to illustrate how the past socially recognized, two-gender-only way of seeing the physical sex and gender of an adolescent does not encompass the bodies and life experiences of all youths. Research presented describes shifts around the language used by many youths to describe their gender and sexual identity as well as offering a deep dive into a seminal longitudinal study about sexual and gender identity development that still resonates. Caring and inclusive adults have been shown to be an asset for gender and sexually diverse youth (e.g., Ioverno et al., 2025), and thus, adult stakeholders in youth should be informed, competent, and inclusive in their understanding of the diversity of adolescent gender and sexual identity development.

Notes

1 See Bussey (2011) as well as Jackson and Bussey (2023) for more on how gender identity can be measured in ways that are consistent with this theory, as well as for an overview of research studies/findings related to this theory.
2 See Dillon et al. (2011) and Rosenberg et al. (2024) for more details on supporting measurement approaches and research studies/findings related to this theory about sexual identity development.
3 This chapter was not designed to provide a comprehensive narrative summary of the research literature or an analysis of all theories relevant to adolescent gender and sexual identity development, but rather, the aim of this chapter was to be illustrative and forward-looking. The reader interested in systematic narrative overviews of this research literature is referred to several excellent articles and chapters cited in the reference list of this chapter.

References

Baams, L., & Kaufman, T. M. L. (2023). Sexual orientation and gender identity/expression in adolescent research: Two decades in review. *Journal of Sex Research*, *60*(7), 1004–1019. https://doi.org/10.1080/00224499.2023.2219245
Bishop, M. D., Fish, J. N., & Russell, S. T. (2024). The timing of sexual identity development milestones: Disentangling age from cohort influences. *Psychology of Sexual Orientation and Gender Diversity*. Advance online publication. https://doi.org/10.1037/sgd0000745

Bowleg, L., Malekzadeh, A. N., AuBuchon, K. E., Ghabrial, M. A., & Bauer, G. R. (2023). Rare exemplars and missed opportunities: Intersectionality within current sexual and gender diversity research and scholarship in psychology. *Current Opinion in Psychology, 49*, Article 101511. https://doi.org/10.1016/j.copsyc.2022.101511

Bussey, K. (2011). Gender identity development. In S. J. Schwartz, K. Luyckx, & V. L. Vignoles (Eds.), *Handbook of identity theory and research (Vols. 1 and 2)* (pp. 603–628). New York, NY: Springer Science + Business Media. https://doi.org/10.1007/978-1-4419-7988-9_25

Cole, E. R. (2009). Intersectionality and research in psychology. *American Psychologist, 64*(3), 170–180. https://doi.org/10.1037/a0014564

Crenshaw, K. (1991). Mapping the margins: Intersectionality, identity politics, and violence against women of color. *Stanford Law Review, 43*(6), 1241–1299. https://doi.org/10.2307/1229039

Diamond, L. M. (2005). A new view of lesbian subtypes: Stable versus fluid identity trajectories over an 8-year period. *Psychology of Women Quarterly, 29*(2), 119–128. https://doi.org/10.1111/j.1471-6402.2005.00174.x

Diamond, L. M. (2008). Female bisexuality from adolescence to adulthood: Results from a 10-year longitudinal study. *Developmental Psychology, 44*(1), 5–14. https://doi.org/10.1037/0012-1649.44.1.5

Diamond, L. M. (2018). Contemporary theory in the study of intimacy, desire, and sexuality. In N. K. Dess, J. Marecek, & L. C. Bell (Eds.), *Gender, sex, and sexualities: Psychological perspectives; gender, sex, and sexualities* (pp. 271–294). Oxford Academic. https://doi.org/10.1093/oso/9780190658540.003.0012

Diamond, L. M. (2020). Gender fluidity and nonbinary gender identities among children and adolescents. *Child Development Perspectives, 14*(2), 110–115. https://doi.org/10.1111/cdep.12366

Diamond, L. M. (2023). What develops in the biodevelopment of sexual orientation? *Archives of Sexual Behavior, 52*(7), 2985–2991. https://doi.org/10.1007/s10508-023-02542-5

Diamond, L. M., & Butterworth, M. (2008). Questioning gender and sexual identity: Dynamic links over time. *Sex Roles: A Journal of Research, 59*(5–6), 365–376. https://doi.org/10.1007/s11199-008-9425-3

Diamond, L. M., Pardo, S. T., & Butterworth, M. R. (2011). Transgender experience and identity. In S. J. Schwartz, K. Luyckx, & V. L. Vignoles (Eds.), *Handbook of identity theory and research* (Vols. 1 and 2, pp. 629–647). Springer Science + Business Media. https://doi.org/10.1007/978-1-4419-7988-9_26

Dillon, F. R., Worthington, R. L., & Moradi, B. (2011). Sexual identity as a universal process. In S. J. Schwartz, K. Luyckx, & V. L. Vignoles (Eds.), *Handbook of identity theory and research (Vols. 1 and 2)* (pp. 649–670). Springer Science + Business Media. https://doi.org/10.1007/978-1-4419-7988-9_27

Erikson, E. H. (1968). *Identity: Youth and crisis*. Norton.

Feinstein, B. A., Hurtado, M., Jr., Dyar, C., & Davila, J. (2023). Disclosure, minority stress, and mental health among bisexual, pansexual, and queer (Bi+) adults: The roles of primary sexual identity and multiple sexual identity label use. *Psychology of Sexual Orientation and Gender Diversity, 10*(2), 181–189. https://doi.org/10.1037/sgd0000532

Garrett-Walker, J., & Montagno, M. J. (2023). Queering labels: Expanding identity categories in LGBTQ + research and clinical practice. *Journal of LGBT Youth, 20*(4), 865. https://doi.org/10.1080/19361653.2021.1896411

Ghavami, N., Katsiaficas, D., & Rogers, L. O. (2016). Toward an intersectional approach in developmental science: The role of race, gender, sexual orientation, and immigrant status. In S. S. Horn, M. D. Ruck, & L. S. Liben (Eds.), *Equity and justice in developmental science: Theoretical and methodological issues* (Vol. 1, pp. 31–73). Elsevier Academic Press. https://doi.org/10.1016/bs.acdb.2015.12.001

Hammack, P. L., & Cohler, B. J. (2011). Narrative, identity, and the politics of exclusion: Social change and the gay and lesbian life course. *Sexuality Research & Social Policy: A Journal of the NSRC, 8*(3), 162–182. https://doi.org/10.1007/s13178-011-0060-3

Hammack, P. L., Hughes, S. D., Atwood, J. M., Cohen, E. M., & Clark, R. C. (2022). Gender and sexual identity in adolescence: A mixed-methods study of labeling in diverse community settings. *Journal of Adolescent Research, 37*(2), 167–220. https://doi.org/10.1177/07435584211000315

Hammack, P. L., & Manago, A. M. (2025). The psychology of sexual and gender diversity in the 21st century: Social technologies and stories of authenticity. *American Psychologist, 80*(3), 375–388. https://doi.org/10.1037/amp0001366

Hammack, P. L., & Wignall, L. (2023). Sexual and gender diversity in the twenty-first century. *Current Opinion in Psychology, 52*, Article 101616. https://doi.org/10.1016/j.copsyc.2023.101616

Ioverno, S., Sherwood, S. H., Costa, S., Van Houtte, M., Dewaele, A., O'Higgins Norman, J., Gato, J., Mazzone, A., Pezzella, A., Huic, A., Šolinc, M., Richard, G., Papathanasiou, N., Aparicio-García, M. E., Wilhelm, W., & Russell, S. T. (2025). Linking inclusive school practices and mental health in sexual and gender minority youth in Europe. *European Child & Adolescent Psychiatry, 34*(10), 3125–3135. https://doi.org/10.1007/s00787-025-02733-6

Jackson, E. F., & Bussey, K. (2023). Broadening gender self-categorization development to include transgender identities. *Social Development, 32*(1), 17–31. https://doi.org/10.1111/sode.12635

Magnusson, E., & Marecek, J. (2018). Setting the stage: Gender, sex, and sexualities in psychology. In N. K. Dess, J. Marecek, & L. C. Bell (Eds.), *Gender, sex, and sexualities: Psychological perspectives* (pp. 3–28). Oxford Academic. https://doi.org/10.1093/oso/9780190658540.003.0001

McCauley, P. S., Eaton, L. A., Puhl, R. M., & Watson, R. J. (2025). Support from school personnel and in-school resources jointly moderate the association between identity-based harassment and depressive symptoms among sexual and gender diverse youth. *Journal of Educational Psychology, 117*(3), 445–465. https://doi.org/10.1037/edu0000945

Mitchell, L. L., Adler, J. M., Carlsson, J., Eriksson, P. L., & Syed, M. (2021). A conceptual review of identity integration across adulthood. *Developmental Psychology, 57*(11), 1981–1990. https://doi.org/10.1037/dev0001246

Moffitt, U., Katsiaficas, D., Ghavami, N., Minor, I., Padilla, D., & Rogers, L. O. (2023). Intersectionality and identity: A systematic review and qualitative analysis of U.S. research in psychological science. *Identity: An International Journal of Theory and Research, 23*(4), 288–313. https://doi.org/10.1080/15283488.2023.2223647

Morgan, E. M. (2013). Contemporary issues in sexual orientation and identity development in emerging adulthood. *Emerging Adulthood, 1*(1), 52–66. https://doi.org/10.1177/2167696812469187

Morgenroth, T. (2025). Language about gender/sex should be used intentionally and flexibly. *British Journal of Psychology, 116*(2), 499–502. https://doi.org/10.1111/bjop.12769

Parent, M. C., DeBlaere, C., & Moradi, B. (2013). Approaches to research on intersectionality: Perspectives on gender, LGBT, and racial/ethnic identities. *Sex Roles: A Journal of Research, 68*(11–12), 639–645. https://doi.org/10.1007/s11199-013-0283-2

Quintana, G. R., & Pfaus, J. G. (2024). Do sex and gender have separate identities? *Archives of Sexual Behavior, 53*(8), 2957–2975. https://doi.org/10.1007/s10508-024-02933-2

Real, A. G., Sherwood, S. H., Ioverno, S., & Russell, S. T. (2024). Strategies to promote safety for sexual and gender minority youth in secondary schools: A longitudinal analysis. *Journal of Research on Adolescence, 34*(4), 1642–1652. https://doi.org/10.1111/jora.13032

Rosenberg, B. A., Dillon, F. R., Eklund, A., & Ebersole, R. (2024). Traditional machismo, caballerismo, and sexual identity development among Latino sexual minority men. *Journal of Latinx Psychology, 12*(4), 362–374. https://doi.org/10.1037/lat0000259

Rosette, A. S., Li, X., Samuel, N., & Petsko, C. D. (2025). From primary to pluralistic: A typology of intersectionality. *Current Opinion in Psychology, 61*, Article 101944. https://doi.org/10.1016/j.copsyc.2024.101944

Russell, S. T., Bishop, M. D., & Fish, J. N. (2023). Expanding notions of LGBTQ+. *Annual Review of Sociology*, *49*, 281–296. https://doi.org/10.1146/annurev-soc-030320-032256
Savin-Williams, R. (2011). Identity development among sexual-minority youth. In S. J. Schwartz, K. Luyckx, & V. L. Vignoles (Eds.), *Handbook of identity theory and research (Vols. 1 and 2)* (pp. 671–689). Springer Science + Business Media. https://doi.org/10.1007/978-1-4419-7988-9_28
Srivastava, A., Green, D., O'Brien, R. P., Parra, L. A., Schrager, S. M., & Goldbach, J. T. (2024). A proposed taxonomy for categorizing sexual identities in adolescence. *Psychology of Sexual Orientation and Gender Diversity*, *12*(3), 477–487. https://doi.org/10.1037/sgd0000685
Stewart, A. J., & McDermott, C. (2004). Gender in psychology. *Annual Review of Psychology*, *55*, 519–544. https://doi.org/10.1146/annurev.psych.55.090902.141537
Syed, M., & McLean, K. C. (2016). Understanding identity integration: Theoretical, methodological, and applied issues. *Journal of Adolescence*, *47*(1), 109–118. https://doi.org/10.1016/j.adolescence.2015.09.005
van Anders, S. M. (2015). Beyond sexual orientation: Integrating gender/sex and diverse sexualities via sexual configurations theory. *Archives of Sexual Behavior*, *44*(5), 1177–1213. https://doi.org/10.1007/s10508-015-0490-8
van Anders, S. M., Schudson, Z. C., Beischel, W. J., & Chadwick, S. B. (2025). Feminist and queer science: Principles for research with gender, sex, and sexuality in psychology and beyond. *Psychology of Sexual Orientation and Gender Diversity*, *12*(2), 181–200. https://doi.org/10.1037/sgd0000646
Watson, R. J., Wheldon, C. W., & Puhl, R. M. (2020). Evidence of diverse identities in a large national sample of sexual and gender minority adolescents. *Journal of Research on Adolescence*, *30*(S2), 431–442. https://doi.org/10.1111/jora.12488
White, A. E., Moeller, J., Ivcevic, Z., & Brackett, M. A. (2018). Gender identity and sexual identity labels used by U.S. high school students: A co-occurrence network analysis. *Psychology of Sexual Orientation and Gender Diversity*, *5*(2), 243–252. https://doi.org/10.1037/sgd0000266

7 Forging a Brave New Digital Identity

> My personality is too big to fit into just one site. People have to meet me. I am an experience.
>
> (Anne, 21-year-old writer and singer)[1]

The trepidation as well as optimism over young people's digital life is undeniable (e.g., APA, 2019; Wols et al., 2024). For example, digital technologies can be used in ways that can cause harm, such as violent video games (APA, 2019) or competitive observations on social media sites concerning what others excel at or have (Yang et al., 2018). Paradoxically, the scope and possibilities of life contexts widen as digital technologies become more available (Maheux et al., 2025; United Nations Children's Fund, 2023). The use of digital technologies has become so widespread among adolescents that three targets within the 2030 Sustainable Development Goals concern digital life/skills and expanded access to key technologies (i.e., targets: 4.4, 5b, and 17.8; United Nations Children's Fund, 2023). Sustainable Development Goals are priorities agreed on by United Nations member states and designed to be a guide to global and beneficial actions.

Digital environments are also increasingly being integrated into health and social care, as well as educational and work opportunities (Zimmermann & Tomczyk, 2025). Like other interventions, some identity interventions have undergone digitalization and further testing to see if these identity interventions can yield benefits while opening up new frontiers to reach more people (e.g., Berman et al., 2025; Soh et al., 2025). These and other developments make digital environments a key arena for developing new ways to enhance positive youth development, including identity development, as well as to support health and well-being (Zimmermann & Tomczyk, 2025).

This chapter describes an extension of identity research that examines digital environments and adolescent identity development. Like Chapters 5 and 6, this chapter is unique in focus and organization and represents a novel extension of identity theory and research. By exploring this up-and-coming area, we show where the edges of our knowledge are and in what directions this field is likely to go.

In terms of its organization, this chapter starts with a description of digital environments. Then, there is a summary and analysis of a theory that offers an

DOI: 10.4324/9781003486336-7

explanation for how hybrid environments provide a context for adolescent identity development. These chapter sections are followed by selected research exemplars. A summary statement concludes the chapter.

The Digital Environment as Pervasive

As a whole, digital technology use is increasingly commonplace. In 2024, the percentage of Internet users in the overall global population among 15–24-year-olds was 79%, while the overall global rate for all ages combined was 66% (ITU, 2024). So, more people are now using the Internet, to some degree, relative to those who are completely offline. Further, there are generational differences in Internet use. For example, for those 55–64 years old, the average daily time spent on the Internet was about five hours, and for those 65 and older, the average time was about three and a half to four hours (Data Reportal et al., 2025). Thus, relative to those 55 years and older, 15–24-year-olds (average daily time spent: seven hours and 23 minutes) and 25–34-year-olds (average daily time spent: seven hours and 15 minutes) are more likely to spend more time online (Data Reportal et al., 2025). Let's stop for a minute and reflect on the number of about seven hours and some minutes spent online daily by the typical adolescent and emerging to young adult. The pervasive reach and time engaged with the Internet make digital environments impossible to ignore by scholars interested in human development.

Yet, despite high global engagement with the internet and other digital environments, there remain substantial variations in Internet use across nations and within demographic subgroups, with variations by gender and educational level. For example, a report on the digital life of 15–24-year-olds living in 54 nations found a range in Internet use, with the lowest levels among youth living in low-income nations (22% males and 10% females) and more prevalent Internet use among young people living in lower-middle-income nations (61% males and 38% females; United Nations Children's Fund, 2023). Report authors also stressed the need for greater access to digital technologies/skills for youth living in low- and lower-middle-income nations in general and for girls living in these nations in particular (United Nations Children's Fund, 2023).

In other global regions, digital life can trend toward very high levels of engagement, and the gender-related concerns take on a different character. As a case in point, a report on digital life among youth living in Organisation for Economic Co-operation and Development (OECD) nations, which are high-income to upper-middle-income economies, noted that as of 2023, the vast majority of households in OECD nations had Internet access (92%), and in 2022, 98% of 15-year-olds living in OECD nations had an Internet-connected smartphone (OECD, 2025). The gender disparities addressed in this report (OECD, 2025) concerned how digital technologies were used; female adolescents were more likely to be frequent social media users, and male adolescents were more likely to be frequent video game users. Each gender had a greater respective risk for problematic use of the more commonly used digital media (OECD, 2025).

Clearly, part of what makes adolescents of today distinguishable from older generations is defined, in part, by how their lives are lived in digital environments (Dimock, 2023; Höfrová et al., 2024). Today's adolescents consist of two generations: Generation Z, born from 1997 to 2009, and Generation Alpha, born from 2010 to 2025, with the older members of Generation Alpha now coming into adolescence (Höfrová et al., 2024). Many members of Generations Z and Alpha are digital natives who view the Internet as fundamental to daily existence (Höfrová et al., 2024). Today's adolescents may also be further distinguished by largely coming of age before (Generation Z) or during the global integration of artificial intelligence with digital environments (Generation Alpha).

With several technologically infused historical shifts all happening at the same time, how adolescent identity development relates to digital environments has garnered substantial attention from multiple scientific disciplines such as psychology, developmental science, computer science, and language and communication studies. Given how essential digital life is for many of today's adolescents (Poushter et al., 2024), what are digital environments like, in detail, for Generations Z and Alpha as well as the rest of us?

Digital Environments Demystified

Soh and colleagues (2024) proposed a useful framework for describing the elements and processes of change that can be characteristic of a wide range of digital environments. These scholars proposed that central elements include media, platforms, and content. Mediums can be the technology itself, such as a virtual reality headset or a smartphone as well as generic digital channels like social media and video games (Soh et al., 2024). Platforms are digital spaces that primarily companies have provided for people to use and can include platforms for dating (e.g., "Tinder"), playing video games (e.g., "Minecraft, World of Warcraft"), video and music streaming, as well as social media (e.g., "Instagram, Snapchat, TikTok, Twitter/X, YouTube"; Soh et al., 2024, p. 4). Content is the information that is shared and interacted with on mediums and platforms (Soh et al., 2024).

Some of the change mechanisms thought to be involved in the person–environment interactions that take place within digital environments are what Soh and colleagues (2024) called affordances. These affordances can include editability (e.g., creating/modifying content, such as being able or not to put a filter on a photo), persistence (e.g., how long content exists before it disappears on a platform), and anonymity (e.g., the ability to share or interact with content in secret or not). Other scholars have identified affordances associated with video games such as "social cue absence," "shared structured activity" (posited to facilitate a greater sense of social identity in a group), and "customizability" (e.g., the ability to get more engaged in a game by discussing and/or selecting outfits and accessories for one's game character/avatar; Maheux et al., 2025, p. 6).

The concept of an affordance, as proposed by J. J. Gibson (1979/2014) in the 1970s and elaborated on and used widely in psychology, human development, and other sciences (e.g., Gibson, 2000; Mangalam et al., 2024), implies that there is a universe of possible interactions that a person can have with an object. As an illustration, consider a young child learning, for the first time, to use a zipper that opens and closes the top of a plastic bag with snacks in it, and think about how the many affordances of this zipper may not be immediately evident and could be more of a nuisance than a help to accessing a snack to the novice user (e.g., Rachwani et al., 2021).

In essence, an affordance in a person–object interaction involves the person's perception of what can be done with an object, a person's goals, the design properties of an object, and then what ends up happening when person–object interactions take place over time (Mangalam et al., 2024). Affordances allow for objects to be used in ways well beyond their intended purposes and open up a space for human creativity. Affordances also add consideration of the individual differences in goals that people bring with them, specifically when they use, turn off, or delete a digital platform (e.g., Agai, 2022). One can further add to the complexity of the person–digital platform interaction by considering what other people on a platform would add to the experience for the user as well as the level of interactivity between people and the digital medium, many of which are designed to provide tailored responses to a user's actions (e.g., video games).

Social Media

The term "social media" covers a great deal of ground, and this term is used in this chapter to refer to the online activities that people engage in for social interaction and connecting to others through the use of social networking sites/platforms (SNS/P) such as Snapchat and/or games. For some SNS/Ps, people can make virtual profiles that contain images, entertainment, and other novel user-made content including information about one's mood, wishes, and opinions as well as reactions to what others have shared through the platform (Maheux et al., 2025).

Social media can range from profiles and activities on for-profit SNS/Ps such as Instagram to more user-cocreated "digital campfires" like the community platforms dedicated to video games or other special interests (Granic et al., 2020a, p. 261). Research in this area is moving more toward a functional/affordance-based approach (e.g., Griffioen et al., 2021). As a case in point, in a qualitative interview study about digital life and narrative identity with 17 Norwegian adolescents, study participants reflected on their evolving views about their perception of the utility of SNS/P use (Agai, 2022). For example, one participant noted:

> . . . It's so that among us young people, there is an expectation to maintain streaks and liking photos, but gradually I began to think that a number does not mean that it is a deep relationship. . . . It made me realize that you, sort

of, need more self-confidence and self-respect from within yourself and build that up rather than getting likes, you know.

(Lilja, 16 years; Agai, 2022, p. 7)

Video Games

Children's and adolescents' video game use represents another main digital medium that has attracted substantial research and public attention.[2] Video games can be played on or off the Internet as well as alone or with other players joining in the same game, which has been called "social gaming" (Maheux et al., 2025, p. 4). Video games are played with a variety of technologies, such as smartphones, computers, or gaming consoles. These games can range from simple to complex as well as be on a continuum from nonsocial, which are played alone, to social games, which are played with other people and may even be dependent on social cooperation (Granic et al., 2014).

Examples of video games that can be complex and social are massive multiplayer online role-playing games (MMORPGs) such as League of Legends or World of Warcraft. MMORPGs involve "virtual worlds in which players interact with each other in the online gaming environment" (Bacchini et al., 2017, p. 191). MMORPGs can have elements of SNS/P integrated within the game, such as the ability to chat (text) or speak with other known or unknown players during gameplay (Maheux et al., 2025). Players, in addition to their gameplay, may also be active on an SNS/P dedicated to the game, for example, as a member of a community on Reddit dedicated to a video game such as Red Dead Redemption (2.4 million community members) or Pokémon Go (5.6 million community members).

Narrative Identity Model in Hybrid Reality

Even though the research literature on adolescent identity development in relation to digital environments is growing, the field remains fragmented (Avci et al., 2024). Furthermore, what we know about this subject also remains only representative of the experience of a minority of youth in the global population of today's adolescents (Sirin et al., 2024). Explanatory and empirically actionable theoretical models can lead to advances that solve problems. Therefore, Granic and colleagues' (2020a, 2020b) model is described here as illustrative of the types of promising theories[3] about identity development that are needed, as digital environments are increasingly entering into everyday life and being considered in identity theory and research.

Granic and colleagues' (2020a, 2020b) model aims to explain the intersections among adolescents' mental health, narrative identity development, and hybrid reality. Hybrid reality was posited by these scholars to be the fusion of digital and offline environments in the lives and worldviews of today's adolescents and represents a "developmental ecosystem that seamlessly combines digital and physical worlds" (Granic et al., 2020b, p. 199). A comment from a participant in a qualitative interview study of 20 adolescents and emerging adults regarding video games and identity illustrates how some young people may resonate with the idea of a hybrid reality, as follows:

> Then I got to the point where I started to think "I'm like a character." I started going to the gym more so I could be strong like my character. I started to study and read and all this more and tinker with stuff so I could be smart like them (Brian, age 20 years).
>
> (Forsyth et al., 2017, p. E7)

For the identity development part of this model, Granic and colleagues (2020b) drew on an Eriksonian view of identity as a key developmental task of adolescence. They went on to describe their view of identity as narrative identity (McAdams & McLean, 2013). Granic et al. proposed that narrative identity intrapersonal processes consist of a developmental sequencing of the fulfillment of three primary needs: coherence, communion, and agency. The first, temporal coherence, is a chronologically consistent life story developed over time. Communion involves a sense of belonging to important others. Finally, agency implies a rejection of conformity and a formulation of what one thinks is right, aims to do, and does so. During early adolescence, communion needs are thought to take precedence, and in middle to later adolescence, the need for communion becomes better balanced with agency and temporal coherence needs (Granic et al., 2020b).

In the Granic and colleagues (2020b) model, individuals are working on their narrative identity in the context of social interactions and relational processes of change by asking for and providing elaboration (e.g., What do you mean by that? Tell me more), active listening (e.g., truly paying attention and taking in what another person has to say), and coming to terms with inconsistencies when self-narrating (e.g., I am bold and unapologetic when talking about my life with friends, but unsure and vulnerable when talking about the same events and feelings about life with a romantic partner). In this model, the intrapersonal and interpersonal factors essential to narrative identity development are recognized to also be embedded in a cultural context. Bidirectional influences are thought to occur at the cultural, interpersonal, and intrapersonal levels of this model. Digital environments, in synergy with offline physical environments (i.e., hybrid reality), can either promote or put a damper on needs fulfillment (see Table 7.1), as well as have importance to other levels of the model (Granic et al., 2020b). The Barsigian and colleagues (2025) study in the research exemplars section of this chapter provides an illustration of how culturally rooted master and alternative narratives are operating and have bearing on how a person's narrative identity development progresses. Also, see Chapter 3 for more on narrative identity as well as master and alternative narratives.

Analysis: Narrative Identity Model in Hybrid Reality

The Granic et al. (2020b) model is a step forward that has high potential to accelerate the empirical research literature on adolescent identity development in digital

Table 7.1 Example Identity/Hybrid Reality Interactions as Proposed by Granic et al. (2020a, 2020b)

Digital environment	*Interaction: Intrapersonal need and digital medium*
Social media and social video games	Can **promote communion** by reinforcing ties to known peers and opening up new social interactions with like-minded peers who are rarer in offline settings.
Competitive video gameplay	**Agency can be strengthened** by the redemptive potential of experiencing failures interspersed with successes in gameplay.
Selection and use of more private and less permanent social media platforms	**Agency can be fostered** by taking charge of one's own digital footprint. **Communion and temporal coherence can be promoted** by more authentic communication with peers.
Social media	**Can inhibit agency and temporal coherence** by posting inauthentic, false content about oneself as well as social media giving in to a sea of goals, values, and choices that a person can get lost in without any guidance.
	Temporal coherence can be weakened by not having a way to connect our identity work across digital platforms that go in and out of use over time (e.g., Myspace or Skype do not exist anymore; all of that information is lost) as well as digital platforms not being connected to one another to provide a holistic view of oneself across digital platforms.

Note. **Bold** added to highlight the interpersonal need involved and whether the interaction is thought to foster or inhibit identity development in this model.

environments. This model considers intrapersonal (psychological), interpersonal (relational and dialogical), and wider contextual factors, interacting with one another to coproduce identity development. This model attempts to explain identity development as a process rather than being satisfied with describing a static snapshot of identity at a single point in time.

In regard to theoretical aspects that could be further developed in the Granic et al. (2020b) model, communion, agency, and temporal coherence needs are conceptualized as intrapersonal processes at the heart of narrative identity development. Needs fulfillment as an explanation for developmental change does appear in models of personality development like the three-layer framework but as its own layer in the model (McAdams & Olson, 2010; see Chapter 3). Communion and agency needs also figure prominently in self-determination theory (SDT; Ryan & Deci, 2000). In a response to critiques of their model, Granic and colleagues (2020a) noted that SDT was not used as an overarching theory in their model due to their view of SDT as lacking a strong consideration of developmental change and dialogical processes. Arguments in favor of some degree of attention to agency and communion needs in a theory of identity development include the frequent appearance of agency and communion themes in narrative identity studies (e.g., Adler et al., 2016) as well as clear intersections between agency and communion with the affordances of several digital mediums. In sum, there are conceptual points against and in favor of the inclusion of needs fulfillment in a model of identity development. The Granic et al. (2020a) model has yet to fully address the necessity

Table 7.2 Examples of Identity Process/Digital Interactions Proposed by Diverse Scholars

Digital environment	*Interaction: Identity process and digital medium*
Social media	Could foster identity exploration through less adult-supervised, low-stakes ways to try out roles/values by content creation (e.g., Hughes et al., 2016), provide a way to better connect and deepen ties to like-minded friends/peers (Manago, 2014; Spies Shapiro & Margolin, 2014), and thereby increase exposure to identity agents[4] (Schachter & Marshall, 2010) and allow for opportunities for self-disclosure and peer feedback (Spies Shapiro & Margolin, 2014).
Social video gaming	Could promote identity exploration by trying out different personality characteristics online (e.g., leadership roles), customization of game avatars (including gender bending), and exposure to gaming subcultures and peer processes (Di Cesare et al., 2024; Maheux et al., 2025).

of needs, particularly agency and communion needs, within their explanation of narrative identity development.

In terms of future directions, the Granic et al. (2020b) model could also benefit from a consideration of an even broader range of narrative identity and other identity change processes – addition of other types of coherence, autobiographical reasoning, narrative and interpretative skills, and exploration and commitment (see Table 7.2 for suggestions from other scholars). Yet, even with the noted areas for further development, the Granic et al. model is timely and promising as an identity theory tailored to advancing what we know about the experience of young people across digital environments.

Some Empirical Lessons Learned So Far from the Research Literature

Relative to the past, more research studies are focusing on how social media use and/or video games are fitting into the life experiences and identity development of adolescents and emerging adults (e.g., Coyne et al., 2023; Eklund & Roman, 2017; Forsyth et al., 2017; Manago et al., 2025). Identity development processes in the context of social media use appear to be more frequently investigated than identity development and video game use.[5]

Social Media Use and Identity: So Far and in Brief

A comprehensive, systematic review was conducted by Avci and colleagues (2024) on social media use and adolescent identity. Identity-related indices included in the review were identity exploration, identity commitment, identity distress, and self-concept consistency. These scholars identified 32 studies with adolescent samples relevant to social media use and the aforementioned identity development process and/or outcomes. Some main conclusions from this review were that inconsistent study results were found for identity commitment as well as identity distress and social media use (Avci et al., 2024). Identity exploration was more likely when social media use was characterized by active engagement in creating content and interacting on SNS/Ps. Presenting a more realistic/authentic version of oneself on social media was associated with greater self-concept consistency (Avci et al., 2024). These scholars recommended more use of longitudinal research designs, a research focus on the motivations behind adolescents' social media use with attention to possible age-related variations within the adolescent period, and a focus on a wider range of SNS/Ps, such as TikTok and YouTube, which have different affordances relative to other SNS/Ps.

Video Games and Identity: So Far and in Brief

Few studies and reviews have specifically been published on video games and adolescent identity development. One relevant review was conducted by Di Cesare and colleagues (2024). This review concerned what role video games played in the well-being, mental health, and resilience of sexual- and gender-diverse youths. These scholars found 27 peer-reviewed journal articles and diverse gray literature studies (Di Cesare et al., 2024).

Identity came up as a theme in the results of reviewed studies, and some conclusions made by Di Cesare and colleagues (2024) were that avatar customization and gameplay with preferred pronouns were perceived by youth as ways to engage in identity exploration. In a study about game streaming through a digital platform called Twitch, it was found that Twitch was perceived as allowing for greater exposure to gender and/or sexually diverse gamers who broadcast their gameplay and interacted/discussed with other gamers' identity questions (Di Cesare et al., 2024). In sum, ways that video gameplay and streaming were posited to contribute to identity development, based on this emerging literature, were by providing opportunities for identity exploration self-expression, and fostering agency in picking digital environments and platform use (Di Cesare et al., 2024).

Research Exemplars

A take-home message from the previous chapter sections is that even though more theories are being developed and increasing research evidence is accumulating, it remains premature to make strong conclusions about the associations between adolescents' use of social media as well as video games and their identity development. The particular findings of the research exemplars in this chapter are noteworthy and illustrate innovative directions for future research (see Table 7.3). Although these studies deserve our attention, the results of these individual research exemplars should be viewed as preliminary and in need of replication by additional research studies.

Crowe and Watts (2014): A Video Game – Social Gaming and Gender Bending

As a researcher, one can focus on a particular SNS/P, such as Instagram, or a given video game, such as Undertale. The advantage of this approach is that knowing

Table 7.3 Overview of Selected Features of Research Exemplars

Study citation	*Type of digital medium/platform*	*Study design*	*Study sample*
Crowe and Watts (2014)	MMORPG Runescape	Five-year ethnographic study	Child and adolescent players in the United Kingdom and globally (estimated age: 11–16 years old)
Yang et al. (2018, 2020)	Use of social networking sites for social comparison and identity-related constructs	Longitudinal	219 freshman university students in the U.S. (average age: 18)
Barsigian et al. (2025)	Social networking sites and narratives about gender and sexuality	Cross-sectional, go-along method with semi-structured interview	20 sexually and gender-diverse adolescents (16–19 years old) in the U.S.

how a digital platform is organized lends itself to deeper insight into that platform's affordances. An exploratory ethnographic study conducted by Crowe and Watts (2014) remains a seminal study in that it is a methodologically diverse illustration of a research approach with a social media game-specific focus.

The Crowe and Watts (2014) study concerned an MMORPG called Runescape. The game is a role-playing fantasy genre game first played in 2001, with a substantial gamer community that has been active for more than two decades; the game has been played in different editions/versions (Chalk, 2021). Crowne and Watts' study aimed to map out how young people encountered this online space, what practices they used, and how they formed a social community around Runescape. A particularly innovative feature of this study is the diverse combination of online and offline data collection. For example, researchers noted that their fieldwork across a five-year period consisted of the following data:

1628 separate recorded in-game virtual interaction/observation sessions;
3247 online in-game virtual interviews/interactions;
50 forum threads;
140 extended peer-to-peer virtual interviews/discussions;
20 material focus group interviews; and
23 game observations in the material world.

(Crowe & Watts, 2014, p. 219)[6]

These researchers were based in the United Kingdom, with some adolescents from the United Kingdom and others from the global gaming community of Runescape players. Researchers observed that Runescape players (who were mostly children and adolescents) were sometimes flexible about taking on a gender different than their offline gender in the game (i.e., in the creation of their game avatar). This "gender bending" approach to the use of game avatars was interpreted by the researchers to be a function of the game design itself, which not only allowed one to play as a girl or boy and yielded some perceived advantages to players in terms of gameplay but also provided an opportunity for players' gender identity exploration (Crowe & Watts, 2014, p. 217). Two male adolescent players of Runescape who participated in this study said the following:

> I know plenty of guys that are girls and a few girls that are guys. No one cares who you are in RL [real life], it's who you are and what you do in Rune that matters. Why would I want to play as something I am in real life? I thought that was the whole point of it being a RPG!
>
> (Crowe & Watts, 2014, p. 223)

In the quote above, RPG refers to a role-playing game. A female adolescent player described the advantages of playing Runescape with a male avatar as follows: "Playing as a guy lets you just get on with the game. If I wanna feel sexy I just go back to the face-mage and swap back" (Crowe & Watts, 2014, p. 225).

Crowe and Watts' (2014) study on Runescape is valuable in that it is documenting the phenomenon of gender bending with game avatars, which shows the ways that adolescents, through their gameplay, may question the utility of the gender conventions common in fantasy-oriented video games and in other media in which female and male physical features are regularly exaggerated or differentially portrayed (e.g., in the game, female avatars lack similar amounts of clothing and armor relative to male avatars; Crowe & Watts, 2014).

It would be a promising future study to longitudinally examine changes in players' gender identity (which was not measured in the Crowe & Watts study) relative to changes in players' gameplay over time, as it relates to gender. Researchers could also have an intentional systematic recruitment of participants from a few different online multiplayer role-playing games that treat gender in the game storyline, activities, and avatar possibilities in different ways. While the Crowe and Watts (2014) study is clearly interesting and important to a field in which few studies exist, the study also raises the ethical concern about the full scope of what researchers should consider when conducting online virtual ethnography with children and adolescents and how research findings generated from a game-specific study can remain relevant as adolescents' online tastes and game activities change over time.

The Yang et al. (2018, 2020) Study: Social Media, Social Comparison, and Identity

Yang and colleagues' (2018) study concerns social comparison and identity development. Because social comparison can be complex, it is explained here in some detail. The type of social comparison that people do offline and online appears to matter. The more beneficial type of social comparison is called social comparison of opinion, which involves observation of the ways that other people meet life's challenges and solve problems such as learning from others' life hacks or engaging in information seeking (Yang et al., 2020). Social comparison of ability is a competitive observation concerning where other people are better or what others have relative to oneself (Yang et al., 2020). This type of comparison of ability has been found to leave most individuals worse off in terms of self-evaluation and mood (Yang et al., 2018).

Returning back to the Yang and colleagues (2018) study, this was a short-term longitudinal study (approximately one year) with 219 entering university students in the United States (U.S.) who reported regular SNS/P use (at least once a week, e.g., Facebook, Instagram, Twitter, and/or Snapchat). Participants were on average 18 years old. Surveys were used to measure several constructs. The identity-related constructs were identity processing style, which is an information processing-oriented index of how people approach identity questions/issues (Berzonsky, 1989), as well as identity coherence as measured by the Erikson Psychosocial Stage Inventory (Rosenthal et al., 1981) and global self-esteem (Rosenberg et al., 1989). Other constructs measured were participants' engagement in social comparison of opinion or ability when using SNS/Ps. Across the two time points, 62% of the sample remained in the study (136 participants; Yang et al., 2018).

Yang and colleagues (2018) found that participants who engaged frequently in social comparison of ability (the more detrimental type of social comparison) while using SNS/P were likely to also have a diffuse-avoidant identity style. The diffuse-avoidant identity style is characterized by being more likely to forestall identity work (Yang et al., 2018). Specifically, time one social comparison of ability and a diffuse-avoidant identity style were prospectively related to less identity coherence at time two (i.e., at the longitudinal follow-up). Conversely, social comparison of opinion, the typically more beneficial type of social comparison, on SNS/P, was not significantly associated with changes in identity coherence or global self-esteem (Yang et al., 2018).

A later published analysis, also using self-report surveys with the same longitudinal sample (Yang et al., 2020, p. 435), showed that identity distress (i.e., being "severely upset or worried about one's identity-related commitments and decisions") and social comparison of ability were positively associated with rumination at time one (at the beginning of the study). Rumination at time one was directly and positively associated with time two compulsive social media use. In other words, identity distress and social comparison of ability were indirectly connected with increases over time in compulsive social media use by way of rumination, which had a direct positive association with the outcome across time (Yang et al., 2020).

A strength of the Yang and colleagues' study (2018, 2020), beyond the use of a longitudinal study design, was the use of several identity-related constructs such as identity processing style, identity coherence, and identity distress, as indexed by well-established instruments. A broad take-home message across the analyses for this study is that social comparison of ability does not appear to benefit a person in terms of attaining a sense of identity coherence (Yang et al., 2018). Further, that social comparison of ability mixed in with being worried about one's identity and being inclined to ruminate can contribute to an increased detrimental use of social media in ways that start to spin outside of a person's control.

The Barsigian et al. (2025) Study: A Go-Along Method Focused on Master and Alternative Narratives

The next research exemplar used a qualitative approach (i.e., reflexive thematic analysis) to identify patterns across the content and participants' reports about several of their public social media platforms (Barsigian et al., 2025). Study participants were 20 sexually diverse and/or gender-diverse adolescents aged 16–19 years living in the U.S. This study was innovative in several ways. For example, it used a go-along method combined with a semi-structured interview in which researchers ". . . asked adolescents to give us a tour of their three most used public social media platforms while answering questions about their experiences navigating norms around gender and sexuality" (Barsigian et al., 2025, p. 415).

Adolescents often have several social media platforms and use these platforms for different purposes; thus, the polymedia focus of this study provided insight into the offerings of the different platforms in the eyes of the study participants (Barsigian et al., 2025). Input into the qualitative analyses included actual posts (text and images) on platforms with explanations of those posts by study participants (recording of visual information on participants' phones) and interview responses from participants during a one-to-three-hour interview. Deductive analyses of the data collected showed participants' engagement with 12 narratives about gender and/or sexuality. For instance, three frequently occurring narratives were about loving someone of the same sex as not morally right or associated with indignity (code: Sin, 136 occurrences), gender considered in relation to biology (code: Biology, 72 occurrences), and the need for gender equality (code: Should-be-equal; 73 occurrences). Inductive analyses identified three affordances participants reported when in these online spaces and included "seeking and sharing information, creating queer community, and choices about visibility and permanence" (Barsigian et al., 2025, p. 429).

For example, in regard to the sense of queer community and joy, one participant noted:

> I didn't really care that I wasn't super attractive in this . . . I didn't care about what other people thought of me. I'm happy here. I'm with my partner who loves me very much, and who respects me and my gender identity, and that's great for me. (Non-binary, 17, bisexual, white).
>
> (Barsigian et al., 2025, p. 431)

The Barsigian et al. (2025) study shows the varied potentials of social media. This study was geared to unpack the identity-related content and lived experience of study participants who were encountering both the unwelcoming and hostile aspects of online spaces as they relate to gender and sexuality, as well as actively creating and managing social medium platforms in ways that were agentic and positively served participants' goals and identity development.

Research Exemplars: Patterns, Priorities, and Innovations

Several patterns of findings emerged across the exemplar studies. The results of the Crowe and Watts (2014) study were exploratory and valuable in highlighting the practice of gender bending by players, which has also been found in other studies (e.g., Forsyth et al., 2017). The Crowe and Watts (2014) and the Barsigian et al. (2025) studies both had online and offline data collection. The Crowe and Watts (2014) study did not have direct assessments of participants' identity development as an a priori study aim, yet identity-related findings came up in the study results. These findings alert us as to how identity-related constructs can be important to exploratory studies with adolescents. From the Yang et al. (2018) study, results showed that when individuals were delaying identity work (diffuse-avoidant identity style), they may also be using online spaces (e.g., use of SNS/Ps for comparisons of ability) in ways that may not ultimately serve them in terms of their later, prospective identity development. The Barsigian et al. (2025) study showed both the negative and positive potentials of social media platforms and illustrated adolescents' agentic use of these online spaces for their own aims and identity development.

A research priority that has already become evident from these early studies is that it is vital to unpack what social media and video game use actually mean to the young person, using a functional/affordance focus as well as a balanced research approach – examining both possible risks and benefits of being in digital environments. These research exemplars also highlight innovations in the methods used and how research questions are being refined and demonstrate how researchers are encountering and working to solve many practical research problems.

Summary

Some virtual spaces are thought to encourage the spread of a global youth culture, individual self-expression, and the enhancement of social networks (Manago, 2014; Sirin et al., 2024). An adolescent's interaction with social media and/or video games can serve as a context for identity development. In these virtual spaces, people can access and provide information (fact and opinion) as well as encounter a range of values and lifestyle possibilities (e.g., Barsigian et al., 2025; Manago et al., 2025). Social media and video games have diverse uses and meanings to people. Because of this diversity, how development unfolds in relation to social media and video game use is undoubtedly complex (Granic et al., 2020a, 2020b; Manago et al., 2025). Research studies and theory specifically about adolescent identity development in digital environments are likely to grow substantially in the future. Much more research is needed to determine how positive and negative forms of identity development interface with digital life. As these associations are clarified in future research studies, new ways to leverage online social interactions and experiences to the benefit of adolescent identity development should be at the forefront of research efforts. The digital adolescent identity field is an exciting work in progress, with researchers launching novel studies as well as digitalizing identity interventions (e.g., Berman et al., 2025;

Soh et al., 2025), all in order to show proof of concept and expand our knowledge of this exciting field.

Notes

1 This passage comes from pilot interviews undertaken by Laura Ferrer-Wreder in 2025 to obtain background information about digital life and identity development; a pseudonym was used in this quote.

2 In this chapter, it is also noted in the subsection titled "Video Games and Identity: So Far and In Brief" that there are a few published research studies on video games and adolescent identity development. However, there are many research studies about video games and adolescent development and behavior more generally (e.g., APA, 2019; Maheux et al., 2025). Interactions with video games and social media use connected to video gameplay represent key future growth areas for adolescent identity development research.

3 See Sirin et al. (2024) and Soh et al. (2024) for other theories about identity development in digital environments.

4 The concept of an identity agent highlights how identity is developed in relationships and how other people may knowingly, or work explicitly, to support another person's identity development (Schachter & Marshall, 2010). Identity agents can be a sounding board for adolescents' identity work (e.g., reinforcing and dismissing identity-related activities or decisions), and in the case of peers, they may also jointly engage in identity exploration and meaning-making together (Schachter & Marshall, 2010).

5 An examination of existing empirical studies using a search engine often used in psychology called PsycINFO yielded 58 results or hits when the search criteria required that the word "identity" be in the document title and the word "internet" be referenced anywhere in the abstract. Other search criteria were that the search result be an English-language peer-reviewed empirical study with a child or adolescent study sample. The same search criteria were used, but the word "Internet" was replaced with "social media" and then "video game." These two additional searches yielded 39 (social media) and seven (video game) articles, respectively. Even though there are limitations to these non-systematic literature searches of the scholarly research literature, the results are illustrative because they give the reader a sense of the empirical evidence in this field and where research attention has generally been focused so far. It should be noted that the chapter is not a comprehensive narrative research summary nor an analysis of all theories relevant to this topic. This chapter aims to be illustrative and forward-looking. The reader interested in systematic reviews in this area is referred to several excellent articles and chapters cited in the reference list of this chapter.

6 Bullet points were in the original quoted text by Crowe and Watts (2014).

References

Adler, J. M., Lodi-Smith, J., Philippe, F. L., & Houle, I. (2016). The incremental validity of narrative identity in predicting well-being: A review of the field and recommendations for the future. *Personality and Social Psychology Review*, *20*(2), 142–175. https://doi.org/10.1177/1088868315585068

Agai, M. S. (2022). Disconnectivity synced with identity cultivation: Adolescent narratives of digital disconnection. *Journal of Computer-Mediated Communication*, *27*(6), 1–11. https://doi.org/10.1093/jcmc/zmac025

APA (2019, October). *APA task force report on violent video games*. https://www.apa.org/science/leadership/bsa/report-violent-video-games.pdf

Avci, H., Baams, L., & Kretschmer, T. (2024). A systematic review of social media use and adolescent identity development. *Adolescent Research Review*, *10*(2), 219–236. https://doi.org/10.1007/s40894-024-00251-1

Bacchini, D., De Angelis, G., & Fanara, A. (2017). Identity formation in adolescent and emerging adult regular players of Massively Multiplayer Online Role-Playing Games (MMORPG). *Computers in Human Behavior*, *73*, 191–199. https://doi.org/10.1016/j.chb.2017.03.045

Barsigian, L. L., Howard, C., Quintero, D. A., Walsh, A. S., & Manago, A. M. (2025). Engagement with master and alternative narratives of gender and sexuality among LGBTQ+ youth in the digital age. *Journal of Adolescent Research*, *40*(2), 413–447. https://doi.org/10.1177/07435584221150223

Berman, S. L., Hall, J., Andrion, C., & Stuckey, A. L. (2025). Making life choices: An evaluation of a university-based identity intervention program. *Identity: An International Journal of Theory and Research*, *25*(2), 305–315. https://doi.org/10.1080/15283488.2024.2389431

Berzonsky, M. D. (1989). Identity style: Conceptualization and measurement. *Journal of Adolescent Research*, *4*(3), 268–282. https://doi.org/10.1177/074355488943002

Chalk, A. (2021, January 5). *Runescape celebrates its 20th anniversary with a 'Grand Party' and special rewards*. PC Gamer. https://www.pcgamer.com/runescape-celebrates-its-20th-anniversary-with-a-grand-party-and-special-rewards/

Coyne, S. M., Weinstein, E., Sheppard, J. A., Spencer, J., Gale, M., Megan, V. A., Ririe, N., Monson, C., Ashby, S., Weston, A., & Banks, K. (2023). Analysis of social media use, mental health, and gender identity among US youths. *JAMA Network Open*, *6*(7), 1–12. https://doi.org/10.1001/jamanetworkopen.2023.24389

Crowe, N., & Watts, M. (2014). 'When I click "ok" I become sassy – I become a girl': Young people and gender identity: Subverting the 'body' in massively multi-player online role-playing games. *International Journal of Adolescence and Youth*, *19*(2), 217–231. https://doi.org/10.1080/02673843.2012.736868

Data Reportal, We Are Social, & Meltwater (2025, February 5). *Average daily time spent using the internet by 3rd quarter 2024, by age and gender (in hours. minutes) [Graph]*. Statista. https://www.statista.com/statistics/1378510/daily-time-spent-online-worldwide-by-age-and-gender/

Di Cesare, D. M., Craig, S. L., Brooks, A. S., & Doll, K. (2024). Setting the game agenda: Reviewing the emerging literature on video gaming and psychological well-being of sexual and gender diverse youth. *Games and Culture: A Journal of Interactive Media*, *19*(7), 933–953. https://doi.org/10.1177/15554120231178883

Dimock, M. (2023, May 22). *5 things to keep in mind when you hear about Gen Z, Millennials, Boomers and other generations*. Pew Research Center. https://www.pewresearch.org/short-reads/2023/05/22/5-things-to-keep-in-mind-when-you-hear-about-gen-z-millennials-boomers-and-other-generations/

Eklund, L., & Roman, S. (2017). Do adolescent gamers make friends offline? Identity and friendship formation in school. *Computers in Human Behavior*, *73*, 284–289. https://doi.org/10.1016/j.chb.2017.03.035

Forsyth, S. R., Chesla, C. A., Rehm, R. S., & Malone, R. E. (2017). "It feels more real": An interpretive phenomenological study of the meaning of video games in adolescent lives. *Advances in Nursing Science*, *40*(4), E1–E17. https://doi.org/10.1097/ANS.0000000000000183

Gibson, E. J. (2000). Perceptual learning in development: Some basic concepts. *Ecological Psychology*, *12*(4), 295–302. https://doi.org/10.1207/S15326969ECO1204_04

Gibson, J. J. (2014). *The ecological approach to visual perception: Classic edition* (1st ed.). Psychology Press. https://doi.org/10.4324/9781315740218 (Original work published 1979)

Granic, I., Lobel, A., & Engels, R. C. M. E. (2014). The benefits of playing video games. *American Psychologist*, *69*(1), 66–78. https://doi.org/10.1037/a0034857

Granic, I., Morita, H., & Scholten, H. (2020a). Young people's digital interactions from a narrative identity perspective: Implications for mental health and wellbeing. *Psychological Inquiry*, *31*(3), 258–270. https://doi.org/10.1080/1047840X.2020.1820225

Granic, I., Morita, H., & Scholten, H. (2020b). Beyond screen time: Identity development in the digital age. *Psychological Inquiry, 31*(3), 195–223. https://doi.org/10.1080/1047840X.2020.1820214

Griffioen, N., Scholten, H., Lichtwarck-Aschoff, A., van Rooij, M., & Granic, I. (2021). Everyone does it – Differently: A window into emerging adults' smartphone use. *Humanities & Social Sciences Communications, 8*(1), 1–11. https://doi.org/10.1057/s41599-021-00863-1

Höfrová, A., Balidemaj, V., & Small, M. A. (2024). A systematic literature review of education for generation alpha. *Discover Education, 3*, Article 125, 1–20. https://doi.org/10.1007/s44217-024-00218-3

Hughes, J., Morrison, L., & Thompson, S. (2016). Who do you think you are? Examining the off/online identities of adolescents using a social networking site. In M. Walrave, K. Ponnet, E. Vanderhoven, J. Haers, & B. Segaert (Eds.), *Youth 2.0: Social media and adolescence: Connecting, sharing and empowering* (pp. 3–19). Switzerland: Springer International Publishing. https://doi.org/10.1007/978-3-319-27893-3_1

ITU (2024, May 31). *Age distribution of internet users worldwide as of 2024, by region [Graph].* Statista. https://www.statista.com/statistics/209101/age-distribution-internet-users-worldwide-by-region/

Maheux, A. J., Garrett, S. L., Fox, K. A., Field, N. H., Burnell, K., Telzer, E. H., & Prinstein, M. J. (2025). Adolescent social gaming as a form of social media: A call for developmental science. *Child Development Perspectives, 19*(1), 3–13. https://doi.org/10.1111/cdep.12518

Manago, A. M. (2014). Identity development in the digital age: The case of social networking sites. In K. C. McLean & M. Syed (Eds.), *The Oxford handbook of identity development* [E-reader version] (pp. 1–33). Oxford University Press. https://doi.org/10.1093/oxfordhb/9780199936564.013.031

Manago, A. M., Perez de la Torre, M. M., & de la Torre Sánchez, M. C. (2025). Cultural identity as worldviews: A natural experiment with Maya adolescents before and after community adoption of digital communication. *Developmental Psychology.* Advance online publication. https://doi.org/10.1037/dev0001945

Mangalam, M., Barrett, L., & Fragaszy, D. M. (2024). From Turing to Gibson: Implications of affordances for the sciences of organisms. In M. Mangalam, A. Hajnal, & D. G. Kelty-Stephen (Eds.), *The modern legacy of Gibson's affordances for the sciences of organisms* (pp. 249–267). Routledge.

McAdams, D. P., & McLean, K. C. (2013). Narrative identity. *Current Directions in Psychological Science, 22*(3), 233–238. https://doi.org/10.1177/0963721413475622

McAdams, D. P., & Olson, B. D. (2010). Personality development: Continuity and change over the life course. *Annual Review of Psychology, 61*, 517–542. https://doi.org/10.1146/annurev.psych.093008.100507

OECD (2025). *How's life for children in the digital age?* Paris: OECD Publishing. https://doi.org/10.1787/0854b900-en

Poushter, J., Gubbala, S., & Austin, S. (2024, February 5). *8 charts on technology use around the world.* Pew Research Center. https://www.pewresearch.org/short-reads/2024/02/05/8-charts-on-technology-use-around-the-world/

Rachwani, J., Kaplan, B. E., Tamis-LeMonda, C. S., & Adolph, K. E. (2021). Children's use of everyday artifacts: Learning the hidden affordance of zipping. *Developmental Psychobiology, 63*(4), 793–799. https://doi.org/10.1002/dev.22049

Rosenberg, M., Schooler, C., & Schoenbach, C. (1989). Self-esteem and adolescent problems: Modeling reciprocal effects. *American Sociological Review, 54*(6), 1004–1018. https://doi.org/10.2307/2095720

Rosenthal, D. A., Gurney, R. M., & Moore, S. M. (1981). From trust on intimacy: A new inventory for examining Erikson's stages of psychosocial development. *Journal of Youth and Adolescence, 10* (6), 525–537. https://doi.org/10.1007/BF02087944

Ryan, R. M., & Deci, E. L. (2000). Self-determination theory and the facilitation of intrinsic motivation, social development, and well-being. *American Psychologist*, *55*(1), 68–78. https://doi.org/10.1037/0003-066X.55.1.68

Schachter, E. P., & Marshall, S. K. (2010). Identity agents: A focus on those purposefully involved in the identity of others. *Identity: An International Journal of Theory and Research*, *10*(2), 71–75. https://doi.org/10.1080/15283481003711676

Sirin, S. R., Brauer, S. Z., & Tugberk, R. C. (2024). Reframing adolescent identity: A global perspective for the digital age. *Annual Review of Developmental Psychology*, *6*, 301–322. https://doi.org/10.1146/annurev-devpsych-010923-101059

Soh, S., Cruz, B., Meca, A., & Harari, G., M. (2025). A digital identity intervention incorporating social media activities promotes identity exploration and commitment among emerging adults. *Identity: An International Journal of Theory and Research*, *25*(2), 330–346. https://doi.org/10.1080/15283488.2024.2404004

Soh, S., Talaifar, S., & Harari, G. M. (2024). Identity development in the digital context. *Social and Personality Psychology Compass*, *18*(2), 1–22. https://doi.org/10.1111/spc3.12940

Spies Shapiro, L. A., & Margolin, G. (2014). Growing up wired: Social networking sites and adolescent psychosocial development. *Clinical Child and Family Psychology Review*, *17*(1), 1–18. https://doi.org/10.1007/s10567-013-0135-1

United Nations Children's Fund (2023). *Bridging the gender digital divide: Challenges and an urgent call for action for equitable digital skills development*. UNICEF. https://data.unicef.org/resources/ictgenderdivide/

Wols, A., Pingel, M., Lichtwarck-Aschoff, A., & Granic, I. (2024). Effectiveness of applied and casual games for young people's mental health: A systematic review of randomised controlled studies. *Clinical Psychology Review*, *108*, 1–20. https://doi.org/10.1016/j.cpr.2024.102396

Yang, C., Carter, M. D. K., Webb, J. J., & Holden, S. M. (2020). Developmentally salient psychosocial characteristics, rumination, and compulsive social media use during the transition to college. *Addiction Research & Theory*, *28*(5), 433–442. https://doi.org/10.1080/16066359.2019.1682137

Yang, C., Holden, S. M., & Carter, M. D. K. (2018). Social media social comparison of ability (but not opinion) predicts lower identity clarity: Identity processing style as a mediator. *Journal of Youth and Adolescence*, *47*(10), 2114–2128. https://doi.org/10.1007/s10964-017-0801-6

Zimmermann, E., & Tomczyk, S. (2025). Using social media to promote life skills among adolescents: A debate on opportunities, challenges, and implications for health and education. *Journal of Prevention*, *46*(2), 201–211. https://doi.org/10.1007/s10935-025-00826-1

8 Identity Beyond Adolescence

> I think since adolescence, my sense of identity has only grown stronger and more solid over time. There haven't been any earth-shattering changes along the way. It's just now I'm far less concerned about what others might think of me and far more trusting of myself and doing what feels right.
>
> (John, 51-year-old teacher)

> For me, the accidental death of my older brother when I was 21 just completely shattered my sense of myself and my certainty about the way the world was "supposed" to be. You just aren't supposed to die so young. That single event has, to this day, made me so very aware of just how fragile life is and how I can never take anything for granted.
>
> (Sarah, 30-year-old computer programmer)

Many years ago, when I (JK) first began teaching a university course on lifespan development, a 19-year-old student came up to me after class one day and asked why she had to learn about adult development – why didn't the class just end at that "terminal point of marriage"? After all, not much of consequence really happened after that, she pointed out. (And whatever really *did* happen to Cinderella through those many years of life after she met her Prince Charming and lived happily ever after?) The formation of identity is not restricted to adolescence, as Erikson (1980, p. 122) pointed out: "[I]dentity formation neither begins nor ends with adolescence: it is a lifelong development." This final chapter will focus on some of the normative changes in identity that are likely to occur beyond adolescence. The chapter will also address how adolescent identity resolutions are likely to impact major psychosocial challenges of adulthood.

The primary reason for the focus of the final chapter is to help readers anticipate what may lie ahead – to appreciate how initial identity resolutions formed at the end of adolescence/emerging adulthood can have rather long-term consequences. Certainly, identity-defining choices and life directions can change over time, but beyond emerging adulthood, major identity changes become far less common (as the research presented ahead will show).

DOI: 10.4324/9781003486336-8

For some individuals, there may be just a growing sense of internal coherence or self-certainty that characterizes identity as it evolves beyond adolescence, while for others, there may be more dramatic "life course changes" to one's place in the world and understandings of oneself. These individual differences in the identity formation process beyond adolescence lead to a number of identity-related questions. What dimensions of one's identity formed during adolescence and young adulthood are likely to remain stable over time, and what dimensions are likely to change? Are there different types of contexts that may be associated with different patterns of identity stability or change during adult life? Where identity does markedly change, are there particular types of events generally associated with specific identity change pathways during adult life? And how are adolescent resolutions to identity related to one's capacity for intimacy, generativity, and integrity during adulthood?

It is the theory and research originating in the psychosocial framework of Erik Erikson that has perhaps offered the most prolific insights into ongoing identity development beyond adolescence. Erikson took special care to emphasize how identity, once formed and stabilized by the end of adolescence, will likely continue to develop through young, middle, and later adulthood years as well:

> Such a sense of identity [developed during adolescence], however, is never gained nor maintained once and for all. Like a "good conscience," it is constantly lost and regained, although more lasting and more economical methods of maintenance and restoration are evolved and fortified in late adolescence.
> (Erikson, 1980, p. 128)

Erikson also wrote extensively about how adolescent identity resolutions may become reactivated and revised during post-adolescent phases of the lifespan. Indeed, Erikson and his colleagues have devoted an entire book to examining the ways in which identity resolutions of adolescence become reconsidered, particularly during later adulthood: "Old age's reconciling of the tension between identity and identity confusion reinvolves the individual in the psychosocial process that dominated adolescence" (Erikson et al., 1986, p. 129). It is thus important to appreciate the impact that identity resolutions undertaken during adolescence may have on various dimensions of adult life in the years beyond identity's primary time of formation.

This volume has reviewed different perspectives on how identity forms and develops during adolescence and emerging adulthood in preparation for entry into adult life, and research from within these varied traditions has begun to supply answers to some of the questions noted earlier. In this final chapter, we explore these questions and conclude with reflections on how identity-related research and practice might be optimized for future developments in the field.

Stability and Change in Identity Beyond Adolescence: Theory

Erikson (1968, 1980; Erikson et al., 1986) has given considerable attention to the epigenesis of identity beyond adolescence through the ensuing psychosocial tasks of adult life. Among the important themes Erikson discussed in identity's onward journey were the importance of identity continuity and the preservation of a sense of self-sameness through the inevitable biological, psychological, and social changes that life invariably brings. In the words of one research participant, I (JK) interviewed as a midlife adult:

> [O]h, I am the same person who I was when I was 7. To other people, my body has changed, and their expectations of me have changed, but I feel the same. Except now I do behave as I feel . . . and people sometimes find it a little odd. But in the long run it's better to be true to yourself than to be true to other people's expectations of you.
>
> (Kroger, 1993, p. 213)

Erikson et al. (1986, p. 130) also made general comments about ongoing identity development through midlife: "During adulthood, the individual struggles to balance a faithfulness to some commitments with an inevitable confusion and abandonment of others, all the while living a life that, in turn, both represents and reflects an underlying sense of self." And Erikson himself continued to highlight resolutions to the identity-versus-role confusion task of adolescence as the foundation for working through the psychosocial tasks of *intimacy versus isolation, generativity versus stagnation*, and *integrity versus despair* during adult life.

With these comments by Erikson in mind, Marcia (2002) developed a cyclical model of ongoing identity development during adulthood. He proposed that following initial identity resolutions of adolescence and young adulthood, there were likely to be normative life events that could shake people at their psychological foundations (i.e., cause disequilibrium), and such life experiences would be associated with some kind of identity reformulation. He conceptualized a conical structure whereby the phases of adolescence, early adulthood, middle adulthood, and late adulthood represented increasingly large elliptical cycles within the cone (pointed downward), as one reexperienced one or more ongoing, disequilibrating cycles of identity foreclosure (and/or diffusion) through moratorium through achievement during each subsequent phase of adulthood as one grappled with issues of *intimacy versus isolation, generativity versus stagnation*, and *integrity versus despair*. Marcia noted that in the case of adults exhibiting stable foreclosure patterns, in which the identity structure was designed to prevent disequilibrium, those ongoing cycles of identity development might or might not occur. When development did occur for the foreclosed individual, the disequilibrium experienced was likely to be quite shattering. Identity-diffuse adults were also unlikely to experience identity disequilibrium during ongoing phases of adult life, according to Marcia, because they lacked a solid identity structure at the outset.

Marcia and colleagues (Stephen et al., 1992) had initially proposed a sequence of moratorium–achievement–moratorium–achievement (MAMA) cycles through adult life, in which one might regress to earlier modes of functioning at times of identity distress. Through his later model, Marcia tried to capture the cycles of identity disequilibrium and reconstruction that had the potential to emerge through ongoing phases of adult identity development in more detail. In order for a new identity structure to emerge, an old one needed to disintegrate, which was likely to be a very confusing and painful experience.

More recently, Mitchell et al. (2021) proposed a conceptual view of how identity, established during adolescence, is both maintained and adapted during adult life. They relied on the concept of identity integration that draws on both narrative analysis and Erikson's writings to propose identity maintenance and reestablishment processes throughout adulthood and across all of Erikson's adult psychosocial development tasks. Given these theoretical propositions, what does the research show about ongoing patterns of identity development beyond adolescence? While adult identity research having origins in Erikson's and Marcia's models has now produced a number of investigations, findings from other related theoretical models discussed in this volume will also be presented, where possible, to illustrate ongoing changes in identity through adulthood.

Stability and Change in Identity Beyond Adolescence: Research

In order to address the question of stability and change in identity's evolution beyond adolescence, one must look, ideally, to longitudinal studies of identity over time as well as cross-sectional and retrospective studies (important but not as ideal as longitudinal studies). Marcia's identity status approach and its elaborations, described in Chapter 2, have been used extensively to identify various pathways that identity status change may take over the course of adulthood. The direction of change and/or stability that these pathways take has now been the focus of a number of longitudinal and cross-sectional as well as retrospective studies involving young, middle-aged, and later-life adults. While a number of longitudinal studies of college-age youths and emerging adults have now been undertaken, the studies reviewed in the following sections all involve longitudinal data collection from individuals followed at least through their 20s and 30s, and often beyond. Findings generally illustrate the following trends:

- When identity status change does occur in adult life, the most common pathway of movement is from foreclosure to moratorium to achievement.
- The highest probability of identity status change occurs during emerging adulthood in comparison with the later part of young adulthood and midlife.
- Different types of lifestyle contexts appear associated with different patterns of identity development from adolescence/emerging adulthood through midlife.
- Identity achievement remains elusive for approximately half of individuals as they enter adult life, at least among those sampled from research conducted in primarily Western contexts.
- The likelihood of movement from the identity diffusion status between the end of adolescence and young to middle adult life is low.
- Narrative studies point to increasing levels of meaning-making over adolescence/young adulthood and of increasing self-concept clarity from adolescence through adulthood for those showing progressive identity development.

Longitudinal Studies

Several longitudinal studies of identity status change during adulthood have emerged over the last two decades. As noted in Chapter 2, different measures have also been devised for determining the identity statuses, and somewhat different time intervals between measurement points have been used in longitudinal identity status assessments. Thus, one must be somewhat cautious in making comparisons across studies of adolescent or adult identity status changes without attention to the actual measures used and the time intervals between assessments that were involved. Carlsson et al. (2024) pointed to the potential conceptual drift between identity status interview and questionnaire measures, for example.

Marcia's ISIs have been employed in several long-term longitudinal studies of identity status change and stability during adult life. In Finland, for example, Fadjukoff and colleagues (Fadjukoff. Pulkkinen, & Kokko, 2016; Fadjukoff et al., 2024) evaluated identity status patterns of stability and change at ages 27, 36, 42, 50, and 61 years in a representative sample of 172 adults from the general population of a large Finnish city (by age 61, 5% of women and 10% of men were deceased). Findings showed considerable variation in identity status ratings given across identity domains. However, the developmental trend from age 27 to age 61 was moderately progressive toward identity achievement within all but the religious identity domain; overall identity commitment to either the foreclosure or achievement statuses was over 90% for both men and women of this sample; by age 61, some 68% of the women and 49% of the men were identity achieved (Fadjukoff. Pulkkinen, & Kokko, 2016).

In Sweden, Eriksson and colleagues (2020) and Larsson et al. (2024) also evaluated identity status change and stability from the mid-20s through the late 30s, at four data collection points (ages 25, 29, 33, and 39 years), with the ISI. By age 39, there were significant increases in identity achievement and significant decreases in identity diffusion; there were no changes in the numbers of those in the identity foreclosure status, however. Stability in identity commitments via achievement and foreclosure statuses was by far the most common identity pattern across early adulthood (Eriksson et al., 2020; Larsson et al., 2024). A qualitative analysis of interview data between ages 33 and 39 (when achievement and foreclosure stability were high) will be discussed in a later section.

Helson et al. (1995) as well as Helson and Mitchell (2020) assessed three cohorts of women who had been young adults in the 1950s and early and late 1960s through to their mid-adulthood years on a number of personality measures, and a Q-sort measure of identity status was included in part of the study. While it was not possible to follow individual pathways of identity status change over time in this study, midlife brought a time of reevaluation of life directions for some, similar to the time of exploration and questioning that many underwent as they entered young adulthood. However, there was generally high stability in all of the women's identity status vectors from their early forties throughout mid-adulthood, suggesting that major identity changes were primarily a phenomenon of late adolescence and emerging adulthood, as well as early midlife to a more limited extent. At the same time, one-third of the sample were foreclosed at midlife, and 11% were diffused. Beyond midlife, identity statuses tended to remain more stable relative to earlier developmental periods.

Several additional longitudinal studies of identity status change from late adolescence to early and mid-adulthood have also been conducted using paper-and-pencil measures. Cramer (2017) undertook a longitudinal study evaluating identity status at ages 18, 22, and 35 years among a group of individuals initially drawn as part of a random sample of entering freshmen at a small American college. Results showed a modest increase in identity achievement scores over this time interval as well as a large decrease in moratorium scores. Group mean scores showed little change in diffusion status scores over the 17-year time interval (although there was individual variability in this status).

Whitbourne and colleagues (Sneed et al., 2006) used a paper-and-pencil measure of identity achievement and diffusion only to study identity status stability and change between college and the age of 54 years, with data collected every 11 years, at ages 20, 31, 42, and 54. Results indicated a general increase in identity achievement scores between the ages of 20 and 31; additionally, the rate of increase in the *identity-versus-role confusion* resolution slowed at each data collection point between the ages of 31 and 54.

Several narrative studies have also made use of Marcia's identity status groupings and have followed individuals through their 20s and 30s and, in several cases, through their 40s, 50s, and 60s. Josselson (2017, 2019) reported on the lives of 25 college women over the course of 45 years (interviews were conducted around the time of their graduation from college at 21 years and again at ages 33, 43, 56, and 67 years). Josselson documented how many of these women went about finding and revising their identities over time and noted how late midlife often brought subtle but important changes to how the women came to see and understand themselves and the world.

Josselson (2017, 2019) found that in their 20s and early 30s, most women focused on trying to develop a sense of competence in the world, while their late 30s and early 40s brought concerns with whether or not they were really pursuing the identity-defining directions they had envisaged and becoming the people they wished to be; the decade of their 40s often became a time of major identity revisions for those who achieved a sense of their own identities by young adulthood. By their mid-50s, these women were reaping the benefits of their earlier identity work and enjoying an "age of fulfilment." In their mid-60s, many were retired or trying to reincorporate previous identity elements that had eluded them earlier. Josselson (2019) noted that what had changed the most for many of these women was the meanings assigned to events and parts of the self, manifestations of an underlying identity. She referred to such changes using the metaphor of a kaleidoscope. New events or social roles, previously unimagined, often required new ways of integrating these elements into an ongoing identity configuration, reminiscent of a kaleidoscope.

Josselson (2019) commented, however, on the patterns for six women she identified as drifters (diffusions) as they left college with no clear goals for the future, living entirely in the moment; if they imagined any futures for themselves at all, their hopes were fantasies, and they had no clear thoughts of how to actualize these "dreams." Although there was individual variation among the drifters in college, most by midlife were feeling battered and chastened by their circumstances, drifting in and out of places, relationships, and endeavors, and holding more jobs, using more drugs and alcohol, and trying more religions as they continued to struggle with feelings of frustration and disappointment across their adult lives. Only one of these individuals had shaped a functional identity by midlife.

A further narrative longitudinal study of identity status change from the mid-20s to late 30s attempted to learn more about continuity in identity development after initial identity commitments had been undertaken (Eriksson et al., 2020; Larsson et al., 2024). Some 124 Swedish men and women were given an ISI at ages 25, 29, 33, and 39, as discussed earlier in this chapter. Identity narratives from these individuals indicated important changes in the ways they approached changing life conditions, the extent to which they engaged in ongoing meaning-making, and how they continued to pursue different life directions. It seems that an identity achieved stance was necessary for a solid sense of identity to stay adaptive and flexible over time.

A further investigation of those who remained in the diffusion status from their mid- to late 20s (seven of 124 participants) found a pattern of keeping their lives on hold through decreased or haphazard activity in relation to changing life circumstances, with few attempts to make meaning of these situations as well as attempts by some to try to "dissolve" their personal life directions (Carlsson et al., 2016). Between ages 33 and 39, there were interesting narrative changes, even among those remaining stable in the same identity status. For most of those who were identity achieved over this time span, commitments became increasingly anchored in the self and were more meaningful to identity. There was also an increasingly integrated and clear identity narrative, and identity was more connected to older and younger generations; the opposite was the case for those who were identity diffuse. Among the stable foreclosed individuals, there was a mixture of patterns – either a weakening or deepening of identity commitments, identity integration, and connection to other generations over this time period (Larsson et al., 2024).

Several additional narrative dimensions of identity change and stability have also been examined longitudinally from late adolescence over the course of adult life. Pals (2006) studied narrative identity processes for women from the Mills Longitudinal Study by Helson (1967), described earlier in this chapter. At age 52 years, some 83 of these women provided a narrative of their most difficult time since college, and Pals used additional personality data from the age 21, 52, and 61 assessments in her study of identity narratives over time. She assumed that difficult life experiences were identity challenging, and she wanted to learn more about how participants responded to their difficult challenges through their narrative processing and their resolutions. In general, Pals found that changes and new ways in which people interpreted their lives and life experiences were likely to trigger new but enduring identity-related patterns of thinking, feeling, and behaving in adult life over time. More specifically, two important findings emerged:

- Individuals high in "coping openness" embraced the narrative challenge of addressing their difficult life experiences and engaged in exploratory narrative

processing of their situations that allowed for greater levels of wisdom, self-understanding, and emotional complexity over time.
- A coherent positive resolution to the challenging event predicted increasing ego resiliency over the course of adult life.

Issues of identity clarity and content in adulthood have also been examined longitudinally over a three-year time span during adulthood with a sample of individuals aged 19–86 years at the start of the study (Lodi-Smith et al., 2017). The study found that changes in self-concept clarity over time corresponded to changes in identity contents and role engagements (sometimes brought about by increasing health limitations). Self-concept clarity appeared, from this study, to be an integral marker of identity maturity in adulthood.

Cross-Sectional and Retrospective Studies

A large, meta-analytic study of identity status stability and change over the course of young and middle adulthood was undertaken by Kroger and colleagues (2010). While this study also included identity status patterns of development during adolescence that have been reviewed in Chapter 2, the larger investigation also included material on young adult development during the ages 22–36 years. It is interesting that while the likelihood of being identity achieved was 34% at age 22 (across eight studies and 247 participants) and 31% from 23 to 29 years (across 11 studies with 253 participants), the 30–36-year time span showed approximately half (47%) of the participants to be identity achieved (across nine studies with 310 participants). Noteworthy, however, is the fact that well into the 30s, the incidences of identity achievement were not higher.

Subsequent to this work, a cross-sectional study of identity status change from adolescence to middle adulthood in Trinidad found that the achieved identity status was most common in middle age, compared with adolescence, emerging adulthood, and young adulthood years, while moratorium and diffusion statuses were more characteristic of the younger age-groups (Arneaud et al., 2016). Again, only approximately half of the individuals in this study were identity achieved by midlife, according to the mean ages of participants who had experienced various adulthood transitions (to marriage, parenting, becoming employed, etc.).

When exploration and commitment constructs are considered separately and cross-sectionally across late adolescence and the early years of adulthood, Luyckx and colleagues (Luyckx et al., 2013) found that, despite some minor fluctuations, identity commitment processes increased in a linear fashion for a sample of Flemish high school, university, and working individuals aged 14–30 years. Exploration in breadth and exploration in depth were highest among those in their early to mid-20s. Additionally, exploration in breadth and depth was strongly related to commitment processes in late adolescence and young adulthood but became increasingly linked with ruminative exploration and depression by the late 20s. It remains unknown, at present, how these patterns of identity exploration and commitment evolved over the course of adulthood beyond age 30. These cross-sectional studies of identity status change over time point to only moderate levels of identity attainment by midlife (only about half of those individuals assessed were identity achieved); identity exploration in breadth and depth peaked from the early to mid-20s.

Cross-sectional *narrative* studies of adult identity development also provide some insights into identity from adolescence to adulthood. McLean (2008) examined narrative identity in two age-groups of individuals: those from late adolescence through young adulthood (age 17–35 years) and older adults (age 65–85 years). In an interview, participants reported three self-defining memories – memories that were vivid, emotional, personally important, and/or highly memorable in that they powerfully conveyed how one came to be the person one currently was. After interviews, participants were asked to report their age at the time of the memory and what it meant to their sense of identity. Findings showed that through their memories, younger individuals constructed themselves more in terms of change, while older participants presented themselves more in terms of stability.

McLean (2008) concluded that although the mechanisms for developing narratives about the self and identity may be similar from late adolescence to adulthood, the functions of creating narratives may be quite different. For late adolescents and young adults, narratives appeared to provide a vehicle for self-exploration and understanding, while for older adults, narratives provided a sense of stability and resolution. For both age-groups, however, there was a striving toward identity continuity over time.

Pasupathi and Mansour (2006) also cross-sectionally examined adult differences in autobiographical reasoning about identity-related issues through narratives. Results from their two studies indicated that middle-aged and older adults were more likely than younger adults to demonstrate explicit autobiographical reasoning when constructing their personal, identity-related narratives. The two studies also found age-related increases in the likelihood of autobiographical reasoning into middle age. It may be that there is an increasing emphasis on remembering more meaningful life experiences as well as an increasing need to remember in order to integrate identity elements across one's life with age.

More recently, Fritsch et al. (2023) examined self-defining memories among four age-groups of French adults: young adults (18–30 years), middle-aged adults (31–59 years), young-old adults (60–69 years), and old-old adults (70–97 years). Self-defining memories appeared differentially influenced by age. Young adult self-defining narratives consisted of two main contents that were highly salient for their sense of identity: relationship events and life-threatening events. Integrative meaning among young-old adults was lower than among young or middle-aged adults. Few differences in self-defining memories were found between young-old and old-old adults, suggesting a more stable sense of personal identity in later life.

Cross-sectional and retrospective studies of additional identity-related variables have also been undertaken throughout adulthood. For example, Zucker et al. (2002) used cross-sectional samples of college-educated young, middle, and late adulthood women to find higher levels of self-certainty with age. An additional retrospective study of identity certainty among a group of highly educated women aged 30–50 years also found this variable to increase with age (Stewart et al.,

2001). Higher levels of self-certainty in identity-related issues do appear to be one concomitant of aging beyond adolescence.

Retrospective accounts of identity stability and change over adulthood have been relatively uncommon. However, despite the issues that accurate recall may bring to remembered life transitions, Kroger and Haslett (1987, 1991) undertook a series of ISIs with 100 midlife men and women aged 40–63 years from upper-middle-class backgrounds in New Zealand in an effort to examine patterns of stability and change in identity status over time since mid-adolescence.

Analyses revealed different identity status transition pathways for individuals who had selected different lifestyle options, even when age, education level, parental and marital status, and identity domain were held constant. For example, while men who were full-time workers throughout their adult lives had about a 50% probability of being identity achieved in the vocational domain by age 43, women who were full-time homemakers since having children in their young adult lives had only about a 12% probability of being identity achieved by age 43. By contrast, women who had worked full time outside the home throughout their child-rearing years as well as women who had returned to full-time work following their child-rearing years both had about a 95% chance of being identity achieved by age 43 years. The probability of change from foreclosure and diffusion statuses was very low across all lifestyle groups beyond age 25 years in this vocational identity domain. Additionally, ongoing MAMA cycles of moratorium–achievement were present during young and middle adulthood across all lifestyle subgroups, after initial identity commitments had been chosen for those rated as identity achieved at the end of adolescence. This retrospective study offers important insights into the relationships between lifestyle contexts and various identity status transition patterns and change rates from adolescence to young and middle adult life.

It is difficult to give a definitive statement about the types of events that may be associated with specific types of identity changes over the course of adulthood. While some studies have examined potential precipitators of identity change during late adolescence and young adult life (reviewed in Chapter 2), there is far less information about factors potentially associated with identity change during middle and late adulthood. Some research does suggest, however, that for the identity achieved, it is often internally driven events (e.g., new insights, deepened awareness, or understandings about one's identity-related life circumstances) that may lead to change (Josselson, 2019, 2017; Pals, 2006). Identity clarity does appear to increase with age. Furthermore, where an initial identity commitment has not been formed during adolescence or young adulthood, the likelihood of this development occurring during adulthood is limited. Patterns of identity stability or change during *later* adulthood years have not been examined often, but the few studies that do exist suggest later adulthood to be a time of greater identity stability.

Adolescent Identity Resolutions and the Psychosocial Tasks of Adulthood: Theory

What are the relations between identity resolutions formed by the end of adolescence or emerging adulthood and the ongoing psychosocial tasks of adult life that

Erikson (1968) identified? In his epigenetic scheme, Erikson emphasized the interrelationships among all psychosocial tasks of development. With reference to adolescent identity, Erikson noted how resolutions to the *identity-versus-role confusion* task consolidated during adolescence or young adulthood would continue to impact ongoing psychosocial tasks of *intimacy versus isolation, generativity versus stagnation*, and *integrity versus despair* over the course of early, middle, and later adulthood. Erikson (1985, n.p.) also suggested that identity beyond adolescence was likely to remain under the dominance of psychosocial tasks of adulthood: "Once ascended from its precursors in earlier stages . . . each [identity] quality must be renewed in subsequent stages under the dominance of later crises." Friedman (1999), however, criticized Erikson for failing to clearly elucidate ongoing developments of identity during adulthood.

Recently, Kroger (2018) began to explore what the epigenesis of identity might actually entail during adult development through the examination of individual case studies during each postadolescent psychosocial phase. These case studies suggested that identity and ongoing psychosocial stages of adulthood may continue to codevelop over time. Much remains to be learned about how identity continuity is both retained and transformed through normative psychosocial developments of adulthood. Below is an overview of some research that has explored the relationship between identity and each of Erikson's psychosocial tasks of *intimacy versus isolation, generativity versus stagnation*, and *integrity versus despair* during adulthood. Results point to identity's evolution throughout the Eriksonian tasks of psychosocial development beyond adolescence.

Adolescent Identity Resolutions and the Psychosocial Tasks of Adulthood: Research

Identity and Intimacy

As noted in Chapter 2, *intimacy versus isolation* is a key psychosocial task of young adulthood, with optimal resolution producing the capacity to genuinely love. Erikson (1968) proposed that in order to experience mature forms of intimacy, resolutions to questions of identity needed to be reasonably well consolidated; otherwise, a close relationship with another was most likely to be in the service of addressing identity needs of the individual partners. At the same time, however, Erikson suggested that women may need to hold identity resolutions in abeyance until a suitable partner could be found around which to consolidate one's sense of identity. While Erikson's (1968) ideas on identity development among women fell by the wayside long ago, women, nevertheless, have shown more diverse patterns in their associations between identity and intimacy than men in contemporary research.

A meta-analysis of 21 studies examining the relationship between identity and intimacy among late adolescent and young adult men and women was undertaken by Årseth et al. (2009). For men, there was a strong sequential relationship between identity and intimacy, as Erikson (1968) had suggested. Results for women were more mixed, however. About two-thirds (65%) of identity-achieved and moratorium women were high in intimacy, like the men; however, foreclosed and diffuse women were almost equally likely to be in low as well as high intimacy groups. This finding suggests that for some women, identity and intimacy are codeveloping. One subsequent study, however, has supported the sequential ordering of identity and intimacy in late adolescence and young adulthood for both genders (e.g., Beyers & Seiffge-Krenke, 2010). Further work is needed to understand more fully the relationships between identity and intimacy for both men and women.

Some studies exploring potential links between identity and intimacy have used narrative methods. For example, Laughland-Booy et al. (2018) used longitudinal methods to interview participants at two time points, some six years apart. The interviews took place over the course of emerging adulthood in an Australian context. Using Marcia's identity statuses as a framework, the authors pointed to how not only individual preference and priority were important to identity and intimacy development, but also important were opportunities available as well as broader social and cultural expectations.

There have been additional studies examining links between identity and intimacy further into adult life. For example, Sneed et al. (2012) undertook a longitudinal investigation of identity and intimacy and their associations with subjective well-being among 182 individuals who were alumni of the University of Rochester between the 1960s and the 1980s. Individuals were studied every 11 years at ages 20, 31, 42, and 54 years to examine the predictive power of identity and intimacy to each other over time as well as their associations with feelings of well-being at midlife. Results generally showed strong positive links between identity and intimacy over the course of adult life. Identity issues were likely to be revisited in early midlife, and successful, intimate partnerships during young adulthood were strongly linked with a fulfilling sense of identity during midlife as well as feelings of well-being. The study also pointed to the notion that resolution of the task of *intimacy versus isolation* is critical not only for developing relationships in young adulthood but also for sustaining these relationships through midlife.

In Canada, Beaumont and Pratt (2011) used a measure of identity style (closely associated with the identity statuses) to investigate links between identity and intimacy. Samples of early- and midlife men and women, comparable in educational and ethnic background, were examined in terms of identity style, intimacy, and generativity. Here, identity style was differentially associated with intimacy resolutions. The informational identity style (comparable to identity achievement) positively predicted intimacy resolutions for the two age-groups, while the normative identity style (comparable to foreclosure) in young adulthood predicted a type of pseudointimacy (a partnership more stereotypic in nature, lacking genuine intimacy) with a partner at midlife. These latter studies supported Erikson's (1968) suggestion of an epigenetic relationship between identity and intimacy for both men and women during young and middle adulthood. Further longitudinal studies of these variables for both genders are in great need.

Identity and Generativity

As noted in Chapter 2, Erikson described the task of *generativity versus stagnation* as a key focus for midlife adults. Generativity refers to the desire to genuinely care for and guide the next as well as future generations through such activities as parenting, mentoring those outside the immediate family through work and other social contexts, volunteering in one's community, and wanting to leave behind some kind of legacy or impact on the world in ways small or large. The counterpoint to generativity is stagnation – self-absorption or self-indulgence – so that little, if any, energy is expended in service to the well-being of others. An optimal resolution to this task is the ability to genuinely care, both for the self and for others, across times and places, both near and far. While, increasingly, research during midlife has examined generativity in relation to such factors as mental health outcomes and aging well (i.e., Villar & Zacares, 2024; Villar et al., 2024), investigations that examine the direct association between identity and generativity have been far fewer in number. However, these studies, both quantitative and qualitative, that are described below, have generally shown increasingly positive connections between identity and generativity through midlife.

Bradley and Marcia (1998) were early investigators who looked at the importance of ego development (related to identity) to generativity status, finding a moderately positive association between generativity and ego development and a moderately negative association between conventional forms of generativity (caring for members of their own group or those of similar backgrounds only) and rising levels of ego development.

A longitudinal study in Finland by Fadjukoff, Pulkkinen, Lyyra, & Kokko (2016) examined parental identity status over 14 years during mid-adulthood (ages 36, 42, and 50 years) and found that parental identity achievement increased from ages 36 to 42 and remained stable thereafter. Neither early parenthood nor number of children was related to parental identity status at any age. Parental identity achievement was also more common among women and foreclosure among men throughout midlife. An achieved parental identity status was also linked with higher generativity scores for both men and women at age 42, and this same association between parental identity status and generativity held for the women but not for men in this sample at age 50. Noncommitted parental identity status (diffusion or moratorium) was linked with the lowest levels of nurturance for both genders at ages 36 and 42, when nurturance scores were measured.

Reinila et al. (2023) further investigated the development of generativity at ages 42, 50, and 61 for both men and women in this sample of adults drawn from the general Finnish population. Large individual differences were found, although there was a general trend toward a decrease in generativity scores for both genders with increasing age. Middle age appeared to be a period of primary concern for issues of generativity for both men and women. This study, however, did not attempt to provide links between identity and generativity.

Beaumont and Pratt (2011) found that midlife adults scored higher on a measure of generativity than younger adults; furthermore, there was also a direct positive relation between identity and generativity using a measure of identity style in a cross-sectional sample of early and midlife adults. Those normative in identity style (similar to those in the foreclosed identity status) were likely to be conventional in their generativity (restricted in their caring to those in their immediate social groups or having similar interests and values). A further study by James and Zarrett (2006) pointed to a similar association among participants from the Sears and colleagues (1951) study over time, where identity that was assessed in 1951 predicted generativity in 1996.

Several narrative studies have also explored the relations between identity and generativity. McAdams et al. (1997) found that adults aged 25–72 years who scored high on a measure of generativity were also more likely to narrate life stories with content that showed commitment to personal ideologies and prosocial behaviors than those who scored low on generativity. Merrill and Fivush (2016) turned to intergenerational family narratives or stories that parents and grandparents shared with their children about their own experiences growing up. These researchers showed that intergenerational narratives and the process of sharing these life stories by elders influenced the psychosocial development of both adolescents and adults in their families. These narratives helped to create a sense of identity and generativity among younger generations, contributing both to family identity and to individual well-being. A further narrative study undertaken in Canada examined the relations between trajectories of generative concerns and environmental narrative identity over the course of young adulthood at ages 23, 26, and 32 years (Jia et al., 2016). Among the findings were increased generative concerns through early adulthood. Additionally, those who developed higher levels of generative concern by age 32 years also had more salient environmental narratives (salient environmental narratives were stories told by participants that depicted turning points in their environmental concerns, coded according to the breadth and sophistication of reasoning, vividness, and impact). Further work by Larsson and Frisén (2024) found that progressive identity development over the decade of the 30s seemed to involve making more reflective comparisons with one's parents with greater independence and agency. Generativity concerns predominated during middle adulthood in the studies reviewed here and as suggested by Erikson's developmental tasks of adulthood; furthermore, generativity resolutions were positively linked with resolutions to identity and intimacy resolutions during earlier phases of adult life.

Identity and Integrity

Erikson's (1968) final psychosocial task of *integrity versus despair* normatively has been a primary focus of concern during late adulthood. During this phase, questions commonly have arisen about the meaning that one's life has had, and many identity questions may become reactivated as the end of life feels somewhat more imminent. Integrity, as noted in Chapter 2, involves the ability to accept the life one has lived with peace and satisfaction, rather than enormous regrets about the roads not taken. Despair refers to a general attitude of unhappiness or despondence over one's life course and dread at the way it is ending. Optimal resolution to this final life task resulted in what Erikson termed "wisdom" or the ability to integrate resolutions of all previous life phases to involve a deeper understanding of the human condition and a connection with those of different places and generations, without fear of death.

After her husband's death, Joan Erikson made use of her husband's annotations on an earlier edition of *The Life Cycle Completed* to suggest that with the increasing number of years one is likely to spend in late adulthood, a ninth stage of development may be needed to capture the psychosocial challenges of very late adulthood (Erikson & Erikson, 1997). This stage captured the struggle that growing mental and physical declines may bring to retaining a sense of integrity. Indeed, an investigation of the two phases of *integrity versus despair* has found some age-group distinctions (Brown & Lowis, 2003). Those in their 60s were primarily focused on traditional integrity concerns, while those in their 80s and 90s were preoccupied with concerns of physical and/or mental decline.

Although Erikson et al. (1986) wrote extensively about the theoretical links between identity and integrity in late adulthood, there has been very little longitudinal or cross-sectional research undertaken to examine this relationship. On a longitudinal basis, Sneed et al. (2006) documented that integrity scores increased and identity scores decreased during midlife, in their study of individuals at age 20 years and subsequently every 11 years until age 54 years. However, Marcia and his colleagues have been among the few research teams who have directly examined the relations between integrity and identity in late adulthood (Hearn et al., 2012). The researchers validated a measure of integrity status (the Self-Examination Interview) for late-life adults and examined, cross-sectionally, how integrity was associated with participants' identity statuses. Participants were in their 60s, 70s, and 80s (mean age of approximately 75 years). A significant association between integrity and identity status was found, with some 86% of integrated late-life adults found to be identity achieved, while no despairing persons were identity achieved. Those participants who were non-exploring (i.e., had not examined questions of personal meaning in their lives) and pseudo-integrated (i.e., fit the world into simplistic templates and clichéd meanings) in integrity status tended to be foreclosed in their identity status.

Predictors and precursors to resolutions of *integrity versus despair* have also been undertaken in several studies. James and Zarrett (2006), in their longitudinal study over 45 years of adult women, found that while identity directly predicted generativity over time, it was generativity scores alone that predicted integrity scores in late adulthood; integrity scores were also negatively related to depression during the final assessment of these women when they were 70 years of age and over. Hannah et al. (1996) also examined predictors of *integrity versus despair* in a sample of adults. In their regression analyses, they found that the most parsimonious models for predicting *integrity-versus-despair* scores were generativity, trust, intimacy, identity, and autonomy, with no meaningful gender differences.

Ego integrity has also been positively linked with higher levels of many identity-related characteristics, such as self-acceptance, meaningfulness of life, and life satisfaction (Newton et al., 2022). Additionally, Nusser et al. (2022) used autobiographical memories from adults aged 61–92 years to examine themes of trust, identity, intimacy, and generativity. Regression analyses showed childhood memories to be associated with trust, memories of adolescence and emerging adulthood with identity and intimacy, and adulthood memories to be associated with intimacy and generativity. Those who rated their memories as more positive showed higher levels of life satisfaction in old age. Thus, identity, intimacy, and generativity resolutions have been linked with integrity resolutions as well as life satisfaction in late adulthood.

Summary and Conclusions

One important theme emerging from studies reviewed in this chapter is that identity resolutions adopted during adolescence and emerging adulthood provide critical foundations not only for ongoing identity development during adulthood but also for all subsequent Eriksonian psychosocial adulthood tasks of *intimacy versus isolation*, *generativity versus stagnation*, and *integrity versus despair*. Identity status studies indicated primarily progressive movements toward identity achievement beyond adolescence, *where identity change occurred*; however, identity status change over adulthood has pointed to only moderate levels of identity attainment by midlife. Progressive changes occurred primarily from the 20s to the early 30s and, to some extent, during midlife. Identity exploration in breadth and depth also peaked from the early to mid-20s. Beyond midlife, identity resolutions were shown to be more stable, relative to earlier time periods.

Increasing self-concept clarity through adulthood as well as striving for identity continuity were apparent in narrative studies of ongoing identity development through adulthood. However, some individuals (diffusions) continued to flounder in their life directions well beyond their adolescent years to drift, leading chaotic, frustrating, and often self-destructive adult lives. Those stably foreclosed over young and early middle adulthood have evidenced either a weakening or a strengthening of identity commitments over time. Identity resolutions during adolescence have also been positively linked with resolutions to Erikson's (1968) psychosocial stages of adult life, providing empirical support for Erikson's psychosocial theory of lifespan development.

The approaches to understanding identity development during adolescence and young adulthood that have been reviewed in this volume have *all* recognized the importance of both individual and contextual factors in charting identity's developmental course. However, different emphases have been placed on the role of the individual – biological and socially constructed factors (such as gender, ethnicity, physical strengths, and limitations) as well as personal psychological factors (individual needs, conscious and unconscious, wishes, and preferences) – and the role of the context (familial, social, cultural, and national) across the identity approaches reviewed in this volume, generating different understandings of identity balances between self and other in resultant research.

One obvious recommendation for future research would be to combine forces and integrate the strengths of as many of the general perspectives on identity as are practical into future studies of identity's formative process. Earlier chapters have also called for an integrated model to study identity in context (e.g., Galliher et al., 2017). Here, we would support such recommendations and ask that researchers frame their studies of identity with an awareness of national, regional, and more immediate social contexts and smaller group influences as well as potential historical/cohort effects on an individual's identity development. Additionally, individual variables involving both the process of identity development and other dimensions of identity that are important to maintaining a sense of personal continuity over time should be examined through a combination of research methods.

Longitudinal studies of identity's structure, content, and process evolution over time should be encouraged; at the same time, such work should aim to address these variables at relatively frequent time intervals. During adolescence and young adulthood, studies are beginning to undertake identity evaluations in a greater variety of national settings than a decade ago. However, beyond adolescence, the norm of 10–11-year time intervals between data collection points makes it difficult to follow some of the more nuanced threads of identity formation and revision over time in any meaningful way. Additionally, the dearth of identity studies, longitudinal or otherwise, for late-life adults (when many identity issues are likely to reemerge) makes this last life phase ripe for future identity as well as integrity research.

Further exploration of circumstances associated with the developmental arrest of identity is also essential to undertake, such that contexts may be structured to facilitate development in optimal ways. Steps toward how one might best support identity exploration in contexts where this process is adaptive are also important to undertake in future identity research. Ultimately, however, it is only one's own ease with that process of change itself that will allow one to aid and not hinder others on their own life journeys. Michener (1972) noted that the most important journey a person will make in life is to find his or her own identity – for if one fails in this task, it really doesn't much matter what else one finds.

References

Arneaud, M. J., Alea, N., & Espinet, M. (2016). Identity development in Trinidad: Status differences by age, adulthood transitions, and culture. *Identity: An International Journal of Theory and Research, 16(1)*, 59–71. http://doi.org/10.1080/15283488.2015.1121818

Årseth, A. K., Kroger, J., Martinussen, M., & Marcia, J. E. (2009). Meta-analytic studies of identity status and the relational issues of attachment and intimacy. *Journal of Adolescence*, *9*(1), 1–32. http://doi.org/10.1080/15283480802579532

Beaumont, S., & Pratt, M. (2011). Identity processing styles and psychosocial balance during early and middle adulthood: The role of identity in intimacy and generativity. *Journal of Adult Development*, *18*(4), 172–183. http://doi.org/10.1007/s10804-011-9125-z

Beyers, W., & Seiffge-Krenke, I. (2010). Does identity precede intimacy? Testing Erikson's theory on romantic development in emerging adults of the 21st century. *Journal of Adolescent Research*, *25*(3), 387–415. http://doi.org/10.1177/0743558410361370

Bradley, C., & Marcia, J. E. (1998). Generativity-stagnation: A five category model. *Journal of Personality*, *66*(1), 39–64. http://doi.org/10.1111/1467-6494.00002

Brown, C., & Lowis, M. J. (2003). Psychological development in the elderly: An investigation into Erikson's ninth stage. *Journal of Aging Studies*, *17*(4), 415–426. http://doi.org/10.1016/S0890-4065(03)00061-6

Carlsson, J., Wängqvist, M., & Frisén, A. (2016). Life on hold: Staying in identity diffusion in the late twenties. *Journal of Adolescence*, *47*(1), 220–229. http://doi.org/10.1016/j.adolescence.2015.10.023

Carlsson, J., Wängqvist, M., Syed, M., & Frisén, A. (2024). Lost in translation: The conceptual drift from the identity status interview to questionnaire measures. *Journal of Adult Development*. Advance online publication. https://doi.org/10.1007/s10804-024-09506-6

Cramer, P. (2017). Identity change between late adolescence and adulthood. *Personality and Individual Differences, 104*(1), 538–543. http://doi.org/10.1016/j.paid.2016.08.044
Erikson, E. H. (1968). *Identity, youth and crisis*. W.W. Norton & Company.
Erikson, E. H. (1980). *Identity and the life cycle*. W.W. Norton & Company.
Erikson, E. H. (1985). Fragments, unsorted. Folder 2, *85M–41. *bMS AM* 2031 (1725). Erikson Harvard Papers.
Erikson, E. H., & Erikson, J. M. (1997). *The life cycle completed (extended version)*. W. W. Norton & Company.
Erikson, E. H., Erikson, J. M., & Kivnic, H. Q. (1986). *Vital involvement in old age*. W. W. Norton & Company.
Eriksson, L., Wängqvist, M., Carlsson, J., & Frisén, A. (2020). Identity development in early adulthood. *Developmental Psychology, 56*(10), 1968–1983. http://doi.org/10.1037/dev0001093
Fadjukoff, P., Pulkkinen, L., & Kokko, K. (2016). Identity formation in adulthood: A longitudinal study from age 27 to 50. *Identity: An International Journal of Theory and Research, 16*(1), 8–23. http://doi.org/10.1080/15283488.2015.1121820
Fadjukoff, P., Pulkkinen, L., & Kokko, K. (2024, June 5–7). Identity status over six domains: A longitudinal study from age 27, 36, 42, 50, and 61 for women and men. In P. Fadjukoff (Chair). *Recent Findings and Insights from Long Longitudinal Studies* [Symposium]. 30th Anniversary Conference of the International Society for the Study of Identity, Tilburg, The Netherlands.
Fadjukoff, P., Pulkkinen, L., Lyyra, A. L., & Kokko, K. (2016). Parental identity and its relation to parenting and psychological functioning in middle age. *Parenting: Science and Practice, 16*(2), 87–107. http://doi.org/10.1080/15295192.2016.1134989
Friedman, L. J. (1999). *Identity's architect: A biography of Erik Erikson*. Scribner.
Fritsch, A., Voltzenlogel, V., & Cuero-Lombard, C. (2023). A cross-sectional study using self-defining memories to explore personal identity through adulthood. *Developmental Psychology, 60*(2), 363–375. https://doi.org/10.1037/dev0001611
Galliher, R. V., McLean, K. C., & Syed, M. (2017). An integrated developmental model for studying identity content in context. *Developmental Psychology, 53*(11), 2011–2022. http://doi.org/10.1037/dev0000299
Hannah, M. T., Domino, G., Figueredo, A. J., & Hendrickson, R. (1996). The prediction of ego integrity in older persons. *Educational and Psychological Measurement, 56*(6), 930–950. http://doi.org/10.1177/0013164496056006002
Hearn, S., Saulnier, G., Strayer, J., Glenham, M., Koopman, R., & Marcia, J. E. (2012). Between integrity and despair: Toward construct validation of Erikson's eighth stage. *Journal of Adult Development, 19*(1), 1–20. http://doi.org/10.1007/s10804-011-9126-y
Helson, R. M. (1967). Personality characteristics and developmental history of creative college women. *Genetic Psychology Monographs, 76*(2), 205–256.
Helson, R. M., & Mitchell, V. (2020). *Women on the river of life: A fifty year study of adult development*. University of California Press.
Helson, R. M., Stewart, A., & Ostrove, J. (1995). Identity in three cohorts of midlife women. *Journal of Personality and Social Psychology, 69*(3), 544–557. http://doi.org/10.1037/0022-3514.69.3.544
James, J. B., & Zarrett, N. (2006). Ego integrity in the lives of older women: A follow-up of mothers from the Sears, Maccoby, and Levin (1951) patterns of child rearing study. *Journal of Adult Development, 13*(2), 61–75. http://doi.org/10.1007/s10804-006-9003-2
Jia, F., Soucie, K., Alisat, S., & Pratt, M. (2016). Sowing seeds for future generations: Development of generative concern and its relation to environmental narrative identity. *International Journal of Behavioral Development, 40*(5), 466–470. http://doi.org/10.1177/0165025415611260
Josselson, R. (2017). *Paths to fulfillment: Women's search for meaning and identity*. Oxford University Press.

Josselson, R. (2019). Narrative, identity, and identity statuses: Reflections on the kaleidoscopic self. In D. P. McAdams, R. L. Shiner, & J. L. Tackett (Eds.), *Handbook of personality development* (pp. 448–464). The Guilford Press.

Kroger, J. (1993). On the nature of structural transition in the identity formation process. In J. Kroger (Ed.), *Discussions on ego identity* (pp. 205–234). Lawrence Erlbaum Associates.

Kroger, J. (2018). The epigenesis of identity: What does it mean? *Identity: An International Journal of Theory and Research, 18*(4), 334–342. http://doi.org/10.1080/15283488.2018.1523730

Kroger, J., & Haslett, S. J. (1987). A retrospective study of ego identity status change by midlife adults. *Social and Behavioral Sciences Documents, 17*(Ms. no. 2797), 52.

Kroger, J., & Haslett, S. J. (1991). A comparison of ego identity status transition pathways and change rates across five identity domains. *International Journal of Aging and Human Development, 32*(4), 303–330. http://doi.org/10.1177/009141509103200405

Kroger, J., Martinussen, M., & Marcia, J. E. (2010). Identity status change during adolescence and young adulthood: A meta-analysis. *Journal of Adolescence, 33*(5), 683–698. http://doi.org/10.1016/j.adolescence.2009.11.002

Larsson, H., Carlsson, J., Erikson, P. L., Syed, M., Wängqvist, M., & Frisén, A. (2024, June 5–7). Longitudinal findings on pathways of identity development across emerging and established adulthood. In P. Fadjukoff (Chair), *Recent findings and insights from long longitudinal studies* [Symposium]. 30th Anniversary Conference of the International Society for Research on Identity, Tilburg, The Netherlands.

Larsson, H., & Frisén, A. (2024). Knowing me, knowing you: Changes in parental representations among established adults going through progressive identity development. *Journal of Adult Development.* Advance online publication. https://doi.org/10.1007/s10804-024-09490-x

Lodi-Smith, J., Cologgi, K., Spain, S. M., & Roberts, B. W. (2017). Development of identity clarity and content in adulthood. *Journal of Personality and Social Psychology, 112*(5), 755–768. http://doi.org/10.1037/pspp0000091

Luyckx, K., Klimstra, T. A., Duriez, B., Van Petegem, S., & Beyers, W. (2013). Personal identity processes from adolescence through the late twenties: Age differences, functionality, and depressive symptoms. *Social Development, 22*(4), 701–721. http://doi.org/10.1111/sode.12027

Marcia, J. E. (2002). Identity and psychosocial development in adulthood. *Identity: An International Journal of Theory and Research, 2*(1), 7–28. http://doi.org/10.1207/S1532706XID0201_02

McAdams, D. P., Diamond, A., de St. Aubin, E., & Mansfield, E. (1997). Stories of commitment: The psychosocial construction of generative lives. *Journal of Personality and Social Psychology, 72*(3), 678–694. http://doi.org/10.1037/0022-3514.72.3.678

McLean, K. C. (2008). Stories of the young and the old: Personal continuity and narrative identity. *Developmental Psychology, 44*(1), 254–264. http://doi.org/10.1037/0012-1649.44.1.254

Merrill, N., & Fivush, R. (2016). Intergenerational narratives and identity across development. *Developmental Review, 40*, 72–92. http://doi.org/10.1016/j.dr.2016.03.001

Michener, J. (1972). *The fires of spring*. Random House.

Mitchell, L. L., Adler, J. M., Carlsson, J., Eriksson, P. L., & Syed, M. (2021). A conceptual review of identity integration across adulthood. *Developmental Psychology, 57*(11), 1981–1990. https://doi.org/10.1037/dev0001246

Newton, J. N., Ottley, K. M., Williams, S. K., & Hill, T. (2022). Women coming to terms with aging: The importance of psychosocial factors. *Journal of Women and Aging, 34*(1), 123–137. https://doi.org/10.1080/08952841.2020.1855049

Nusser, L., Zimprich, D., & Wolf, T. (2022). Themes of trust, identity, intimacy, and generativity in important autobiographical memories: Associations with life periods and life satisfaction. *Journal of Personality, 91*(5), 1110–1122. https://doi.org/10.1111/jopy.12786

Pals, J. L. (2006). Narrative identity processing of difficult life experiences: Pathways of personality development and positive self-transformation in adulthood. *Journal of Personality*, *74*(4), 1079–1110. https://doi.org/10.1111/j.1467-6494.2006.00403.x

Pasupathi, M., & Mansour, E. (2006). Adult age differences in autobiographical reasoning in narratives. *Developmental Psychology*, *42*(5), 798–808. http://doi.org/10.1037/0012-1649.42.5.798

Reinila, E., Kekalainen, T., Saajanaho, M., & Kokko, K. (2023). The structure of well-being and its relationship with generativity in middle adulthood and the beginning of late adulthood. *International Journal of Behavioral Development, 47*(4), 328–338. http://doi.org/10.1177/01650254231165837

Sears, R., Maccoby, E., & Levin, H. (1951). *Patterns of child-rearing*. Stanford University Press.

Sneed, J. R., Whitbourne, S. K., & Culang, M. E. (2006). Trust, identity, and ego integrity: Modelling Erikson's core stages over 34 years. *Journal of Adult Development*, *13*(1), 148–157. http://doi.org/10.1007/s10804-007-9026-3

Sneed, J. R., Whitbourne, S. K., Schwartz, S. J., & Huang, S. (2012). The relationship between identity, intimacy, and midlife well-being: Findings from the Rochester adult longitudinal study. *Psychology and Aging*, *27*(2), 318–323. http://doi.org/10.1037/a0026378

Stephen, J., Fraser, E., & Marcia, J. E. (1992). Lifespan identity development: Variables related to Moratorium-Achievement (MAMA) cycles. *Journal of Adolescence*, *15*(3), 283–300. https://doi.org/10.1016/0140-1971(92)90031-Y

Stewart, A. J., Ostrove, J. M., & Helson, R. (2001). Middle aging in women: Patterns of personality change from the 30s to the 50s. *Journal of Adult Development*, *8*(1), 23–37. http://doi.org/10.1023/A:1026445704288

Villar, F., Serrat, R., & Pratt, M. W. (2024). Theory and methods in recent research on generativity across adulthood. In F. Villar, H. H. Lawford, & M. W. Pratt (Eds.), *The development of generativity across adulthood* (pp. 1–36). Oxford University Press. http://doi.org/10.1093/9780191966309.003.0001

Villar, F., & Zacares, J. J. (2024). Generativity, ego integrity, and the achievement of aging well. In F. Villar, H. H. Lawford, & M. W. Pratt (Eds.), *The development of generativity across adulthood* (pp. 79–95). Oxford University Press. http://doi.org/10.1093/9780191966309.003.0005

Zucker, A. N., Ostrove, J. M., & Stewart, J. J. (2002). College educated women's personality development in adulthood: Perceptions and age differences. *Psychology and Aging*, *17*(2), 236–244. http://doi.org/10.1037/0882-7974.17.2.236

Index

Note: Page numbers in **bold** indicate a table on the corresponding page.

For Product Safety Concerns and Information please contact our EU
representative GPSR@taylorandfrancis.com
Taylor & Francis Verlag GmbH, Kaufingerstraße 24, 80331 München, Germany

www.ingramcontent.com/pod-product-compliance
Ingram Content Group UK Ltd.
Pitfield, Milton Keynes, MK11 3LW, UK
UKHW020006200926
475702UK00015B/2503
9781032775807